# KALLIS' iBT
# TOEFL® PATTERN

## Writing 3

**KALLIS' iBT TOEFL® Pattern** Writing 3

**KALLIS EDU, INC.**
7490 Opportunity Road, Suite 203
San Diego, CA 92111
(858) 277-8600
info@kallisedu.com
www.kallisedu.com

**ISBN-10**: 1-5058-8139-0
**ISBN-13**: 978-1-5058-8139-4

**iBT TOEFL® Pattern - Writing III** is the third
of our three-level iBT TOEFL® Writing Exam
preparation book series.

Our **iBT TOEFL® Pattern Writing** series
simplifies each TOEFL writing task into a
series of basic steps, ensuring that students
do not become overwhelmed as they develop
their writing skills. Moreover, our commitment
to minimizing instruction and maximizing
student practice provides students with many
opportunities to strengthen their writing skills
while developing a unique writing style.

**KALLIS**

# KALLIS'

# TOEFL® iBT

# PATTERN

# WRITING 3

## FINAL PREP

# Getting Started

A study guide should familiarize the reader with the material found on the test, develop unique methods that can be used to solve various question types, and provide practice questions to challenge future test-takers. *KALLIS' iBT TOEFL® Pattern Series* aims to accomplish all these study tasks by presenting iBT TOEFL® test material in an organized, comprehensive, and easy-to-understand way.

*KALLIS' iBT TOEFL® Pattern Writing Series* provides in-depth explanations and practices that will help you prepare for the iBT TOEFL writing section. Each writing task is broken down into a series of steps, allowing you to develop reliable and efficient writing strategies.

## Understanding the Writing Tasks

The beginning of Chapters 1 and 2 provide introductory information that is designed to familiarize you with the two types of writing tasks encountered on the iBT TOEFL writing section. These sections will prepare you for the subsequent explanations and practices.

### General Information

The **General Information** section presents the writing skills that you will need to complete iBT TOEFL writing section and provides descriptions of each writing task.

### Response Format

The **Response Format** section provides organizational strategies to help you structure your writing task responses. This section provides general information regarding how many paragraphs a response should consist of, as well as what information should be included in each paragraph.

### Hacking Strategy

The **Hacking Strategy** provides a step-by-step process explaining how to organize and compose responses to a writing task. Each step that is outlined in the **Hacking Strategy** section is elaborated on in detail throughout the chapter.

# Improving Writing Skills through Practice

A combination of explanations and practices breaks down each writing task into simple step-by-step processes.

## Practice Sets

The majority of this book is devoted to 20 **Practice Sets**, each of which contains one Integrated Writing task and two Independent Writing tasks, as well as space to take notes and write a response. These **Practice Sets** provide you with opportunities to develop the skills that you have read about and to strengthen your writing abilities.

# In Case You Need Help

▶ The last two pages of Chapter 1 consist of an **Integrated Writing Checklist** and an **Integrated Writing Task Rubric**. The last two pages of Chapter 2 consist of an **Independent Writing Checklist** and an **Independent Writing Task Rubric**. Reviewing these before you begin writing can help you structure your responses; reviewing them after you have completed a writing task can help you assess the quality of your writing.

▶ A **Model Answer** is located after each task in all **Practice Sets**. These **Model Answers** demonstrate one acceptable way to respond to each prompt, but there will often be many acceptable responses for any given task. So do not feel that your responses must be the same as the **Model Answers**; just use them for guidance when necessary.

# Table of Contents

Write Now!
Right Now!

## Chapter 1

### INTEGRATED WRITING TASK

## Chapter 2

### INDEPENDENT WRITING TASK

# WRITING 3

*FINAL PREP*

## Chapter 3

## WRITING PRACTICE TASK

## INTEGRATED AND INDEPENDENT TASKS

The iBT TOEFL writing section consists of two tasks: one Integrated task and one Independent task.

The first task is called the "Integrated task" because it requires you to incorporate, or integrate, material from spoken and/or written sources into your response. This task will require you to read a passage, listen to a lecture, and then form a response based on what you have read and heard.

The second task is called the "Independent task" because it requires you to produce a response without using any extra written or spoken materials. Thus, you must come up with responses to the second task independently, using your own experiences or opinions.

## TRANSITION WORDS AND PHRASES

**Transition words and phrases** explain how the content of one sentence relates to the rest of your response.

| Meaning | Examples |
|---|---|
| addition | *additionally, furthermore, in addition, in fact, moreover* |
| cause-and-effect | *as a result, consequently, then, therefore, to this end* |
| compare/contrast | *compared to, despite, however, in contrast, on the contrary, on the one hand, on the other hand, nevertheless* |
| conclusions | *finally, in conclusion, in summary, lastly, thus, in short* |
| examples | *for example, for instance, in this case, in this situation* |
| introductions | *according to, as indicated in/by, based on* |
| reasons | *one reason is, another reason is, due to* |
| sequence | *afterward, again, also, finally, first, next, previously, second, third* |

## SYMBOLS AND ABBREVIATIONS

When taking notes to prepare for a written response, save time by using symbols and abbreviations instead of complete words. You can create your own symbols and abbreviations in addition to using those listed in the charts on the following page.

| Symbol | Meaning | Symbol | Meaning |
|---|---|---|---|
| & | and | = | equals, is |
| % | percent | > | more than |
| # | number | < | less than |
| @ | at | → | resulting in |
| ↓ | decreasing | ↑ | increasing |

## ABBREVIATIONS FOR UNIVERSITY ACTIVITIES

| Abbreviation | Meaning | Abbreviation | Meaning |
|---|---|---|---|
| edu. | education | RA | resident assistant |
| GE | general education | stu. | student |
| GPA | grade point average | TA | teaching assistant |
| prof. | professor/professional | univ. | university |

## ABBREVIATIONS FOR ACADEMIC TOPICS

| Abbreviation | Meaning | Abbreviation | Meaning |
|---|---|---|---|
| bio. | biology/biological | exp. | experience/experiment |
| c. | century | info. | information |
| chem. | chemistry/chemical | gov. | government |
| def. | definition | hypo. | hypothesis |
| econ. | economics/economy | phys. | physics/physical |
| env. | environment | psych. | psychology/psychological |
| ex. | example | sci. | science/scientific |

## OTHER ABBREVIATIONS

| Abbreviation | Meaning | Abbreviation | Meaning |
|---|---|---|---|
| abt. | about | pic. | picture |
| b/c | because | ppl. | people |
| comm. | community/communication | pref. | preference |
| e/o | each other | pt. | point |
| fam. | family | ques. | question |
| fav. | favorite | s/b | somebody |
| gen. | general/generation | s/o | someone |
| hr. | hour | sec. | second |
| impt. | important | w/ | with |
| loc. | location | w/i | within |
| lvl. | level | w/o | without |
| min. | minute | yr. | year |

# iBT TOEFL Writing Section: Task Composition

| Task Type | Task Description |
|---|---|
| **Task 1**<br><br>Integrated Task<br><br>(20 minutes to respond) | • **Read** a passage about an academic subject.<br>(passage length: 230-300 words; reading time: 3 minutes)<br><br>• **Listen** to a lecture that approaches the academic subject explained in the passage from different perspective.<br>(listening time: 2 minutes)<br><br>• **Write** a response that summarizes the essential points from the lecture and explain their relationship to the essential points in the passage.<br><br>• Length of Response: generally 150-225 words, but responding with more than 225 words is also acceptable. |
| **Task 2**<br><br>Independent Task<br><br>(30 minutes to respond) | • **Write** an essay that responds to the prompt by presenting your opinion on a certain issue; include explanations and details that support your opinion.<br><br>• Length of Response: at least 300 words |

# iBT TOEFL Writing Score

| Skill | Score Range | Score Calculation Method | Level |
|---|---|---|---|
| **Writing** | 0-30 | • ETS grader + automatic grading technique<br><br>• Each of two tasks is scored between 0 to 5 points. The average of these scores is converted into a grading scale that ranges from 0 to 30 points. | Limited (1-16) |
| | | | Fair (17-23) |
| | | | Good (24-30) |

.

# Chapter 1

# INTEGRATED
# WRITING TASK

# THE INTEGRATED WRITING TASK

## A. GENERAL INFORMATION

### 1. EXPLANATION OF TASK

- You will have 3 minutes to read a 250- to 300-word passage that defines an academic term, process, or concept.
- You will use a headset to listen to a 2-minute lecture that either **supports** or **refutes** the information presented in the passage.
- Given a 20-minute response time, you will connect the information in the lecture to the information in the passage.
- Topics on this writing task include academic subjects commonly studied at universities, such as literature, biology, and psychology.

### 2. NECESSARY SKILLS FOR TASK

To complete the writing task, you must be able to:

- **paraphrase** and **summarize** major points from reading and listening information
- explain the relationships between the major points

### 3. STRATEGIES FOR APPROACHING TASK

You will receive scratch paper for the writing test, so you can use either paper or the computer's word processor to take notes and form an outline.

1) Take notes as you read the academic passage. After 3 minutes, the passage disappears.
2) Take notes as you listen to the lecture.
3) The writing prompt asks you to summarize and connect information in the passage and the lecture. Then the reading passage reappears.
4) Spend approximately 5 minutes organizing your notes into an outline.
5) Use the remainder of your time to compose a response based on your outline. The suggested response length is 150-225 words. A word counter keeps track of your word count.

### 4. TIPS

1) Focus on the lecture; determine how the lecture relates to the passage.
2) Do not simply copy text from the lecture and the passage. Copying exact text from either of the sources will result in the deduction of points. Paraphrase the information instead.
3) Respond using the simple present tense whenever doing so is appropriate: "The lecture says..."
4) Demonstrate your ability to use transitions, citations, and reporting verbs or phrases.
5) Save the last few minutes of your response time to proofread and edit your essay.

### 1. TAKING NOTES

**Take notes** on the passage and the lecture; pay special attention to whether the lecture **supports** or **refutes** the passage.

### 2. OUTLINING

Organize your thoughts by forming a **topic statement** and identifying three points from the lecture that either support or refute the points from the passage.

### 3. ESSAY WRITING

Refer to your outline and add **transition words** to clarify the relationship between the passage and the lecture. Summarize, paraphrase, and cite important information.

### 4. PROOFREADING

**Proofread** and **edit** your Integrated response using our "Writing Checklist" (page 14) for guidance.

## C. NOTE-TAKING TIPS

**Note taking** is writing down information from sources that you encounter from the reading and listening portions of the Integrated Writing task.

**Taking notes involves**:
- identifying the **main ideas** and the **important details**

### 1. ABBREVIATIONS

When taking notes for the Integrated Writing response, save time by using **abbreviations**, which are symbols or shortened forms of words.

| Abbreviation/Symbol | Meaning | Abbreviation/Symbol | Meaning |
|---|---|---|---|
| & | and | @ | at |
| % | percent | # | number |
| ex | example | b/c | because |
| w/ | with | w/o | without |
| > | more than | < | less than |
| = | equal, is | → | resulting in |
| ↓ | decreasing | ↑ | increasing |
| / | or | $ | money |
| + | plus/add | – | negative/subtract |

### 2. LIST FORMAT

Another way to save time is to **condense information** in your notes. For example, try using a list format to summarize and outline information. By doing so, you can leave out transitions, verbs, and other words that you think you will remember anyway.

**Ex** Full sentence: From 1920 until 1933, the United States government enforced prohibition, which made the manufacture, sale, and storage of alcohol illegal.

Notes: *1920-1933 = prohibition in U.S. (no alcohol allowed)*

Full sentence: Jared's brother and sister have birthdays in May; Jared's birthday is in December.

Notes: *Jared bro/sis = May b-day; Jared = Dec. b-day*

# D. CONNECTING INFORMATION

During the reading and listening portions of the Integrated Writing task, you will read a passage about an academic subject and then listen to a lecture on that subject.

Afterward, you will be asked a question about the connection between the lecture and the passage.

The lecture will either provide information that:

- **supports** the information in the passage
- **refutes** the information in the passage

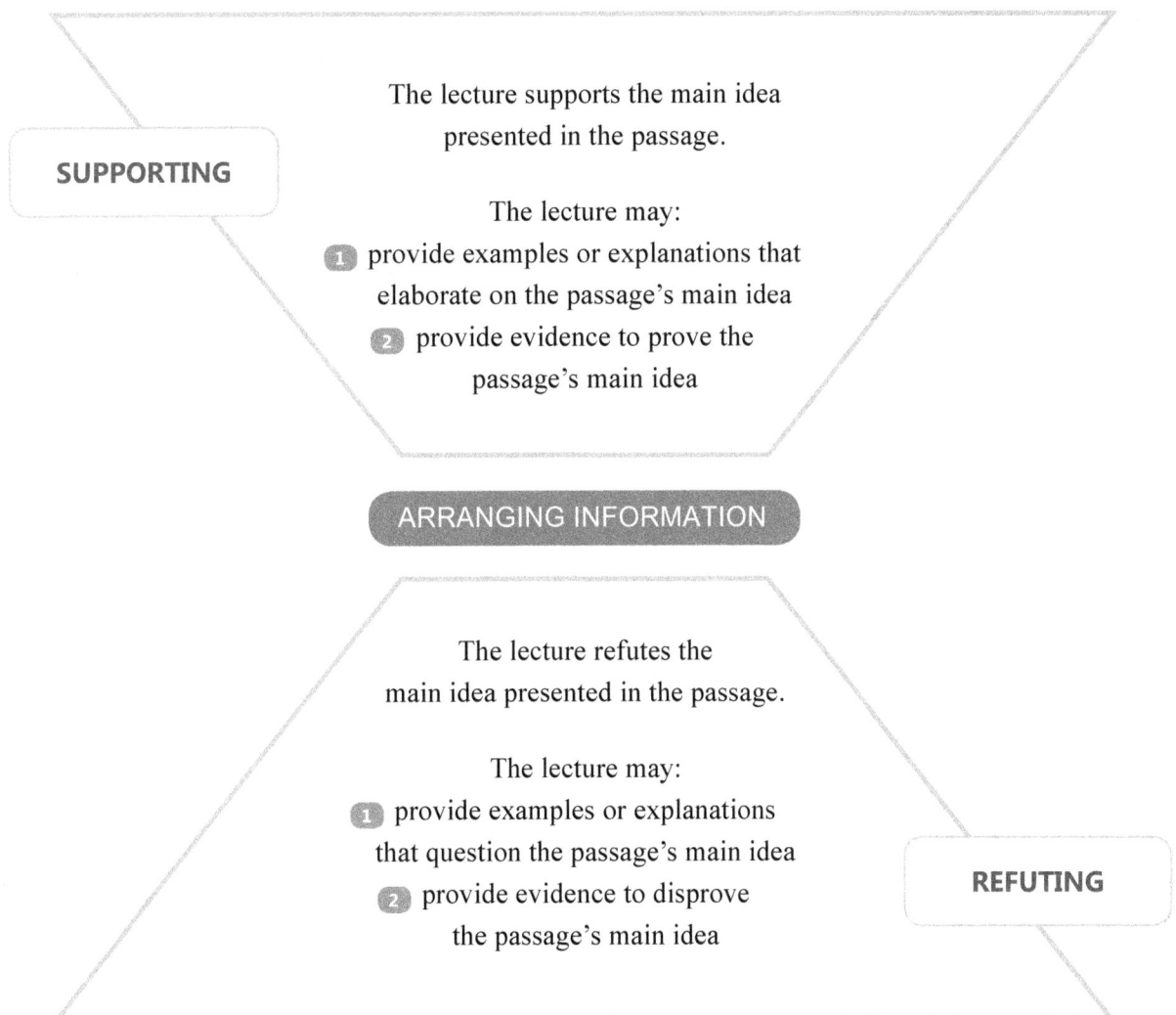

**SUPPORTING**

The lecture supports the main idea presented in the passage.

The lecture may:
1. provide examples or explanations that elaborate on the passage's main idea
2. provide evidence to prove the passage's main idea

**ARRANGING INFORMATION**

The lecture refutes the main idea presented in the passage.

The lecture may:
1. provide examples or explanations that question the passage's main idea
2. provide evidence to disprove the passage's main idea

**REFUTING**

## 1. TAKING NOTES WHILE YOU READ

---

> **PASSAGE**
>
> Many senior citizens, especially those who are single, suffer from feelings of loneliness, boredom, and depression. However, many studies have shown that caring for a pet dog is a great way to combat these problems.
>
> For instance, dogs provide companionship. After all, dogs are intelligent and sensitive animals with many qualities cherished by humans. They can act as non-judgmental listeners, and they enjoy spending time with their owners. Thus, dogs can accompany their owners on walks and provide companionship during household chores.
>
> Caring for a dog also provides a person with a sense of purpose. Because dogs require feeding, playtime, and minor medical care, caring for a dog is the perfect way to battle the boredom faced by so many senior citizens. All of these tasks are challenging enough to hold off boredom, but manageable enough for most senior citizens.
>
> Finally, caring for a dog is the perfect way to lift depression. As mentioned before, dogs are intelligent and sensitive animals. Studies have shown that dogs are sympathetic toward human emotions. As a result, when a senior citizen gets a dog, he or she is getting a therapist, too.

> **PASSAGE NOTES**
>
> benefits of owning dog for senior:
>
> - give companionship
>
> - give purpose
>
> - give happiness

## 2. Taking Notes While You Listen

> **SUPPORTING LECTURE**
>
> As stated in the reading, when senior citizens take on the responsibility of caring for a dog, they receive many benefits.
>
> As mentioned in the reading, dogs provide psychological benefits by acting as friends and companions to senior citizens. And this companionship can have health benefits, too. Taking a dog for a daily walk provides seniors with a means of exercise, and studies have shown that the presence of a dog can decrease blood pressure and stress levels.
>
> Dogs also fight boredom by encouraging seniors to be more social. People in social settings are more likely to approach and talk to someone with a dog because the dog itself is a great conversation starter. Senior citizens can start conversations by talking to others about the dogs breed or temperament, or just by inviting others to pet the dog.
>
> And of course, dogs have many tricks for fighting depression among senior citizens. Dogs can lift their owners' spirits by licking their owners' hands or faces, lying next to their owners during moments of sadness, and encouraging their owners to play games. So ultimately, senior citizens have nothing to lost and everything to gain by caring for a dog.

> **REFUTING LECTURE**
>
> A newly published study, which followed 1,000 senior dog owners for five years, calls into question the idea that caring for dogs is a "cure-all" for the feelings of loneliness and depression experienced by many seniors. In fact, the study showed that dog care often had the exact opposite effect. Let's look at what the study determined.
>
> Unfortunately, the dogs in the study didn't provide stable companionship for many senior citizens. In over half of the reported cases, the dogs wanted to spend most of their time alone, so many of the senior citizens felt unwanted by their pets. In another third of the cases, the dogs were often hostile toward their owners. Sadly, only about 10 percent of the senior citizens established good connections with their dogs.
>
> Additionally, the dogs' many needs proved burdensome to many seniors. In fact, some seniors became sick from fatigue because they spent so much time trying to care for and train their dogs. And about one-fifth of the dogs were given up because their owners couldn't afford the medical and food expenses.
>
> Lastly, dog ownership didn't lift the depression that many senior citizens experience. The unpredictable behaviors of many of the dogs fed into senior citizens low self-esteem, often worsening symptoms of depression. Some seniors even took the situation personally by blaming themselves for their dog troubles.

| SUPPORTING LECTURE NOTES | REFUTING LECTURE NOTES |
|---|---|
| supports reading | refutes reading |
| ● dog = companion, health benefits<br>  walking dog = exercise<br>  dogs ↓ blood pressure & ↓ stress lvls. | ● 50% → dogs wanted to be alone<br>  30% → dogs were hostile<br>  only 10% → dogs were good |
| ● ↓ boredom<br>  ppl. approach dog owners<br>  dog = conversation starter | ● time-consuming → some seniors became sick<br>  owners' high med. costs → 1/5 dogs given up |
| ● ↓ depression<br>  dogs lick/comfort owners<br>  dogs encourage activity | ● most → more depressed<br>  some → self-blame for dog troubles |

# F. INTEGRATED RESPONSE FORMATS

## POINT-BY-POINT RESPONSE

In some Integrated Writing tasks, each detail from the lecture will correspond with a detail in the passage. In such cases, form your response using the point-by-point method.

## BLOCK RESPONSE

In the Integrated Writing task, most lectures that elaborate upon passage information, as well as some refuting lectures, do not contain details that correspond perfectly with the passage information. In these cases, respond using the block method.

### Introduction
**Topic Statement**: presents the main ideas in both the passage and the lecture and states whether the lecture supports or refutes the passage

### Introduction
**Topic Statement**: presents the main ideas in both the passage and the lecture and states whether the lecture supports or refutes the passage

### Body Paragraph 1
provides the first example from the passage and the first example from the lecture that shows contrast or support

### Body Paragraph 1
summarizes the main idea of the passage and summarizes/paraphrases the details, examples, or explanations used to support the main idea

### Body Paragraph 2
provides the second example from the passage and the second example from the lecture that shows contrast or support

### Body Paragraph 2
summarizes the main idea in the lecture and clarifies how the lecture information either supports or refutes the passage's information by summarizing/paraphrasing the details and examples from the lecture

### Body Paragraph 3
provides the third example from the passage and the third example from the lecture that shows contrast or support

# G. THE INTRODUCTION

## 1. IDENTIFYING RELATIONSHIPS

When taking notes for the Integrated Writing task, the two concepts that you should focus on are

- determining the relationship between the passage and the lecture
- condensing the main ideas and supporting details by using abbreviations

## 2. FORMING A TOPIC STATEMENT

Before you outline an entire Integrated Writing response, you must first form a clear and concise *topic statement*. The topic statement should:

- state the main idea discussed in both the lecture and the passage
- state whether the lecture supports or refutes the passage
- include major pieces of information that tell how or why the lecture agrees or disagrees with the passage
- **not** include any specific information that you might want to save for the body paragraphs

▶ TOPIC STATEMENT BUILDING

**TOPIC STATEMENT STRUCTURE 1**

The lecture claims that _____

_____

_____

_____. The lecture provides information that _____ the passage.

**TOPIC STATEMENT STRUCTURE 2**

The lecture primarily talks about _____

_____

_____

_____. The information in the lecture _____ the reading passage.

# H. BODY PARAGRAPHS — POINT-BY-POINT METHOD

▶ TIPS FOR USING THE POINT-BY-POINT METHOD:

- Make sure that you know how each detail or example from the passage corresponds to a detail or example from the lecture.

- This is the preferred method when the lecture refutes the passage.

**RESPONSE FORMAT**

**BODY PARAGRAPH 1**

> first main example or detail from the lecture

For one, the lecture states that _____

_____

This lecture information (**supports / refutes**) the information from the reading passage because the reading asserts that _____

_____

_____

**BODY PARAGRAPH 2**

> second main example or detail from the lecture

Additionally, the lecture asserts that _____

_____

These claims (**support / refute**) the claims made in the passage because the reading passage describes _____

_____

_____

explanation of how the information in the lecture either supports or refutes ideas in the passage

**BODY PARAGRAPH 3**

> third main example or detail from the lecture

Finally, the lecture claims that _____

_____

This lecture information (**supports / refutes**) the information from the reading passage because the passage states _____

_____

# I. BODY PARAGRAPHS — BLOCK METHOD

▶ TIPS FOR USING THE BLOCK METHOD:

• Use this method if you are not sure how each point in the lecture corresponds to information in the passage.

• This method is effective when the information in the lecture elaborates upon or supports information from the passage.

**RESPONSE FORMAT**

**BODY PARAGRAPH 1**

> the main idea from the passage followed by details and examples in the passage that support the main idea

The passage provides a number of details explaining _____

_____

_____

_____

_____

_____

**BODY PARAGRAPH 2**

The lecture (**elaborates upon / refutes**) the information in the reading

passage with several pieces of evidence. For instance, _____

_____

> details and examples from the lecture that show how the lecture either supports or refutes the information from the passage

_____

_____

_____

_____

## MODEL ANSWER

The lecture discusses a study that questions the idea that dogs can help senior citizens emotionally. According to the study, the vast majority of senior citizens were harmed by the experience of pet ownership.

First, the lecture states that dog ownership did not make senior citizens less lonely. The reading suggested that caring for a dog could ease senior citizens' loneliness because dogs provide constant companionship. However, the study showed that this was not true. In over half the reported cases, the dogs did not want to be around their owners. In another third of the cases, the dogs were erratic and sometimes even violent toward their owners.

Second, the professor claims that the amount of effort required to care for a dog overwhelmed many of the seniors. The reading suggested that dog ownership could give senior citizens a sense of purpose by providing them with manageable challenges. However, the study revealed that many seniors became tired and sick from constantly caring for their dogs. Some had to give up their dogs due to high food and medical costs.

Finally, the lecture states that many of the dogs' behaviors increased their owners' symptoms of depression. The reading suggested dogs' ability to sympathize with human emotions could make senior citizens feel better. However, the study showed that most senior citizens were saddened by their dogs' erratic or violent behaviors.

# K. BLOCK METHOD EXAMPLE

## MODEL ANSWER

The passage and the lecture both discuss the benefits of dog ownership for senior citizens. The lecture provides information that supports the reading passage by elaborating on each of the passage's key points.

The passage provides a number of details explaining how caring for a dog can help senior citizens. For one, the passage states that dogs make great companion animals, as they can accompany seniors while running errands or doing chores. Additionally, dogs help keep seniors busy because they must take care of dogs' dietary and medical needs. Moreover, the author states that dogs are very compassionate, so they can help seniors become less lonely and depressed. The passage even states that dogs are often therapeutic to their senior owners.

The lecture provides more details proving that dog ownership is beneficial for seniors. For instance, the lecture states that keeping a dog for companionship encourages seniors to exercise by walking their dogs, and just being around a dog can lower a person's blood pressure and levels of stress. Thus, dog ownership has several health benefits. Dogs also encourage seniors to socialize more, as people often approach dog owners to ask them questions about their dogs. Finally, dogs fight sadness and depression by comforting their owners and encouraging them to stay active.

# L. INTEGRATED WRITING CHECKLIST

Here is a checklist to help you review and proofread your integrated response.

## 1. ESSENTIALS CHECK

| | | |
|---|---|---|
| **Topic Statement** | ✓ | The topic statement in the introduction summarizes the main idea in the passage and the lecture and indicates whether the lecture agrees or disagrees with the passage. |
| **Body Paragraphs** | ✓ | Each paragraph explains how a point from the passage agrees or disagrees with a point from the lecture. |
| **Citations** | ✓ | The source of each borrowed idea is cited. Use citations when you quote, paraphrase, or summarize ideas from another person. |
| **Transitions** | ✓ | Transition words are used effectively between paragraphs and between some sentences to show the relationships between ideas. |

## 2. GRAMMAR CHECK

| | | |
|---|---|---|
| **Subject-Verb Agreement** | ✓ | The correct verb matches the subject of each sentence in terms of number and person. |
| **Pronouns** | ✓ | Each pronoun matches its *antecedent*—the word or words that the pronoun is referring to—in number. |
| **Spelling & Punctuation** | ✓ | Spelling and punctuation are correct. |

## 3. STYLE CHECK

| | | |
|---|---|---|
| **Word/Sentence Variety** | ✓ | Words and sentence structures are varied to avoid repetition; synonyms have been used to avoid copying. |
| **Clarity** | ✓ | Ideas and sentences are clearly stated. Word usage is accurate and appropriate. |

| | |
|---|---|
| **5** | • The response effectively identifies relevant information from the lecture and connects it to the related information in the passage in a logical and skillful manner.<br>• The response is well organized and has few grammatical errors.<br>• Any minor errors do not make the content unclear, including the explanation of the passage and lecture relationships. |
| **4** | • Meaningful information from the passage and the lecture is presented, and connections between the two are generally accurate, but there may be some minor inexact, incorrect, or omitted information.<br>• A response at this level may have more frequent or apparent minor language errors, but the usage and grammar rarely affect the precision, coherency, or connection between ideas. |
| **3** | The response contains important lecture information and relays some critical information between the passage and the lecture. However, the response also contains one or more of the following issues:<br><br>• The connections between the passage and the lecture are vague, unclear, or generalized.<br>• The response may fail to mention one main point from the lecture.<br>• Some main points from the passage or the lecture may be incomplete, incorrect, or imprecise.<br>• Grammatical errors may be more frequent.<br>• Grammar errors may make unclear connections and result in imprecise expressions. |
| **2** | The response provides some important lecture information but reflects major language problems. The response may misstate or omit ideas from the lecture or the connections between the passage and the lecture. One or more of the following may occur:<br><br>• The response inaccurately represents or leaves out the unifying connection between the passage and the lecture.<br>• The response leaves out or misstates main ideas from the lecture.<br>• Language errors or misused expressions make connections or meaning unclear at critical points in the response. |
| **1** | One or more of the following may occur:<br><br>• The response offers no or little important or relevant information from the lecture.<br>• The intended meaning of the response is unclear. |
| **0** | • The response simply copies sentences from the passage.<br>• The response is not related to the topic.<br>• The response is written in a language other than English or only consists of keystrokes. |

# Chapter 2

# INDEPENDENT WRITING TASK

# THE INDEPENDENT WRITING TASK

## A. GENERAL INFORMATION

### 1. NECESSARY SKILLS FOR TASK

To complete the writing task, you must be able to:

- form opinions about personal experiences and events
- organize ideas logically with a clear thesis statement, supporting paragraphs, and conclusion
- convey information clearly using correct grammar and appropriate vocabulary
- use transitions, citations, and reporting verbs or phrases accurately

### 2. STRATEGIES FOR APPROACHING TASK

You will receive scratch paper for the writing test, so you can use either paper or the computer's word processor to take notes and form an outline. You have a total of 30 minutes to complete this task.

1) Spend about 5 minutes planning and outlining your essay.
2) Spend about 20 minutes writing your response.
3) Leave a few minutes to proofread and edit your response.

**PROMPT FORMAT**

- You must state, explain, and support an opinion about a familiar topic.
- You will receive one of three prompt types:

**Type 1**  **Agree or Disagree Prompts**

Do you agree or disagree with the following statement? Use reasons and examples to support your opinion.

Some people believe X. Other people believe Y. Which position do you agree with? Give reasons and details to support your answer.

**Type 2**  **Compare and Contrast Prompts**

Some people believe X. Other people believe Y. Compare these two attitudes. Which attitude do you agree with? Give reasons and details to support your answer.

**Type 3**  **Personal Opinion Prompts**

Describe a time when X happened in your life. Explain why this event/person/object is so important to you. Use reasons and examples to support your answer.

**Note**  Personal opinion topics will vary in format.

Because you only have a few minutes to outline your ideas for the Independent Writing response, you should quickly write down ideas using a format that will help you organize your support and explanations.

Your essay should consist of either four or five paragraphs: an **introduction**, two to three **body paragraphs**, and a **conclusion**.

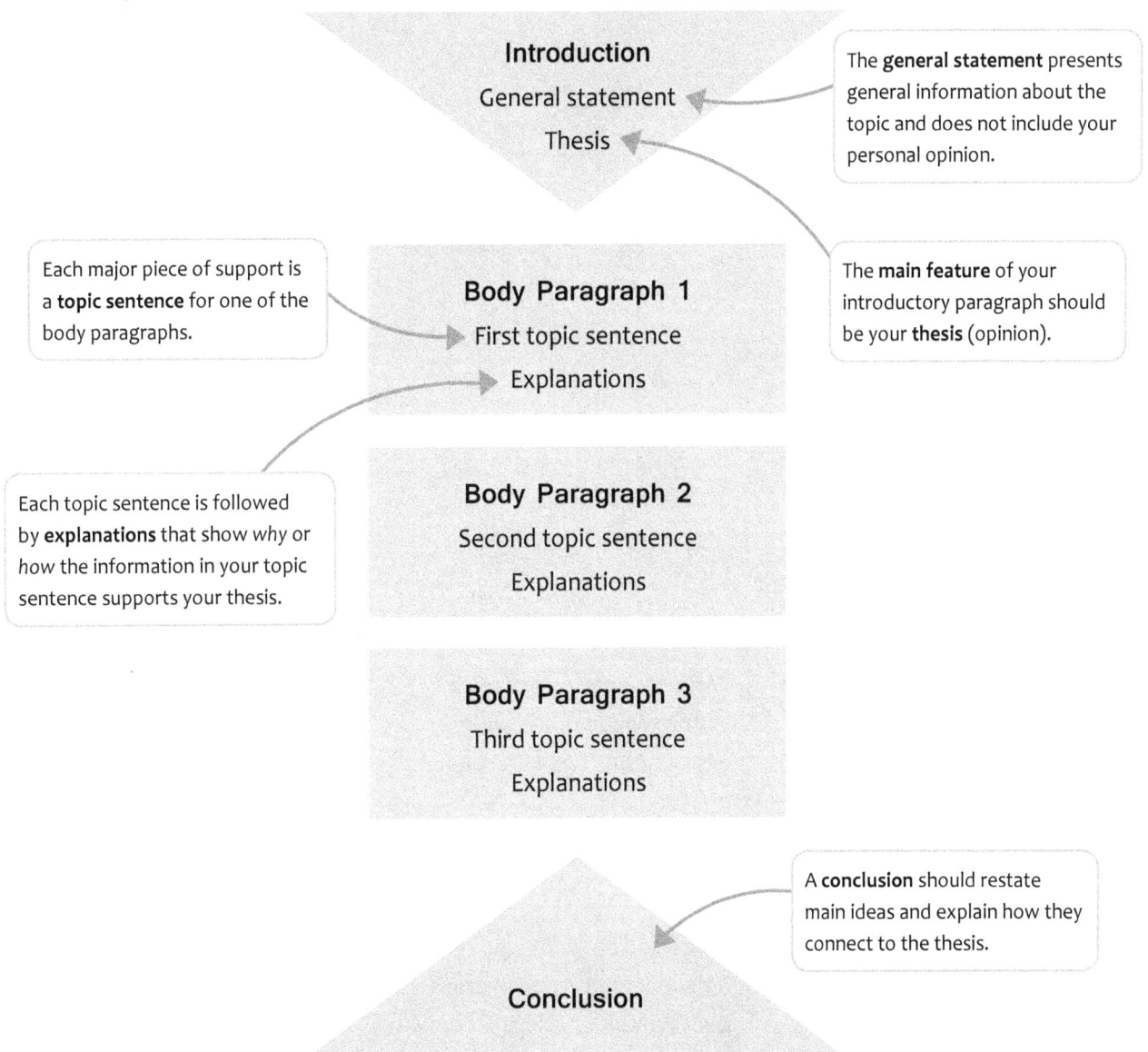

**ESSAY FORMAT**

**Introduction**
General statement
Thesis

The **general statement** presents general information about the topic and does not include your personal opinion.

The **main feature** of your introductory paragraph should be your **thesis** (opinion).

Each major piece of support is a **topic sentence** for one of the body paragraphs.

**Body Paragraph 1**
First topic sentence
Explanations

Each topic sentence is followed by **explanations** that show *why* or *how* the information in your topic sentence supports your thesis.

**Body Paragraph 2**
Second topic sentence
Explanations

**Body Paragraph 3**
Third topic sentence
Explanations

A **conclusion** should restate main ideas and explain how they connect to the thesis.

**Conclusion**

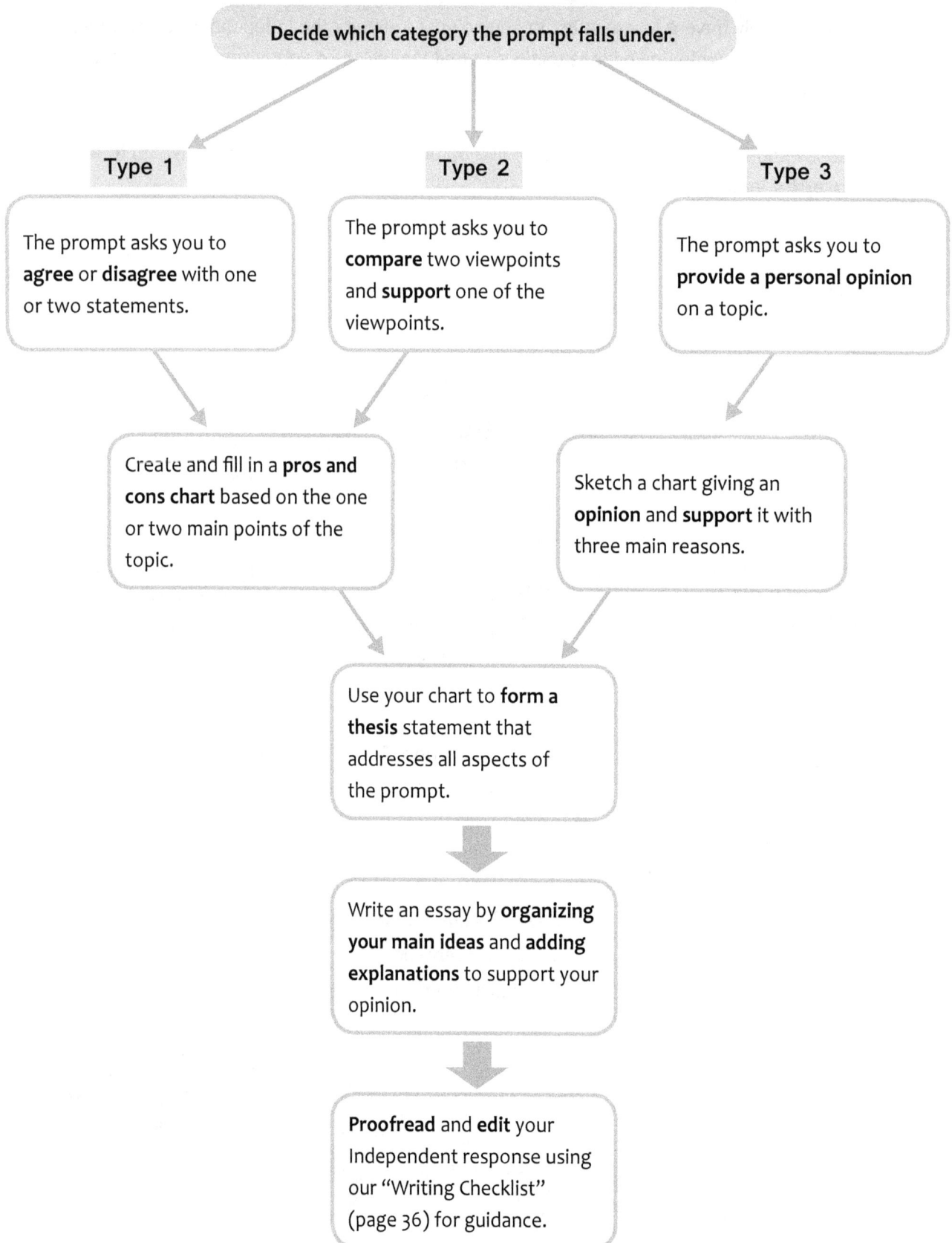

**Decide which category the prompt falls under.**

### Type 1

The prompt asks you to **agree** or **disagree** with one or two statements.

### Type 2

The prompt asks you to **compare** two viewpoints and **support** one of the viewpoints.

### Type 3

The prompt asks you to **provide a personal opinion** on a topic.

Create and fill in a **pros and cons chart** based on the one or two main points of the topic.

Sketch a chart giving an **opinion** and **support** it with three main reasons.

Use your chart to **form a thesis** statement that addresses all aspects of the prompt.

Write an essay by **organizing your main ideas** and **adding explanations** to support your opinion.

**Proofread** and **edit** your Independent response using our "Writing Checklist" (page 36) for guidance.

## D. EXAMPLE PROMPTS

### TYPE 1: AGREE/DISAGREE PROMPTS

**EXAMPLE 1**

Do you agree or disagree with the following statement? People today have less time for physical activity than people did a century ago. Use specific reasons and examples to support your response.

**EXAMPLE 2**

Do you agree or disagree with the following statement? Most students work more effectively in groups than by themselves. Use specific reasons and details to develop your essay.

### TYPE 2: COMPARE AND CONTRAST PROMPTS

**EXAMPLE 1**

Some students enjoy attending large classes with many students. Other students prefer to attend small classes with few students. Discuss the advantages of both types of classroom, and then state which type you prefer. Explain your viewpoint.

**EXAMPLE 2**

Some students like to spend many hours outlining and brainstorming before they begin a writing assignment. Other students prefer to begin writing immediately, with little planning. Compare these two writing methods, and then state which method you prefer. Use specific examples to support your preference.

### TYPE 3: PERSONAL OPINION PROMPTS

**EXAMPLE 1**

What profession do you believe benefits society most? Use specific reasons and examples to support you opinion.

**EXAMPLE 2**

In what government program do you think your country should invest more money? Explain your viewpoint using details and examples.

# E. INTRODUCTION FORMAT

The introduction of an essay is formed by combining a *general statement* and a *thesis*.

The *general statement* introduces the prompt that you will discuss throughout your response. It should be the first one or two sentences of your introduction, and it **should present information broadly.**

**+**

The *thesis* is your response to a writing prompt. A thesis should be a single sentence located in the introduction; it should provide an opinion that fully responds to the essay prompt **without including minor details.**

# F. BRAINSTORMING IDEAS

When brainstorming and writing an Independent response, you must *choose one viewpoint* that you can develop using details and explanations.

When brainstorming your response, address the three steps that follow:

1) Decide on *an opinion* that answers the question in the prompt. If the prompt asks for your personal opinion, make sure that you choose one opinion that you can then build upon. If the prompt asks you to pick a preference or to agree/disagree with a statement, make sure that you choose a position that you can write about in-depth.

2) Choose two or three ideas that support your viewpoint; you will use these ideas to form *topic sentences* for your body paragraphs, which prove why your thesis is valid.

3) Support your ideas with *explanations*, which provide specific information that relates your support to your thesis.

Your *brainstorm chart* should list simplified versions of your viewpoint, topic sentences, and explanations. Thus, you can remember what you want to include in your final response.

# Step 2. The Introduction (1 Paragraph)

The introduction includes a general statement and a thesis.

- The first sentence of your introduction should be the **general statement,** which broadly introduces the main ideas mentioned in the prompt.

### GENERAL STATEMENT EXPRESSIONS

Recently, there has been controversy about whether _____.

Technology has completely changed the way _____.

Some people believe that _____ while other people feel that _____.

There are so many _____.

There are different opinions regarding _____.

There is an expression that _____.

All over the world, _____.

These days, most people _____.

- Your general statement should be followed by a thesis. Your thesis may or may not include the ideas that you will elaborate on in your body paragraphs.

### THESIS STATEMENT EXPRESSIONS

In my opinion, _____.

As far as I'm concerned, _____.

There is no question that _____.

Personally, I believe that _____.

While some people _____, I believe that _____.

However, if you ask me, _____.

However, if I have to choose one thing that _____, I would say that _____.

If someone asked me whether I should _____, I would have to say _____.

I personally prefer to _____.

However, there are other _____.

Do you agree or disagree with the following statement? Businesses should hire employees for their entire lives. Use specific reasons and examples to support your opinion.

## Reasons for Topic Sentences

| agree | disagree |
|-------|----------|
|       | *unmotivated employees* |
|       | *older employees* |
|       | *lose $* |

**BRAINSTORM**

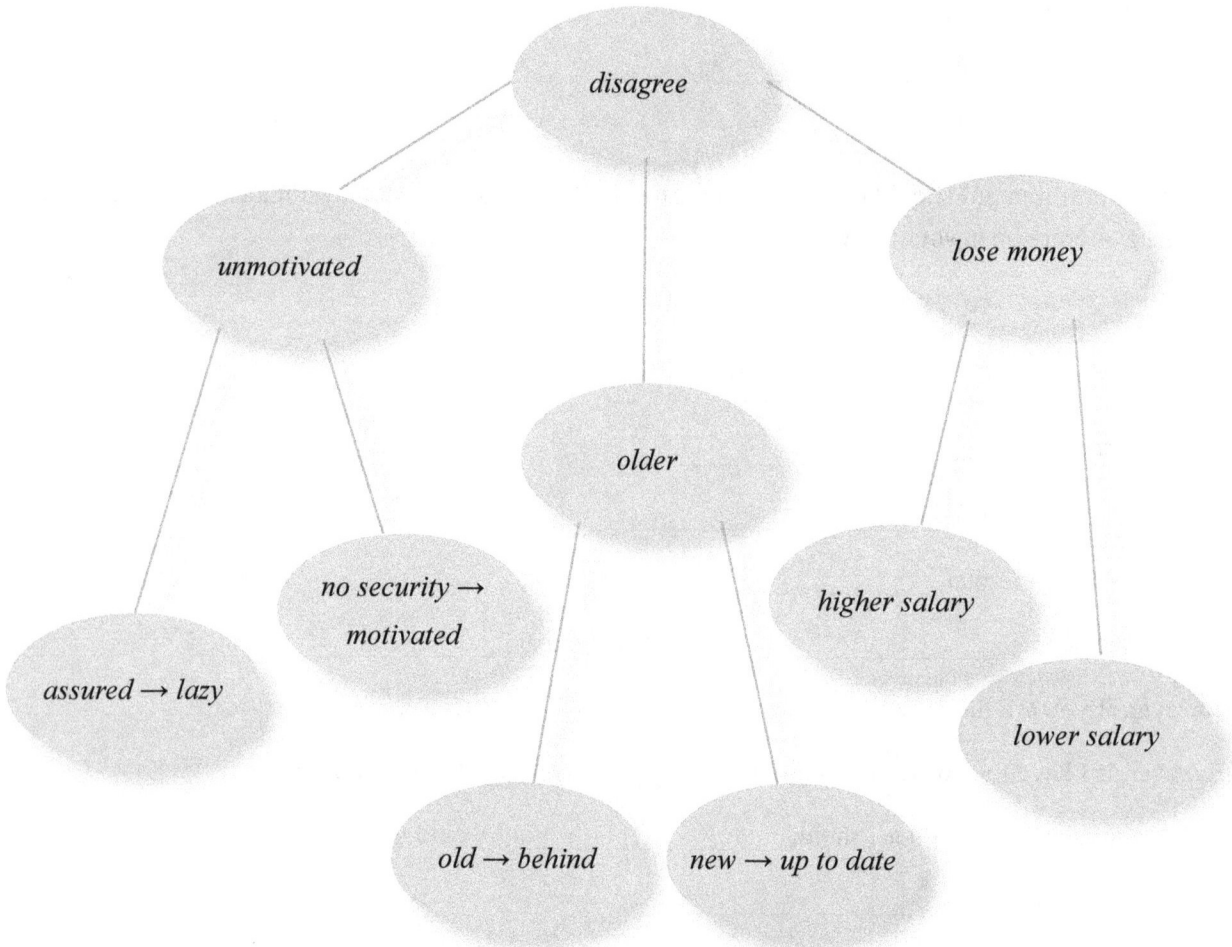

Your thesis statement can include the ideas that you will elaborate on in your body paragraphs.

### Introduction 1 (Thesis *with* reasons listed)

**GENERAL STATEMENT** In some parts of the world, businesses hire employees for their whole lives. Many employers hope that this practice will create stability and loyalty within an organization. **THESIS** However, I believe that guaranteeing lifetime employment is a bad idea. The company will have to deal with unmotivated employees, less skillful employees, and disproportionately high salaries.

If you choose not to introduce your main ideas in your thesis statement, you can add phrases such as "**for several reasons**" and "**for a number of reasons**" at the end of your thesis statement.

### Introduction 2 (Thesis *without* reasons listed)

**GENERAL STATEMENT** In some parts of the world, there are businesses that hire employees for their whole lives. Many employers hope that this practice will create stability and loyalty within an organization. **THESIS** However, I believe that guaranteeing lifetime employment is a bad idea **for a number of reasons**.

# G. THE BODY PARAGRAPHS

To complete a body paragraph, you must provide **explanations** that demonstrate how your topic sentences support your thesis.

> **Prompt**
>
> Do you agree or disagree with the following statement? Businesses should hire employees for their entire lives. Use specific reasons and examples to support your opinion.

### Reasons for Topic Sentences

| agree | disagree |
| --- | --- |
|  | *unmotivated employees* |
|  | *older employees* |
|  | *lose $* |

The **thesis** is the main idea of the entire essay, so it should be placed in the introduction. Each of the "agree" statements in the chart above can be used as the **topic sentences** to the essay's body paragraphs.

**Thesis:** I believe that hiring employees for their entire lives is a bad idea because the company will have to deal with unmotivated employees, less skillful employees, and disproportionately high salaries.

To have enough information to complete your body paragraphs, you must provide **explanations** to prove that your topic sentences are valid points.

**Explanations** are details, examples, or supporting pieces of information. They can be personal experiences that help prove a point, or they can be statistical or scientific pieces of information that provide evidence for an opinion.

**Topic Sentence 1:** Businesses that offer lifetime employment produce unmotivated employees.

### Explanation(s):

1. *When employees feel that they cannot lose their jobs, they become lazy and do as little work as possible.*
2. *Lifetime employees may miss work, arrive late, and neglect assignments because they feel that their job is guaranteed.*
3. *When employees are pressured by the prospect of being fired, they are more motivated.*

## Completed Body Paragraphs

### BODY PARAGRAPH 1

TOPIC SENTENCE  **First**, <u>businesses that offer lifetime employment produce unmotivated employees.</u>  EXAMPLE  When employees feel that they cannot lose their jobs, they become lazy and do as little work as possible.  EXAMPLE  **Therefore**, lifetime employees may miss work, arrive late, and neglect assignments because they feel that their job is guaranteed.  CONTRAST  **However**, when employees are pressured by the prospect of being fired, they are more motivated. They always work hard because they must compete to keep their jobs.

### BODY PARAGRAPH 2

TOPIC SENTENCE  **Second**, <u>businesses that offer lifetime employment must keep older employees regardless of their productivity.</u> Older employees may have health problems, and they are often uninformed about new developments within an industry.  CONTRAST  **However**, many younger employees are healthier and work efficiently. They keep up with the latest trends in business and productivity.  CONSEQUENCE  **Thus**, younger employees help businesses move forward and grow.

### BODY PARAGRAPH 3

TOPIC SENTENCE  **Finally**, <u>businesses that offer lifetime employment lose money by paying older employees higher salaries.</u> The longer an employee works at a company, the more he or she is paid.  CONSEQUENCE  **As a result**, having a company full of lifetime employees is a big drain on a company's revenue.  CONTRAST  **However**, periodically hiring new employees keeps salary costs down, saving companies large amounts of money. After all, a company's goal is to make a profit, so it should not waste money on unproductive workers.

## H. THE CONCLUSION

The last major piece of an Independent Writing response is the conclusion. The **conclusion** is the last paragraph in your essay. In the conclusion, you should summarize the main points presented in your body paragraphs and clarify how each of these main points relates to your thesis.

- Do **not** introduce new main ideas or examples in your conclusion.

### PARAPHRASE → RESTATE → EXPAND

You can create a conclusion by **paraphrasing** and **summarizing** your thesis and main ideas. Then you can conclude your essay by offering further details or examples that demonstrate why your thesis matters or how your essay relates to everyday life.

> **Prompt**
>
> Do you agree or disagree with the following statement? Business should hire employees for their entire lives. Use specific reasons and examples to support your opinion.

**Thesis:** *I believe that hiring employees for their entire lives is a bad idea for a number of reasons.*

| Formula for a Conclusion | Example |
|---|---|
| 1) **Paraphrase** your thesis to remind the reader what your essay focused on. | *In conclusion, I firmly disagree that companies should hire employees for their entire careers.* |
| 2) **Restate** the main ideas that you used to support your thesis throughout the essay. | *Doing so creates an unenthusiastic, unproductive, and unprofitable environment.* |
| 3) **Expand** upon your main ideas by telling the reader how your support might relate to real-life experience. | *I would not recommend a lifetime hiring policy to any company unless it wants to go out of business.* |

**Conclusion:** *In conclusion, I firmly disagree that companies should hire employees for their entire careers. Doing so creates an unenthusiastic, unproductive, and unprofitable environment. I would not recommend a lifetime hiring policy to any company unless it wants to go out of business.*

**MODEL ANSWER**

In some parts of the world, there are businesses that hire employees for their entire careers. Many employers hope that this practice will create stability and loyalty within an organization. **However, I believe that hiring employees for their entire lives is a bad idea for a number of reasons.**

First, businesses that offer lifetime employment produce unmotivated employees. If employees feel that they cannot lose their jobs, they become lazy and do as little work as possible. Therefore, lifetime employees may miss work, arrive late, and neglect assignments because they feel that their job is guaranteed. However, when employees are pressured by the prospect of being fired, they are more motivated. They always work hard because they must compete to keep their jobs.

Second, businesses that offer lifetime employment must keep older employees regardless of their productivity. Older employees may have health problems, and they are often uninformed about new developments within an industry. However, many younger employees are healthier and work efficiently. They keep up with the latest trends in business and productivity. Thus, younger employees help businesses move forward and grow.

Finally, businesses that offer lifetime employment lose money by paying older employees higher salaries. The longer an employee works at a company, the more he or she is paid. As a result, having a company full of lifetime employees is a big drain on a company's revenue. However, periodically hiring new employees keeps salary costs down, saving companies large amounts of money. After all, a company's goal is to make a profit, so it should not waste money on unproductive workers.

In conclusion, I firmly disagree that companies should hire employees for their entire careers. Doing so creates an unenthusiastic, unproductive, and unprofitable environment. I would not recommend a lifetime hiring policy to any company unless it wants to go out of business.

## TYPE 1: AGREE/DISAGREE PROMPTS

If the Independent Writing prompt asks you to *agree* or *disagree* with a viewpoint, your first task should be to choose a side to defend.

**RESPONSE FORMAT**

**Introduction**

General statement
+
Thesis

**Body Paragraph 1**

*First,* **Topic sentence 1**
+
Explanation
+
Explanation

**Body Paragraph 2**

*Second,* **Topic sentence 2**
+
Explanation
+
Explanation

**Body Paragraph 3
(optional)**

*Third,* **Topic sentence 3**
+
Explanation
+
Explanation

**Conclusion**

*To conclude,*
_____
(Paraphrase **introduction** and
expand on main ideas)

Do you agree or disagree with the following statement? A person should never make an important decision alone. Use specific reasons and examples to support your answer.

## SAMPLE RESPONSE

Life is filled with decisions both significant and insignificant. In some cases, we make the decisions ourselves. In other cases, we rely on the help of friends and family. **In my opinion, one needs to strike a balance between listening to oneself and listening to others. Doing so allows one to benefit from important personal and financial decisions.**

For one, it is sometimes best to make important decisions on one's own. For example, when choosing a husband or wife, a person must reflect upon who he or she is most compatible with. Parents and friends might think that they know who will make a good life partner, but they are often wrong. When a decision is very personal, it is often best to make that decision on one's own.

However, it is better to receive input from others in some situations. For instance, when making an important purchase, such as a car or a house, it is often helpful to talk to experts who can help one make a financially and qualitatively sound choice. Failing to do so may result in being cheated by salespeople who simply want to make money. Alternately, one who makes a large purchase without consulting an expert may end up buying a low-quality product and regretting it for a very long time.

Therefore, I believe that the best way for a person to make important decisions is to strike a balance between conferring with oneself and conferring with others. In very personal situations, one must make his or her own decisions. In situations where outside experts can provide assistance, it is best to confer with others. By following these rules, one is likely to make successful decisions.

## TYPE 2: COMPARE AND CONTRAST PROMPTS

Some prompts will ask you to **compare** and **contrast** two viewpoints and then pick a side to support. In these cases, briefly mention the contrasting viewpoints in your introduction, and then use your body paragraphs to discuss each viewpoint in greater detail to better argue why your viewpoint is more valid.

**RESPONSE FORMAT**

**Introduction**

> **General statement**
> **+**
> **Thesis**

**Body Paragraph 1**

> *On the one hand,* **Topic sentence 1**
> **+**
> Explanation
> **+**
> Explanation

**Body Paragraph 2**

> *On the other hand,* **Topic sentence 2**
> **+**
> Explanation
> **+**
> Explanation

**Body Paragraph 3**

> *Moreover,* **Topic sentence 3**
> **+**
> Explanation
> **+**
> Explanation

**Conclusion**

> *In conclusion,*
> _____
> (Paraphrase **introduction** and expand on main ideas)

Some people trust their first impressions about a person's character because they believe that these judgments are generally correct. Other people do not judge a person's character quickly because they believe first impressions are often wrong. Compare these two attitudes. Which attitude do you agree with? Support your choice with specific examples.

**SAMPLE RESPONSE**

Some people argue that trusting your first impressions is dangerous. After all, a person who is shy during a first encounter may become more open during later encounters. Others claim that you can gauge a person's personality after just one encounter. **If I had to choose between the two, I would say that I make better judgments based upon first impressions.**

On the one hand, some people do not judge a person's character immediately because they do not trust their first impressions. These people may believe that relationships should be established slowly and carefully. Those who ignore their first impressions may prove to be just as friendly and trusting as those who trust their first impressions, but it often takes them longer to develop the same level of confidence.

On the other hand, some people trust their first impressions about a person because they believe these judgments are usually accurate. These people may have excellent intuition, and they can sense something about another person's character without thinking. In all likelihood, these intuitive people spend a great deal of time around others. These individuals, with social personalities and familiarity with the feelings of others, are well equipped to gauge people's personalities

Personally, I tend to rely on my first impressions when meeting a person. Generally, I can very accurately determine another person's character. For instance, my girlfriend and I have been together for five years. I knew she was the one for me the first time we met. Likewise, I have known my two closest friends since elementary school. When we first met in the third grade, I knew that they would be my friends for life.

Ultimately, I tend to trust my first impressions because my experiences have proven that I have excellent intuition. Of course, there is no right way to judge a person's character, and everyone must discover his or her own strategy when forming judgments.

## TYPE 3: PERSONAL OPINION PROMPTS

Some prompts will ask for your *personal opinion* about something. The process for outlining these prompts is very similar to the Type 1, agree/disagree prompts discussed earlier.

**RESPONSE FORMAT**

**Introduction**

General statement
+
**Thesis**

**Body Paragraph 1**

*For one,* **Topic sentence 1**
+
Explanation
+
Explanation

**Body Paragraph 2**

*Furthermore,* **Topic sentence 2**
+
Explanation
+
Explanation

**Body Paragraph 3
(optional)**

*Finally,* **Topic sentence 3**
+
Explanation
+
Explanation

**Conclusion**

*Therefore,*
_____
(Paraphrase **introduction** and
expand on main ideas)

You need to travel from your home to a place that is 60 kilometers away. Compare the different kinds of transportation you could use. State which method of travel you would choose. Give specific reasons for your choice.

## SAMPLE RESPONSE

Every person has a preferred method of travel. Many environmentally conscious people choose to ride a bike or take public transportation, while those who prefer speed and privacy might choose the convenience of a car. **My favorite way to travel long distances is by train, but there are also advantages to traveling by car or by bus.**

For instance, traveling from my home to a place 60 kilometers away by car has some benefits. For one, I can make my own schedule because I do not have to wait for the bus or train to pick me up at a certain time. Likewise, I can travel in peace and quiet because I do not have to deal with the crowds that are always gathered at train and bus stations. Instead, I can enjoy my drive by listening to the radio or a CD of my choice.

Moreover, there are advantages to traveling from my home to a place 60 kilometers away by bus. Generally, traveling by bus is cheaper than traveling by car or train, so traveling by bus saves me money. On the road, buses have priority over cars; they travel in lanes that are less crowded than automobile lanes, so they often reach their destinations faster than cars.

However, if I had to choose one method of transportation, I would choose to travel by train. Traveling by train has two significant advantages over traveling by car or bus. For one, trains are faster than both cars and buses. In Korea, the roads are always crowded. Even at its best, the traffic rarely moves quickly. However, trains are not constrained by traffic because they travel on railway tracks. Moreover, I can get work done on a train. In a car, I have to focus my attention on driving, and in buses, it is too noisy to do work. Traveling by train allows me to be productive even when I travel.

Ultimately, if I had to travel from my house to a place 60 kilometers away, I could travel by car, by bus, or by train. Each form of transportation has its unique advantages. However, the advantages of traveling by train outweigh those of traveling by car or bus, so I would choose to travel by train.

# L. INDEPENDENT WRITING CHECKLIST

Here is a checklist to help you review your Independent response.

## 1. ESSENTIALS CHECK

| | | |
|---|---|---|
| **Introduction** | ✓ | The general statement mentions the main topic discussed in the essay, and the thesis in the introduction addresses the prompt and presents a viewpoint. |
| **Topic Sentence** | ✓ | Each body paragraph has a topic sentence that supports the thesis statement and provides a main idea for the paragraph. |
| **Explanations** | ✓ | Each body paragraph contains explanations such as examples, details, or reasons that support the main idea of the paragraph. |
| **Transitions** | ✓ | Transition words are used between paragraphs and between sentences to show the relationship between ideas. |
| **Conclusion** | ✓ | The conclusion summarizes the main points and connects them to the thesis. |

## 2. GRAMMAR CHECK

| | | |
|---|---|---|
| **Subject-Verb Agreement** | ✓ | The correct verb matches the subject of each sentence. |
| **Pronouns** | ✓ | Each pronoun matches its *antecedent*—the word or words that the pronoun is referring to—in number. |
| **Spelling & Punctuation** | ✓ | Spelling and punctuation are correct. |

## 3. STYLE CHECK

| | | |
|---|---|---|
| **Word/Sentence Variety** | ✓ | Words and sentence structures are varied to avoid repetition. |
| **Clarity** | ✓ | Ideas and sentences are clearly stated. Word usage is accurate and appropriate. |

| | |
|---|---|
| **5** | For the most part, the essay accomplishes all of the following points:<br><br>• The response completely addresses the topic and handles the task effectively.<br>• The response is effectively developed and is well organized.<br>• Examples, explanations, and/or details are appropriate and clearly stated.<br>• The response demonstrates coherence, integration, and appropriate organization.<br>• The entire response shows skill in language usage. This includes the ability to vary sentences and use the correct words and idioms. Minor grammatical or vocabulary errors may occur. |
| **4** | For the most part, the essay accomplishes all of the following points:<br><br>• The response addresses the topic and handles the task well. Some points may not be completely addressed.<br>• In general, the response is well organized and well developed.<br>• Explanations, examples, and/or details are appropriate and clearly stated.<br>• The response demonstrates coherence, integration, and appropriate organization. Occasional repetitions or imprecise connections may occur.<br>• The response shows skill in language usage. The response varies sentence structure and vocabulary usage. Occasional minor errors may occur but do not impact meaning. Errors may include those relating to composition, word form, or idiomatic language usage. |
| **3** | The essay is identified by one or more of the following:<br><br>• The essay responds to the topic and handles the task. Explanations, examples, and/or details are somewhat developed.<br>• The response demonstrates coherence, integration, and appropriate organization. Connections between concepts may be vague at times.<br>• Unclear meanings may result from incorrect sentence formation and word choice.<br>• The response may show a limited, although accurate, range of vocabulary and sentence structures. |
| **2** | The essay has one or more of the following issues:<br><br>• The response is limited in development.<br>• The organization is poor, and/or the connections between concepts are weak.<br>• The response has incorrect or too few examples, explanations, or details to support generalizations.<br>• The choice of words or word forms is obviously incorrect.<br>• Sentence structures and/or word usage errors are common. |
| **1** | The essay has serious issues, including one or more of the following:<br><br>• The response is seriously disorganized or not developed enough.<br>• The response does not demonstrate relevant use of details, or it shows a misunderstanding of the prompt.<br>• There are many major errors in the sentence structure or usage. |
| **0** | • The essay does not relate to the topic.<br>• The essay is written in a language other than English, is unwritten, or consists of keystrokes. |

# Chapter 3
# WRITING
# TASKS

# Integrated Writing Task 1

## PASSAGE

Most American states sponsor some form of public lottery. To participate, a person buys one or more low-priced, numbered tickets, which go into a collection containing all other participants' tickets. Then a computer randomly selects one of the ticket numbers, and the owner of that ticket wins most of the money. Everyone hopes to gain something from the lottery: participants hope to win millions of dollars, small shops hope that customers will be lured in by the ticket sales, and states hope that many people will play because states can claim a portion of the ticket money.

Public lotteries benefit the public by supporting state government programs. For example, in California, a percentage of lottery earnings is earmarked, or set aside, for schools. In Pennsylvania, a majority of the money goes toward programs for senior citizens. Many states collect tens of millions of dollars through lotteries.

Moreover, lotteries help boost local economies. In the United States, small retail stores are the largest distributors of lottery tickets. By selling tickets, the retailers draw customers who spend more money on merchandise, benefiting the small businesses. In addition, when lottery winnings are distributed, winners tend to spend much of their money on various products and services. In particular, the real estate market profits from big winners.

But most of all, lotteries benefit the participants. Many lottery winners in the U.S. have low incomes. Thus, lotteries give a few individuals the chance to break multi-generational patterns of poverty. More than half of the winners polled in a recent study said that they were happier after winning; many had moved from apartments into single-family homes, traveled, and given money to family members. The lottery improves the lives of those who win.

🔊 Now listen to part of a lecture on the topic you just read about.

## Notes

| P: | L: |
|---|---|
| | |
| | |
| | |

**Prompt**

Summarize the points made in the lecture, being sure to explain how they oppose specific points made in the reading passage.

_____

_____

_____

_____

_____

_____

_____

_____

_____

_____

_____

_____

_____

_____

_____

_____

_____

_____

_____

_____

# Model Answer

Most American states sponsor some form of public lottery. To participate, a person buys one or more low-priced, numbered tickets, which go into a collection containing all other participants' tickets. Then a computer randomly selects one of the ticket numbers, and the owner of that ticket wins most of the money. Everyone hopes to gain something from the lottery: participants hope to win millions of dollars, small shops hope that customers will be lured in by the ticket sales, and states hope that many people will play because states can claim a portion of the ticket money.

Public lotteries benefit the public by supporting state government programs. For example, in California, a percentage of lottery earnings is earmarked, or set aside, for schools. In Pennsylvania, a majority of the money goes toward programs for senior citizens. Many states collect tens of millions of dollars through lotteries.

Moreover, lotteries help boost local economies. In the United States, small retail stores are the largest distributors of lottery tickets. By selling tickets, the retailers draw customers who spend more money on merchandise, benefiting the small businesses. In addition, when lottery winnings are distributed, winners tend to spend much of their money on various products and services. In particular, the real estate market profits from big winners.

But most of all, lotteries benefit the participants. Many lottery winners in the U.S. have low incomes. Thus, lotteries give a few individuals the chance to break multi-generational patterns of poverty. More than half of the winners polled in a recent study said that they were happier after winning; many had moved from apartments into single-family homes, traveled, and given money to family members. The lottery improves the lives of those who win.

## LECTURE

*Those who market public lotteries praise their benefits. But when you scrutinize the evidence, are these praises justified? Well, not always. In fact, I'll even make the argument that lotteries harm more people than they benefit.*

*To start, the public programs that are supposed to benefit from the lotteries don't usually receive extra funding from increased lottery sales. One reason is that state legislatures may use the lottery money in place of tax-generated money, not in addition to it. So legislators support the lottery because they can claim to oppose taxes while still having lottery money to spend on government programs.*

*Next, lotteries don't help small businesses and local economies. While many small retail outlets sell lottery tickets, studies show that their overall earnings don't improve as a result of lottery sales. Since nearly all convenience stores offer the tickets, there's no real competitive advantage. In terms of benefiting from the windfall, the biggest lottery winners tend to spend their winnings outside of their communities, on travel and housing in other areas.*

*Finally, there are two reasons that lotteries don't benefit individuals. One is that the lottery is a prime example of a regressive tax, or a tax that weighs more heavily on the poor as a percentage of income. Because of their relatively low income, poor people spend a larger portion of their money on lottery tickets. And as poorer people hand over their hard-earned wages, the chance of anyone winning remains almost nonexistent. Some sources have figured that one is more likely to become a parent to identical quadruplets or to become president of the United States than to win the lottery. And even if you do win, wealth is not guaranteed. The federal government takes a big slice of the prize as a tax, you may struggle to manage spending, and friends and family may bombard you with requests for money. Up to one-third of winners end up bankrupt within a few years.*

Notes

| P: benefits of lotteries | L: refutes reading |
|---|---|
| support state programs | state programs don't get extra $ |
| boost local econ. | no benefit to small business/local econ. |
| break poverty patterns | financially harmful to poor<br>bankruptcy among $1/3$ of winners |

The lecture refutes each claim stated in the reading, arguing that public lotteries are not beneficial and, in fact, may be harmful. The reading asserts that public lotteries are beneficial to government programs, local economies, and lucky individuals.

In the reading, public lotteries are praised as a source of supplementary income for the government, providing additional funding for government programs. Also, the passage states that public lotteries support local small business, because people often buy other goods when they stop in to buy lottery tickets. Finally, the reading claims that public lotteries are good because random, individual taxpayers can change their lives in positive ways by winning a lottery.

The lecture refutes each claim in turn. According to the lecture, governments do not use lottery ticket sales to provide extra funding to government programs. Rather, they replace government money with lottery earnings, a system that does nothing to benefit these programs. Moreover, local businesses do not profit significantly from the sale of lottery tickets; so many retail outlets offer lottery tickets that any financial benefit from selling the tickets is diluted among tens of thousands of businesses. Finally, the odds of winning enough in a public lottery to live on the proceeds are incredibly low. Among the very few people who do win big, up to a third wind up bankrupt within a few years.

# Independent Writing Task I

> **Prompt**
>
> Do you agree or disagree with the following statement? People who develop many different skills are more successful than those who master just one skill. Use specific details in your discussion.

**Brainstorm**

▸ **Prompt** ◂
Do you agree or disagree with the following statement? People who develop many different skills are more successful than those who master just one skill. Use specific details in your discussion.

**Brainstorm**

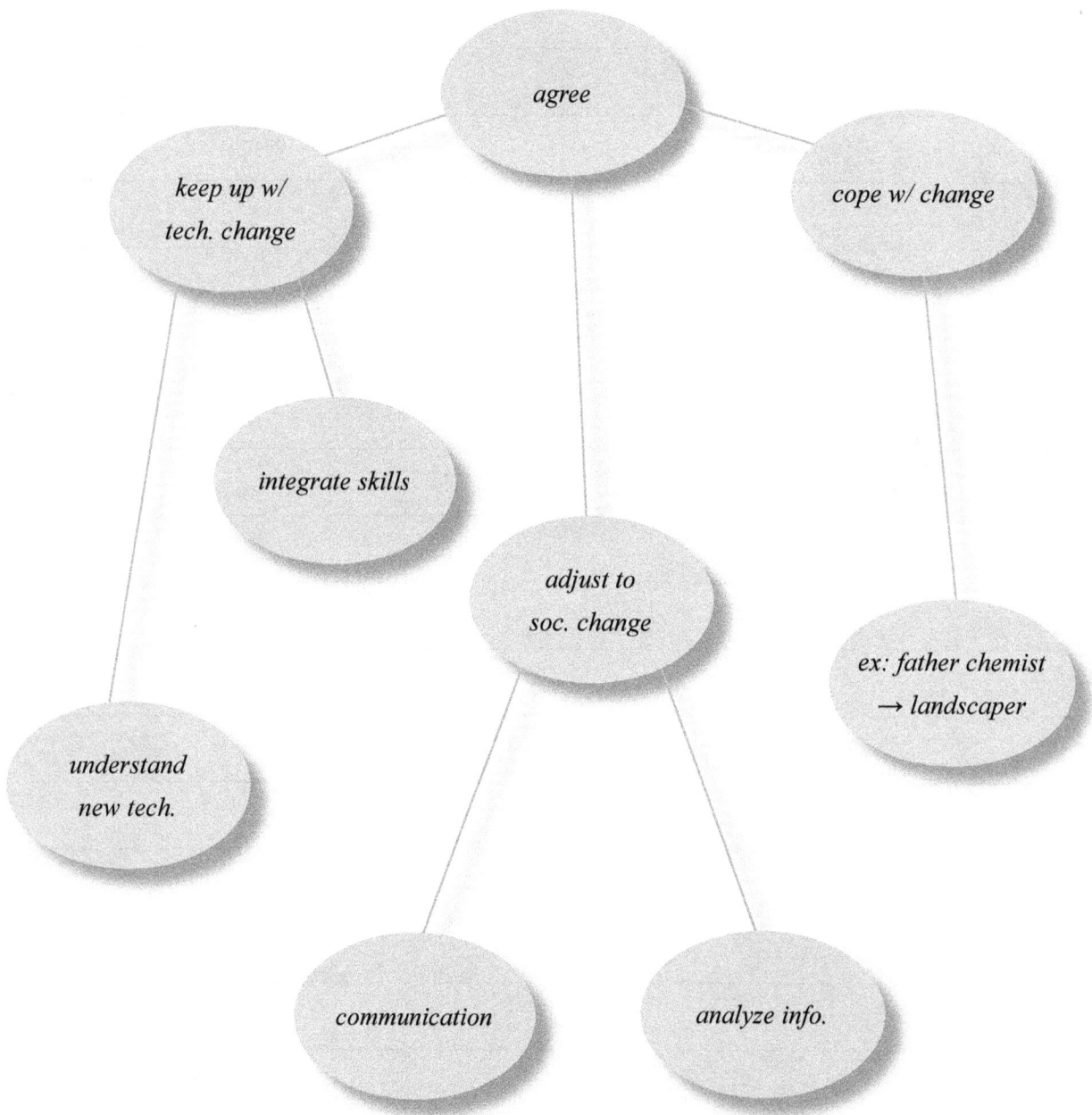

Specialization used to be the best way to ensure long-term employment and success. However, technology is reshaping many industries and rendering once-crucial skills obsolete. Thus, specialization has become impractical rather than necessary. **Developing just one skill does not allow a person to adapt. People who develop a variety of basic skills can successfully cope with changes in technology, society, and their personal lives.**

For one, learning many basic skills can help a person keep up with technological change. A person with many skills will have basic knowledge of numerous subjects, which leads to a clearer understanding of cross-disciplinary fields, such as bioengineering and science writing. Besides boosting general understanding, possessing a variety of skills also helps one in specific technological tasks. For example, a teacher with wide-ranging knowledge and a variety of skills could create an educational website after brief technical training.

A variety of skills also helps a person adjust to societal changes. For instance, online communication such as emails, blogs, Tweets, and text messages increasingly influences human interactions, a person needs to be able to communicate in many different ways to express himself or herself clearly. Additionally, as society is saturated with information, general analytical abilities may help individuals define where they stand on political issues and personal values.

Finally, developing many skills helps one cope with dramatic changes in life, such as career crises. For example, my father worked as a chemist for over a decade, but a few years ago his lab closed down and he lost his job. While he searched for a new lab job, he spent much of his free time on his hobby—landscaping the yard. A few of our neighbors were impressed with his work, and they hired him to landscape their yards as well. Because my father minored in business and accounting in college, he was able to start his own landscaping business. Now his hobby is also his profession.

Clearly, succeeding in today's society depends upon intellectual flexibility. People have to be able to transform and change themselves to fit the moment. No one can see into the future, but it is certain that society and technology will never stop changing, and success comes from changing with them.

# Independent Writing Task II

Are people with ambitious goals more likely to succeed than people with realistic goals are?
Use specific examples and reasons to support your opinion.

## Brainstorm

_____

_____

_____

_____

_____

_____

_____

_____

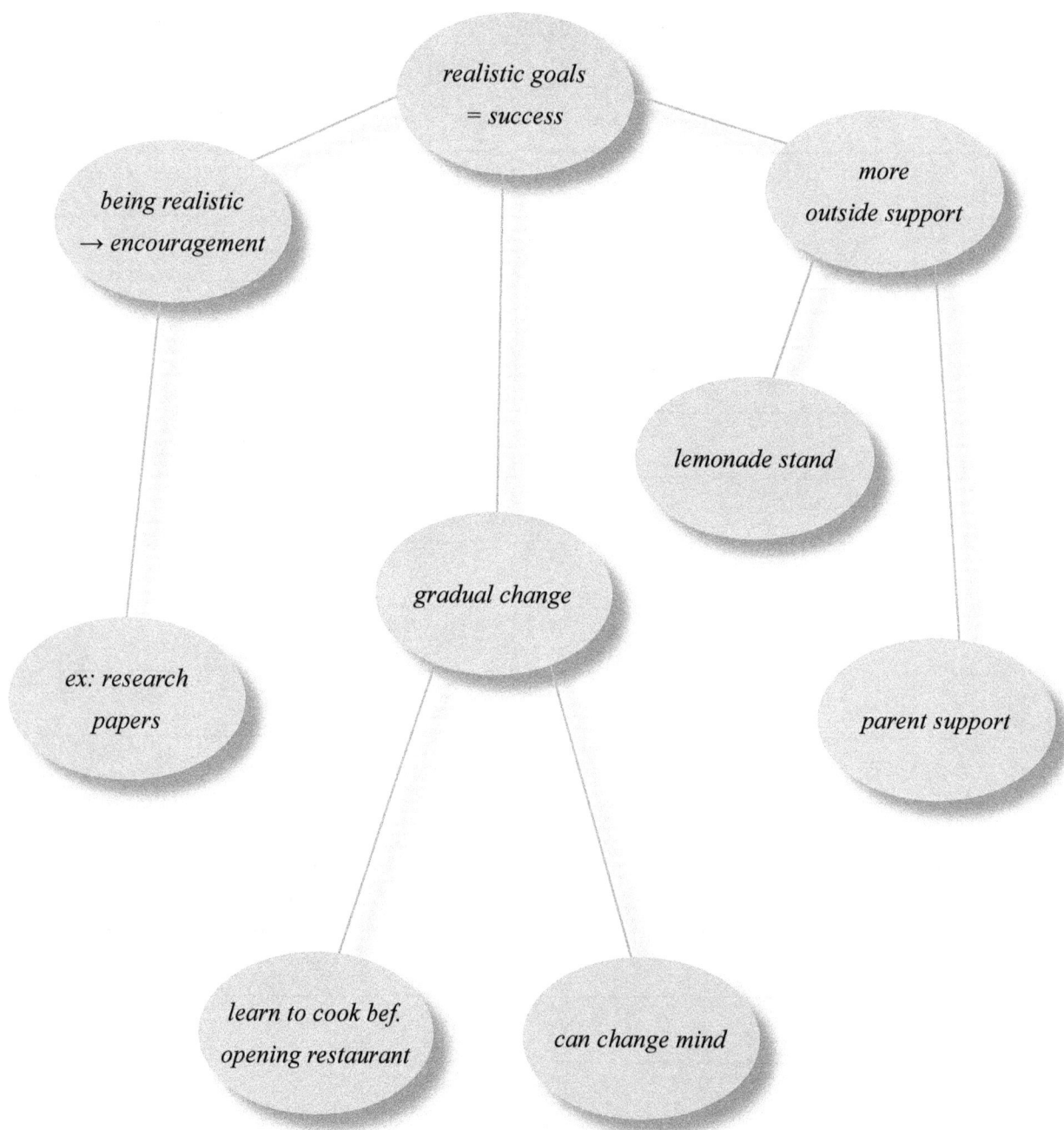

# Model Answer

Prompt

**Prompt**

Are people with ambitious goals more likely to succeed than people with realistic goals are?
Use specific examples and reasons to support your opinion.

**Brainstorm**

*realistic goals
= success*

*being realistic
→ encouragement*

*more
outside support*

*lemonade stand*

*gradual change*

*ex: research
papers*

*parent support*

*learn to cook bef.
opening restaurant*

*can change mind*

A wise problem-solving strategy is to divide a problem into smaller pieces, which can be solved one at a time. **The same can be said for goals. A person is more likely to find success if he or she sets small, realistic goals and accomplishes these goals one at a time.**

By pursuing realistic goals, a person is more likely to succeed, and success is encouraging. Beginning research papers used to overwhelm me, as I never knew where to begin my research or my writing. However, I discovered that creating a list of everything I had to do helped me organize my thoughts. Using this step-by-step process made my papers much more organized, which resulted in better grades and improved confidence. Breaking a large project into a series of realistic goals encouraged me to become a better, more organized writer.

Setting realistic goals allows people to make small, gradual changes to their lives, allowing them to confirm that they are taking their desired paths in life. For instance, suppose that someone dreams of opening a restaurant. The first realistic goal may be learning how to cook. If the person truly enjoys cooking, he or she can then take restaurant jobs and see what the restaurant industry is like. Finally, the person can look for a small site and develop a short menu. Thus, one seemingly impossible, ambitious goal can be achieved gradually, with opportunities along the way to change course.

A final reason for setting small, realistic goals is that others may be more willing to help or invest. For example, if a child declares that he wants to create a new brand of lemonade, adults are not likely to take him seriously. But if the child wants to set up a lemonade stand on the sidewalk for a day, most parents would be happy to provide the lemonade, as well as the cups and the table.

In conclusion, ambition is a strong quality, but it is only useful when balanced by practicality. Therefore, people should be ambitious, but they should pursue their ambitions by setting a series of small, realistic goals.

# Integrated Writing Task 2

## PASSAGE

Many species, including humans, possess the ability to recognize danger and react with extra strength or speed—the "fight or flight" response. Unfortunately, the worries and fears of modern life may unnecessarily trigger the same physical responses that helped save early humans from predators. These stress responses cause a host of physical and mental problems over time. Yet there is also a timeless, simple way to soothe the body's stress responses: meditation.

Medical research largely supports the health benefits of meditation. Even sitting quietly in a chair for 5 to 20 minutes to calm one's thoughts, and basic breathing exercises can lower blood pressure and heart rate, and boost the immune system. One typical objective of meditation is to remove judgment and criticism from one's thoughts and actions. Perhaps for this reason, meditation has also been shown to decrease feelings of anxiety and depression in many people.

Additionally, meditation is more effective than other stress-reducers such as prescription medication and therapy. While meditation is accessible to everyone and has immediate effects, other methods are much more problematic. For example, not everyone can take up exercise programs or attend therapy sessions for scheduling and financial reasons. And in terms of mental health, not everyone can tolerate the side effects of medicine for anxiety and depression. Meditation, however, is available to people of all income levels and mental states.

Another reason to meditate is that it often makes people more receptive to new experiences and unfamiliar viewpoints. Meditation improves a person's awareness of the needs of others as well as his or her ability to empathize. Thus, meditation benefits the meditator and the people he or she interacts with.

🔊 Now listen to part of a lecture on the topic you just read about.

### Notes

| P: | L: |
|---|---|
|  |  |
|  |  |
|  |  |

**Prompt**

Summarize the points made in the lecture, being sure to explain how they oppose specific points made in the reading passage.

_____

_____

_____

_____

_____

_____

_____

_____

_____

_____

_____

_____

_____

_____

_____

_____

_____

_____

_____

_____

## Model Answer

Many species, including humans, possess the ability to recognize danger and react with extra strength or speed—the "fight or flight" response. Unfortunately, the worries and fears of modern life may unnecessarily trigger the same physical responses that helped save early humans from predators. These stress responses cause a host of physical and mental problems over time. Yet there is also a timeless, simple way to soothe the body's stress responses: meditation.

Medical research largely supports the health benefits of meditation. Even sitting quietly in a chair for 5 to 20 minutes to calm one's thoughts, and basic breathing exercises can lower blood pressure and heart rate, and boost the immune system. One typical objective of meditation is to remove judgment and criticism from one's thoughts and actions. Perhaps for this reason, meditation has also been shown to decrease feelings of anxiety and depression in many people.

Additionally, meditation is more effective than other stress-reducers such as prescription medication and therapy. While meditation is accessible to everyone and has immediate effects, other methods are much more problematic. For example, not everyone can take up exercise programs or attend therapy sessions for scheduling and financial reasons. And in terms of mental health, not everyone can tolerate the side effects of medicine for anxiety and depression. Meditation, however, is available to people of all income levels and mental states.

Another reason to meditate is that it often makes people more receptive to new experiences and unfamiliar viewpoints. Meditation improves a person's awareness of the needs of others as well as his or her ability to empathize. Thus, meditation benefits the meditator and the people he or she interacts with.

### LECTURE

*At one point or another, we all deal with stress in our lives. So people are constantly looking for medical, social, or spiritual methods for battling this stress. As you've seen in the reading, meditation is often advertised as one of the "simple" solutions to getting rid of stress. And while it may work for some people, meditation is not effective for everyone.*

*First, meditation does not always improve physical and mental health. Some people who try meditating actually find clearing their minds to be very stressful. Those who can't completely clear their minds feel that they are not meditating correctly, which may bring about feelings of failure and only increase their anxiety. If they do not have the time or patience to keep trying, they may criticize themselves, which is of course the opposite of the intended effect. Also, for people struggling with mental health problems, meditation may worsen their symptoms.*

*Although meditation is easily accessible, it's not widely practiced. In other words, meditation remains fairly unpopular. Whether people become quickly discouraged because they can't seem to "get it," or whether few people have enough time and a quiet place to meditate, fewer than one in 10 people meditate in the U.S., according to a government survey.*

*Finally, I know this sounds crazy, but sometimes it's important to experience feelings of stress or discomfort. People may misuse meditation to numb feelings of sadness and anger that might motivate them to solve the problems that caused these negative feelings to begin with. That'd be a sad outcome indeed.*

## Notes

| P: meditation fights stress | L: med. not best method for everyone |
|---|---|
| benefits = lower blood pressure/heart rate, boost immune system | doesn't always boost health; may create stress |
| accessible, free; immediate effects | fairly unpopular, not widely practiced in U.S. |
| increased awareness; empathy | impt. to feel stress sometimes; med. may decrease motivation |

The lecture counters the advantages of meditation described in the reading. The lecture maintains that meditation can be helpful to some people, but it does not automatically benefit everyone.

To start, meditation itself can be a stressor. People who try meditation may hope to find relief from their worries, as promised in the reading. Instead, beginners sometimes feel an increase in anxiety if they cannot achieve the desired state of mind. For many people, trying to clear the mind is very challenging. When people fail to clear their minds, they often judge themselves as failures, and that may make them feel worse instead of better. Also, meditation might not be appropriate for people with certain types of mental health issues.

Second, while meditation may seem cheaper, easier, and safer than some other methods of controlling stress, an apparent downside is that few people actually practice meditation. The lecture states that a government survey found that fewer than 10 percent of Americans meditate. Whatever the reason, meditation is unpopular, so it is unlikely to prove helpful to most of the population.

Third, the lecture points out that some people may use meditation as a way to avoid feeling unpleasant emotions. A person who suppresses upsetting feelings through meditation may be less inclined to make necessary changes in his or her life. He or she may also feel less empathy for others.

Therefore, the lecture demonstrates that meditation has pitfalls. Individuals may find it stressful, may not want to do it, and may misuse it. While good for some people, meditation is not a simple cure-all for society's stresses.

# Independent Writing Task I

> **Prompt**
>
> In a certain company, employees have the choice of working in a traditional office with other employees or working alone at home, connected to other employees by computer. Which situation do you prefer? Use specific examples and reasons to explain your view.

## Brainstorm

_____

_____

_____

_____

_____

_____

_____

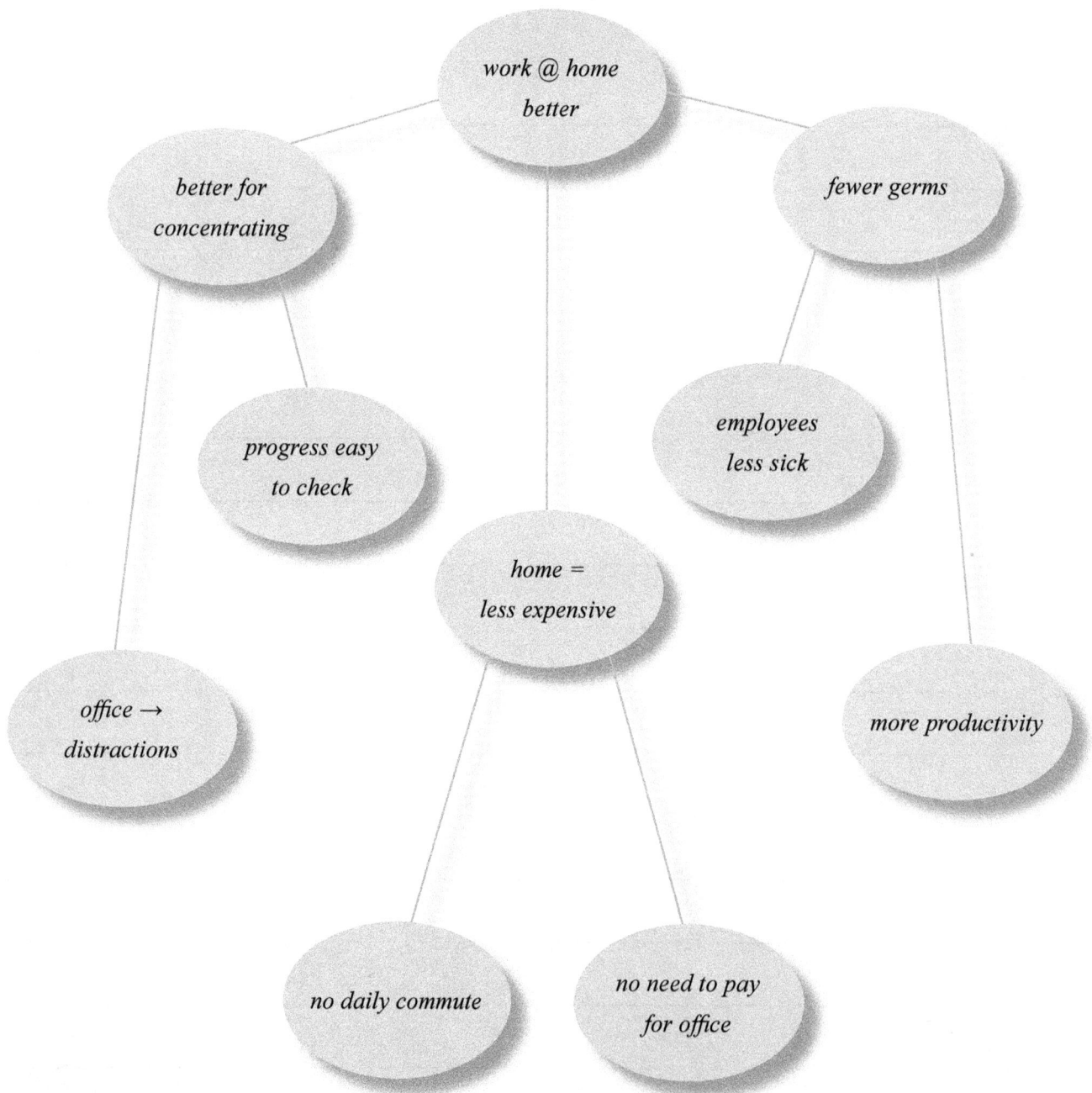

**Prompt**

In a certain company, employees have the choice of working in a traditional office with other employees or working alone at home, connected to other employees by computer. Which situation do you prefer? Use specific examples and reasons to explain your view.

**Brainstorm**

work @ home better

better for concentrating

fewer germs

progress easy to check

employees less sick

home = less expensive

office → distractions

more productivity

no daily commute

no need to pay for office

Computers are increasingly present in homes worldwide, transforming society in many ways. One of the most noticeable changes is that many people can now work from home rather than in an office while remaining linked to coworkers via computer. It is true that some people prefer working with other people in a traditional office setting. **However, working from home is preferable for many jobs because it allows an employee to concentrate, it saves resources, and it helps maintain employees' health.**

Working from home is more efficient than working in an office because offices usually have more distractions. When working at home, an employee may occasionally be tempted to watch television or cook a meal, but these distractions are minimal compared to the amount of time spent at an office celebrating coworkers' birthdays, taking coffee breaks, or chatting with coworkers and clients. Although an employee who works from home cannot be constantly supervised, his or her hard work will be evident when assignments are turned in.

Working from home also eliminates an employee's daily commute, resulting in financial and environmental benefits. Employees save time and money by not having to commute using a car, bus, or train. Employers also save money and natural resources because they are not required to provide office space and then to heat, cool, and equip the office.

Finally, working at home may keep employees healthier, causing them to use fewer sick days than they would while working in an office. Fewer face-to-face interactions between coworkers will prevent the spread of viruses and harmful bacteria. Home-based employees with young children may find that their children do not need to be in daycare as long, so the children are also exposed to fewer germs. In all, if workers and their families are healthier, workers will need less time off and companies will be more efficient.

In short, working at home allows employees to remain focused, save money, and stay healthy. Therefore, working at home provides far more benefits than does working in a traditional office, for workers and employers alike.

# Independent Writing Task II

Some people believe that developing a good reputation is more important than seeking financial success. Other people seek financial success, even if doing so jeopardizes their personal reputations. Explain which of these attitudes you prefer. Use specific reasons and examples to support your opinion.

## Brainstorm

---

---

---

---

---

---

---

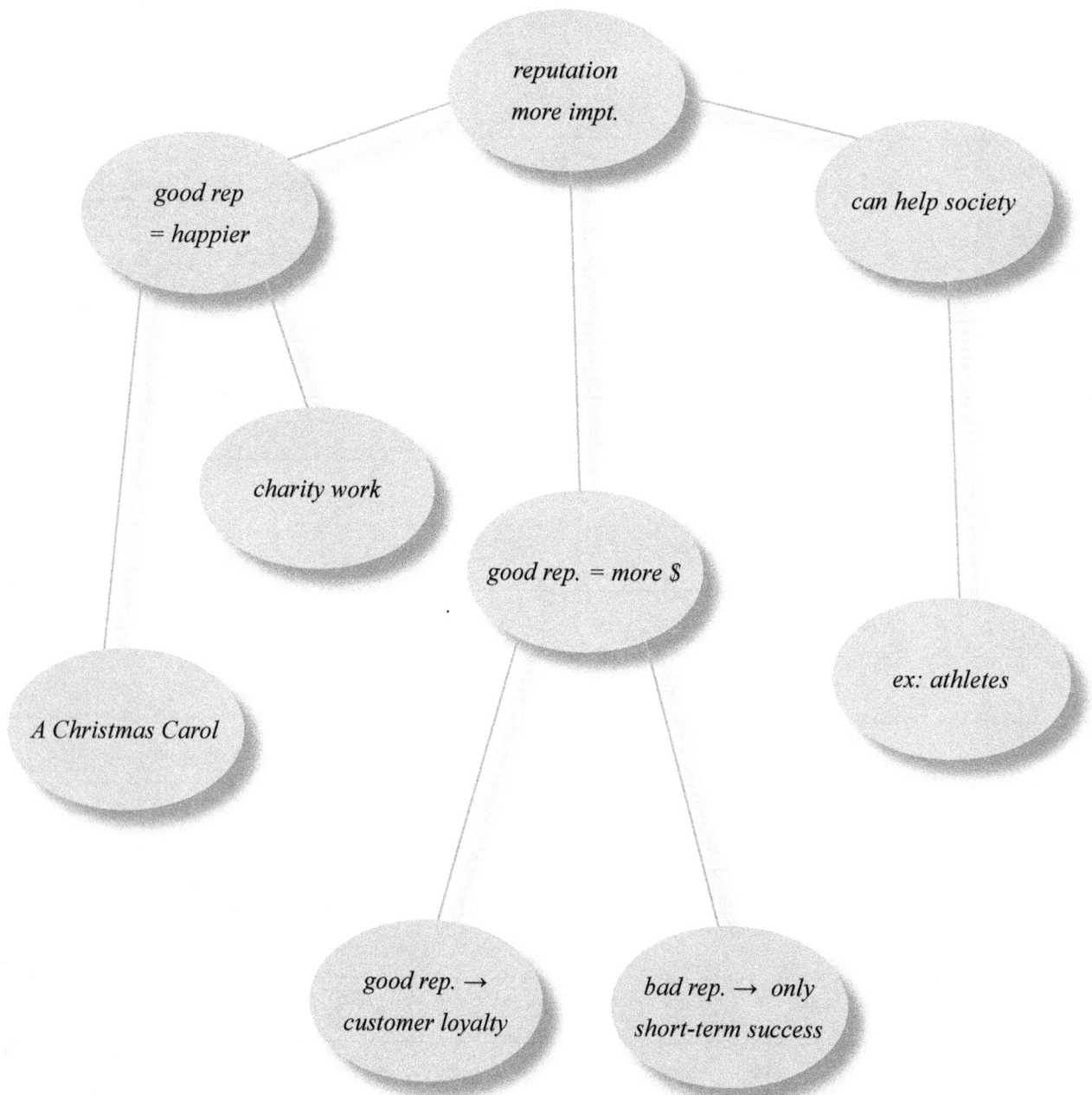

Prompt

Some people believe that developing a good reputation is more important than seeking financial success. Other people seek financial success, even if doing so jeopardizes their personal reputations. Explain which of these attitudes you prefer. Use specific reasons and examples to support your opinion.

**Brainstorm**

reputation more impt.

good rep = happier

can help society

charity work

good rep. = more $

A Christmas Carol

ex: athletes

good rep. → customer loyalty

bad rep. → only short-term success

Everyone can agree that earning money is important. At the same time, one's reputation in the community is priceless. Thinking only about financial gains has more costs than benefits if doing so results in developing a reputation as a dishonest, mean, or selfish person. **In contrast, acting admirably and earning a good reputation has many rewards, even if it does not make a person rich.**

<u>People who develop good reputations tend to be happier than those who are primarily concerned with earning money.</u> Literature is full of stories about how much more satisfying it is to be loved and respected than to have money. In Charles Dickens' tale *A Christmas Carol*, a rich man named Scrooge is hated by everyone because of his greed; Scrooge finds joy only when he becomes openly generous and kind. In my own life, I found that when I took a low-paid job at a nonprofit agency helping others, I felt appreciated and happy, even though I was not earning much money.

Moreover, <u>maintaining a good reputation can often contribute to one's financial success.</u> This is especially true among businesses. If a salesperson has developed a reputation as an honest, reliable individual, he or she will have no trouble attracting loyal customers. Conversely, disreputable businesspeople may succeed temporarily by cheating and lying to others. However, such a businessperson will not be able to earn customers' trust, which is crucial for long-term financial success. Thus, building a good reputation may be a prerequisite for, not an obstacle to, achieving financial success.

Third, <u>focusing on reputation allows one to have a more meaningful impact on society.</u> For example, some professional athletes focus only on the skills necessary to win games. While they may set records statistically and earn good contracts with teams, they are seldom the athletes that fans remember. The athletes who demonstrate good sportsmanship, good teamwork, humor, and generosity towards their community end up serving as role models, especially for children.

In the end, a person's reputation reflects the story of his or her life. Making choices that strengthen one's reputation brings more happiness to oneself, one's family, and one's community.

# Integrated Writing Task 3

One reason that earthquakes are dangerous is that they occur without warning. People have long wished for a way of predicting earthquakes so that they could reach shelter in a safer place before the ground starts shaking. Fortunately, there are several promising methods of predicting earthquakes.

One method is the "animal early warning." Since ancient times, people have noticed that animals' behavior was abnormal before an earthquake. In mid-1970s, Chinese researchers determined that a large earthquake would likely strike in the area of Haicheng sometime within the next two years. Hoping to avoid a disaster, researchers trained volunteers to recognize and report unusual animal behaviors. Soon after this training, reports of odd animal behavior flooded in. After a series of small earthquakes and many more reports about wild and domestic animals acting oddly, officials evacuated Haicheng just in time to save hundreds of thousands of people from the effects of a large earthquake.

Another way of predicting earthquakes is to apply mathematical algorithms to determine the probability of a large earthquake striking a particular region during a particular period. Russian geophysicist Vladimir Keilis-Borok championed the mathematical approach, collaborating with many other scientists. The predictions generated using his methods are said to be 70 percent accurate.

Many researchers believe that it is possible to analyze patterns to predict earthquakes. For example, the "Mogi doughnut" hypothesis, proposed in 1969 by Kiyoo Mogi, held that if researchers find a circular pattern of high seismic activity around an area of low seismic activity, a large earthquake is likely to occur in the center. Other researchers have found correlations between earthquakes and the gravitational pull of the Moon. The idea is that the pull of gravity on the Earth's crust and on the ocean tides may trigger earthquakes. Eventually, researchers may be able to predict large earthquakes based upon the movements of the Moon.

🔊)) Now listen to part of a lecture on the topic you just read about.

Notes

| P: | L: |
|---|---|
| | |
| | |
| | |

**Prompt**

Summarize the points made in the lecture, being sure to explain how they oppose specific points made in the reading passage.

_____

_____

_____

_____

_____

_____

_____

_____

_____

_____

_____

_____

_____

_____

_____

_____

_____

_____

_____

_____

# Model Answer

One reason that earthquakes are dangerous is that they occur without warning. People have long wished for a way of predicting earthquakes so that they could reach shelter in a safer place before the ground starts shaking. Fortunately, there are several promising methods of predicting earthquakes.

One method is the "animal early warning." Since ancient times, people have noticed that animals' behavior was abnormal before an earthquake. In mid-1970s, Chinese researchers determined that a large earthquake would likely strike in the area of Haicheng sometime within the next two years. Hoping to avoid a disaster, researchers trained volunteers to recognize and report unusual animal behaviors. Soon after this training, reports of odd animal behavior flooded in. After a series of small earthquakes and many more reports about wild and domestic animals acting oddly, officials evacuated Haicheng just in time to save hundreds of thousands of people from the effects of a large earthquake.

Another way of predicting earthquakes is to apply mathematical algorithms to determine the probability of a large earthquake striking a particular region during a particular period. Russian geophysicist Vladimir Keilis-Borok championed the mathematical approach, collaborating with many other scientists. The predictions generated using his methods are said to be 70 percent accurate.

Many researchers believe that it is possible to analyze patterns to predict earthquakes. For example, the "Mogi doughnut" hypothesis, proposed in 1969 by Kiyoo Mogi, held that if researchers find a circular pattern of high seismic activity around an area of low seismic activity, a large earthquake is likely to occur in the center. Other researchers have found correlations between earthquakes and the gravitational pull of the Moon. The idea is that the pull of gravity on the Earth's crust and on the ocean tides may trigger earthquakes. Eventually, researchers may be able to predict large earthquakes based upon the movements of the Moon.

## LECTURE

*We've just read some convincing theories about earthquake prediction. Unfortunately, none of these theories has proven consistently effective. No earthquake predictor has ever worked effectively and consistently at any time in history.*

*The first theory mentioned—animal early warning—sounds plausible. It would make sense that animals could hear or otherwise sense disasters before humans could. But as the reading materials mention, the Haicheng earthquake of 1975 followed a series of foreshocks. These smaller advance earthquakes were probably the reason the animals were upset in Haicheng. Over the following decades, there has been no documented case of animals "predicting" a quake.*

*The idea of using mathematics to recognize patterns in earthquake occurrences in a particular spot is also quite problematic. For one thing, mathematical probability typically applies to large regions and periods of time. For instance, these mathematical methods might indicate that a large earthquake is probable within five years in an area with a diameter of 1,000 kilometers. Such vague calculations are not helpful for planning evacuations.*

*Furthermore, be it the Mogi doughnut or tide analysis, proving any hypothesis that involves pattern analysis has one major flaw: there are an estimated 3 million small earthquakes around the globe every year. About 10,000 quakes occur annually in the 4.0 magnitude range, as well as about 20 "big ones" in the 7.0 range. Anyone who claims to have analyzed a pattern and predicted an earthquake is likely to have a high rate of success just because there are so many occurring all the time.*

**Notes**

| **P:** *promising earthquake prediction methods* | **L:** *no accurate prediction method* |
|---|---|
| *animal early warning* | *animals upset at foreshocks (not predicting)* |
| *math algorithms* | *calculations too general to be effective* |
| *pattern analysis* | *flawed conclusions: millions of earthquakes each year* |

The lecture refutes the effectiveness of all the earthquake prediction methods mentioned in the reading, claiming instead that an accurate prediction method does not exist at all.

To start, the lecture emphasizes the unreliability of the animal early warning method. Although the reading claims that animals were able to provide advance warning of the powerful Haicheng earthquake, there is another obvious explanation: the animals were not predicting an earthquake. The lecture proposes that the animals were simply scared by the many small quakes that came before it. No other cases of animals predicting quakes have been documented since.

Using mathematical algorithms seems like it would be more reliable, but the lecturer says that mathematical models provide only general predictions for earthquake locations and times. The predictions cannot tell precisely when or where a quake will occur. Using mathematical models, government officials would only be able to guess when to evacuate an area.

The reading also advocates the use of pattern analysis to predict earthquakes. Some researchers hope that mapping the locations of smaller quakes will allow them to predict the location of a larger quake. Pattern-analysis methods also include tracking the way the Moon's gravity pulls on the Earth because the resulting tides may actually cause earthquakes. But the lecture refutes these methods by claiming that any kind of pattern-based analysis can mistakenly claim to work because millions of earthquakes occur each year; most go unnoticed because they are small or occur in remote areas. Large earthquakes in the 7.0 magnitude range occur almost once a month. Because there are so many earthquakes, any prediction has good odds of being accurate.

# Independent Writing Task I

**▸ Prompt ◂**

In some jobs, employees can choose to work long hours for three days a week or to work fewer hours for five days a week. Which situation do you prefer? Use specific reasons to develop your essay.

**Brainstorm**

_____

_____

_____

_____

_____

_____

_____

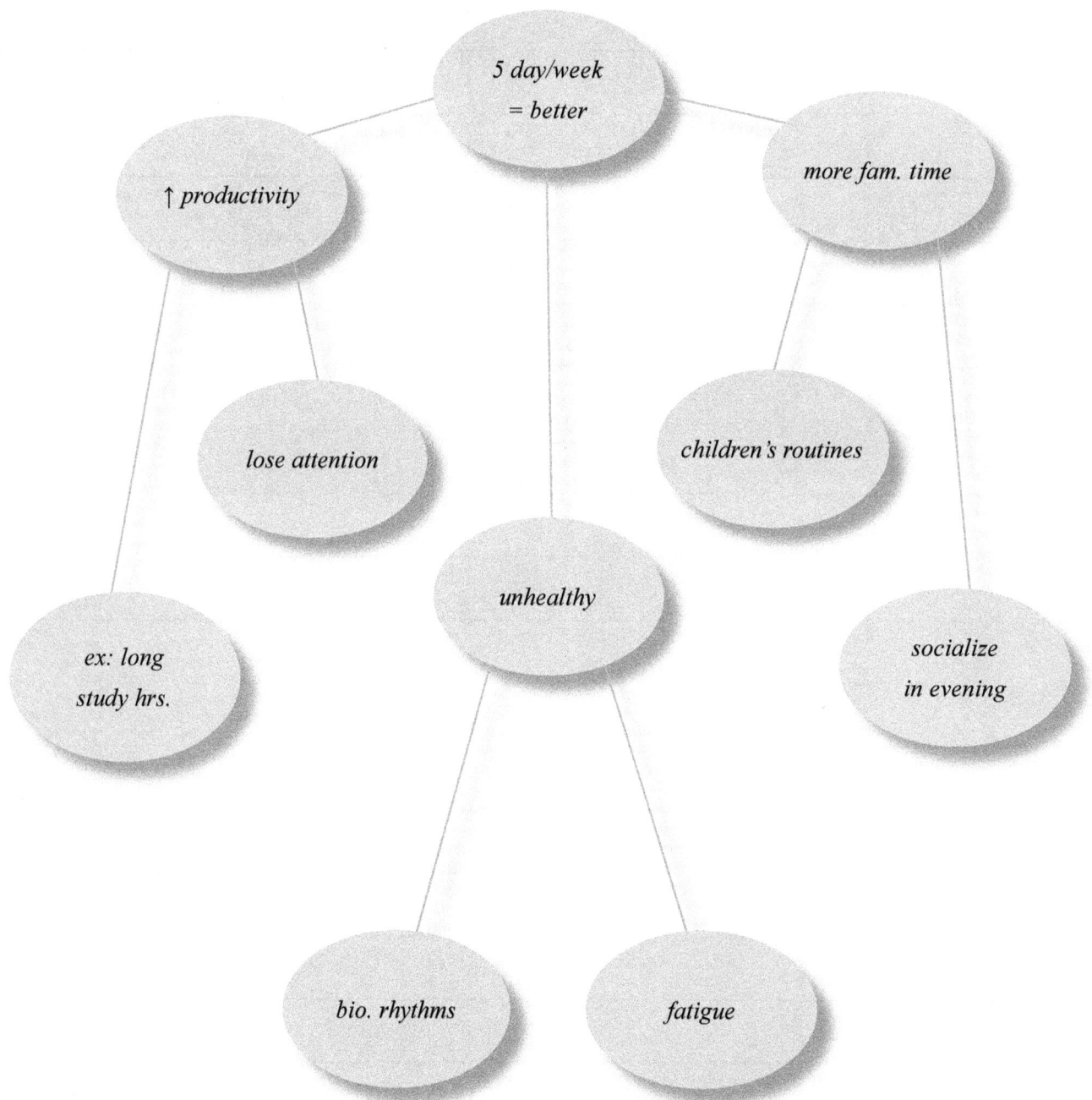

# Model Answer

**➤ Prompt ◄**

In some jobs, employees can choose to work long hours for three days a week or to work fewer hours for five days a week. Which situation do you prefer? Use specific reasons to develop your essay.

## Brainstorm

*5 day/week = better*

*↑ productivity*

*more fam. time*

*lose attention*

*children's routines*

*ex: long study hrs.*

*unhealthy*

*socialize in evening*

*bio. rhythms*

*fatigue*

Everyone appreciates days off from work. Firefighters, nurses, and airline pilots are among the professionals who may be asked to work long hours for fewer days, and many people envy their compact schedules. **However, I prefer working a "normal" work week of eight hours a day for five days a week; doing so allows me to accomplish more at work and also take better care of myself and my family.**

First of all, <u>during the last part of a 10- or 12-hour work day, most people's productivity decreases.</u> For example, I have found that when I try to study for more than eight hours at a time, I reach a point of diminishing returns, when I am too tired to write well or learn many facts. Also, when doing a job that is not as exciting as firefighting, for example, it is hard to stay focused on the work after eight hours. For instance, with typical desk jobs, people are likely to become bored and distracted toward the end of the day.

<u>Another disadvantage of a long workday is that it does not allow one's body to get into a balanced, healthy routine.</u> For example, an airplane pilot may be too tired to cook or exercise upon returning home after a long international flight, or he may feel awake during normal sleeping hours. A nurse who works long, stressful days may feel like she does not receive enough opportunities for rest or relaxation.

<u>The most important reason that regular eight-hour days are preferable is that one can spend regular evening hours with family and friends.</u> For a person with young children, evening hours are particularly important, as children need comforting bedtime routines. Moreover, evening hours are when most social activities take place. I think that most people would prefer to synchronize their schedules with the schedules of the people they care about.

In conclusion, I prefer regular work hours to longer work hours spread over fewer days. On a standard schedule, I am able to be more productive at work, I am not fatigued, and I have more time in the evenings with my family.

# Independent Writing Task II

### Prompt

Do you agree or disagree with the following statement? Although we live in a time when most people have access to an abundance of food, people in the past ate healthier food than do people today. Support your answer with specific examples and reasons.

## Brainstorm

_____

_____

_____

_____

_____

_____

_____

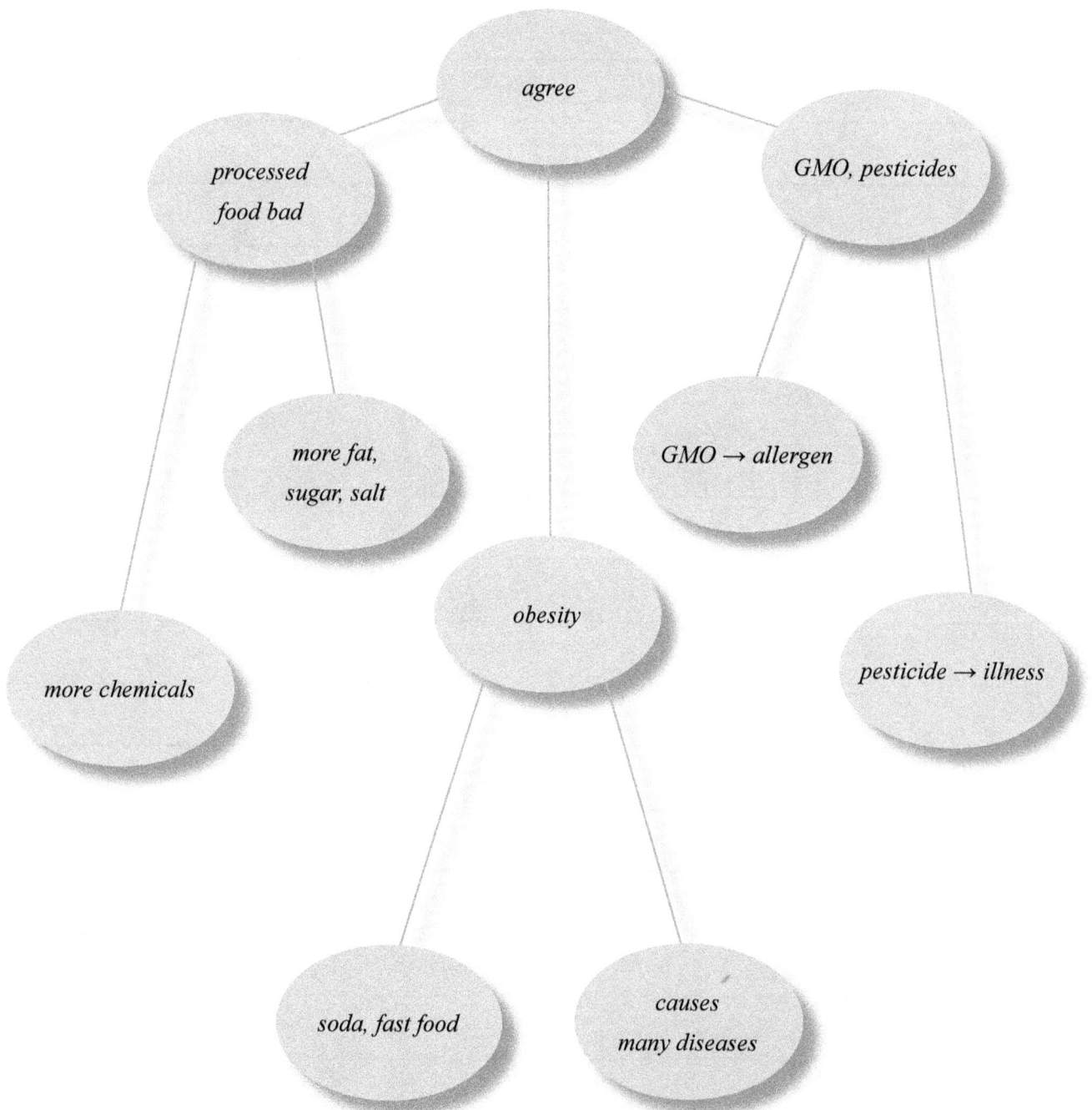

# Model Answer

**▷ Prompt ◁**

Do you agree or disagree with the following statement? Although we live in a time when most people have access to an abundance of food, people in the past ate healthier food than do people today. Support your answer with specific examples and reasons.

## Brainstorm

agree

processed food bad

GMO, pesticides

more fat, sugar, salt

GMO → allergen

more chemicals

obesity

pesticide → illness

soda, fast food

causes many diseases

In developed nations, grocery stores are likely to offer huge numbers of products from all corners of the world. Thus, a person can purchase fresh swordfish from Norway, Peruvian mangoes, and kiwi fruit from New Zealand at any time of year. **Although people have access to more food now than at any other time in history, people in the past actually had healthier diets than people have today. Most modern humans eat too many processed and modified foods that contribute to a variety of health problems.**

First, <u>most people in the developed world rely on processed or prepackaged foods because these choices are more convenient than preparing one's own meals.</u> However, even the simplest foods, such as peanut butter and bread, are modified in factories. Chemicals are often added to preserve freshness, create a desired texture, or color the food. Human bodies may not be adapted to consuming so many chemicals. Even worse, processed foods may contain more fat, sugar, and salt in order to taste and look appealing. For example, most canned soups and packaged ramen contain an excess of salt in each serving.

Moreover, <u>the accessibility of tasty yet unhealthy foods has caused an obesity issue in many countries.</u> Nearly every food establishment serves soda, which is filled with sugar and carbohydrates, and unhealthy fast food restaurants sit on almost every street corner. Before the development of processed foods, people were less likely to overload their bodies with empty calories. And because obesity was less of an issue for previous generations, so too were obesity-related diseases such as high blood pressure and heart failure.

Finally, <u>people today have to worry about whether their food was genetically modified or treated with pesticides.</u> Many researchers are concerned that genetically modified plants may cause unforeseen allergic reactions in some people. Additionally, treating plants with pesticides has long been a controversial practice, as many people have become ill from pesticide exposure. People of the past did not mix chemistry and food as we do today, so their food was less altered and more organic, making it safer for consumption.

To conclude, it is easy to see that people in the past ate healthier food than people do today. Like people in the past, we still eat breakfast, lunch, and dinner, but our meals today are loaded with unnecessary calories and unhealthy additives.

# Integrated Writing Task 4

## PASSAGE

By the time most people are 60 years old, they have some type of back pain. However, no matter how much pain a person experiences, it is unwise to have surgery to correct back pain for several reasons.

To start, surgery cannot fix all back problems, as the causes of back pain vary from person to person. For some people, it is a direct physical problem, such as the deterioration of discs — the pads between the vertebrae. For others, the pain involves cognitive and perceptual processes in the brain. For these individuals, back surgery is of no help. Some do better with antidepressants or anxiety medications. Others do better with an external treatment such as massages or physical therapy.

Additionally, when compared to other types of surgery, most forms of back surgery are relatively new procedures. In other words, every back surgery done is essentially an experimental surgery. As a result, when people have back surgery they are putting themselves at great risk. The nerves in the back are small yet incredibly numerous. Even the smallest surgical mistake can result in even more back pain for a patient.

Finally, even when doctors manage "successful" back surgeries, many patients have a recurrence of pain at the same level within five years. In one study, up to 50 percent of patients over 60 who had surgery returned to the operating table within five years. Sadly, repeat surgeries are even less successful at treating the problem.

◄))  Now listen to part of a lecture on the topic you just read about.

### Notes

| P: | L: |
|---|---|
| | |
| | |
| | |

**Prompt**

Summarize the points made in the lecture, being sure to explain how they oppose specific points made in the reading passage.

_____

_____

_____

_____

_____

_____

_____

_____

_____

_____

_____

_____

_____

_____

_____

_____

_____

_____

_____

PASSAGE

By the time most people are 60 years old, they have some type of back pain. However, no matter how much pain a person experiences, it is unwise to have surgery to correct back pain for several reasons.

To start, surgery cannot fix all back problems, as the causes of back pain vary from person to person. For some people, it is a direct physical problem, such as the deterioration of discs — the pads between the vertebrae. For others, the pain involves cognitive and perceptual processes in the brain. For these individuals, back surgery is of no help. Some do better with antidepressants or anxiety medications. Others do better with an external treatment such as massages or physical therapy.

Additionally, when compared to other types of surgery, most forms of back surgery are relatively new procedures. In other words, every back surgery done is essentially an experimental surgery. As a result, when people have back surgery they are putting themselves at great risk. The nerves in the back are small yet incredibly numerous. Even the smallest surgical mistake can result in even more back pain for a patient.

Finally, even when doctors manage "successful" back surgeries, many patients have a recurrence of pain at the same level within five years. In one study, up to 50 percent of patients over 60 who had surgery returned to the operating table within five years. Sadly, repeat surgeries are even less successful at treating the problem.

LECTURE

You've just read an article that's very critical of back surgery. It suggests that back surgery is too risky, regardless of how much pain a person's back causes. While some back surgeries are risky, it's simply not true that people over 60 should avoid them at all costs. Let me tell you why.

First, the article says that doctors are not sure what causes back pain. To put it mildly, this is an exaggeration. While a small number of back pain cases do involve perceptual and cognitive processing complications, a large number of back problems are clearly caused by ruptured discs, arthritis, and other structural issues. Consequently, doctors recommend that those suffering from back pain receive surgery because it's the most viable option.

Second, the article suggests that all back surgeries are experimental. That's also untrue. Certain types of back surgery, such as those involving artificial discs, are relatively new. But the recommended surgery for most ruptured discs—removal and vertebrae fusion—has been performed successfully for more than 50 years. This is older than other common orthopedic surgeries such as hip and knee replacements.

Lastly, the article suggests that most back surgery patients experience a return of their symptoms within 5 years of receiving the surgery. But this claim is backed up by just one study. In contrast, dozens of other studies show that back surgery is highly successful at reducing pain in patients over the age of 60. So as with all surgeries, there are risks involved. But if your back is causing you large amounts of pain, back surgery may be worth the risk.

Notes

| P: back surgery: bad idea | L: back surgery: worth risks |
|---|---|
| *causes of pain often uncertain* | *causes of pain usually known* |
| *new, risky procedure* | *common back surgeries not experimental* |
| *pain/problems often return in 5 yrs.* | *back surgery reduces pain* |

The lecture refutes the idea that people over 60 should avoid back surgery when they are experiencing great pain. It says that the information in the reading exaggerates the risks and downplays the benefits of back surgery.

To start, the lecture claims that doctors know what causes back pain in most cases. Although the reading states that doctors are not sure what causes back pain in most people, the lecture says that this is the situation in only a small percentage of cases. Generally, there are clear physical causes, such as ruptured discs or arthritis. Doctors recommend that people with these physical ailments should have back surgery.

Next, not all back surgeries are experimental. The reading says that back surgery is a new, experimental type of surgery. The lecture acknowledges that certain back surgeries are new. However, the lecture also states that the most common types of back surgeries have been done successfully for over 50 years. This is longer than other bone- and joint-related surgeries that have become commonplace, such as hip and knee replacements.

Finally, not all back surgeries are unsuccessful. The reading claims that back pain often returns within five years for people over 60 who have surgery. However, the lecture points out that conclusion is based on a single study. The lecture claims that there are many more studies that show the opposite: back pain does not return in five years. The lecture argues that the benefits of back surgery outweigh the risks.

# Independent Writing Task I

---

**Prompt**

It is generally agreed that a well-informed person must obtain information not just only one news source, but rather from many different news sources. Do you agree or disagree with this opinion? Use specific details and reasons to explain your answer.

**Brainstorm**

---

---

---

---

---

---

---

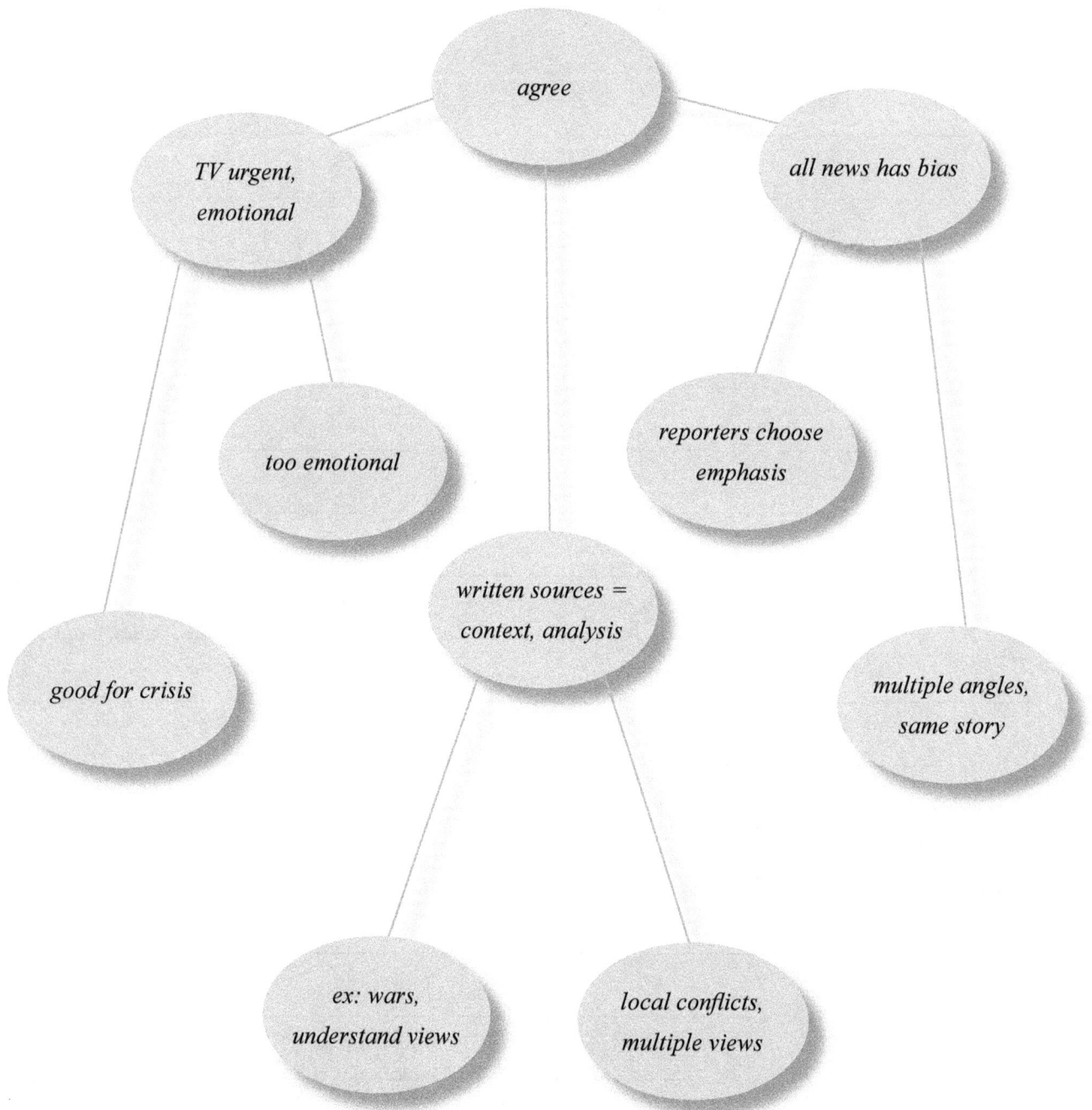

► Prompt ◄

It is generally agreed that a well-informed person must obtain information not only from one news source, but rather from many different news sources. Do you agree or disagree with this opinion? Use specific details and reasons to explain your answer.

**Brainstorm**

agree

TV urgent, emotional

all news has bias

too emotional

reporters choose emphasis

good for crisis

written sources = context, analysis

multiple angles, same story

ex: wars, understand views

local conflicts, multiple views

The most basic function of news is to inform us of the experiences of others. Some people feel that a single news outlet can give them a clear picture of what goes on in the world, while others receive their news from a variety of sources. **I believe that the only way to gain a comprehensive understanding of the experiences of others is by absorbing as many sources and types of media as possible.**

Television news reports offer a way to capture the urgency and emotion of a situation. For example, networks that showed amateur film footage of the Indian Ocean tsunami in 2004 helped generate global sympathy for the victims of the tsunami. However, television news can also focus on emotion at the expense of reason. Candidates debating an issue on television might win or lose based on how people feel about their appearances rather than how well they voice their opinions.

Newspapers and Internet websites tend to provide more context and analysis of a news event. Because written news sources are generally free from the pressure of providing on-the-spot coverage, they can do more research and interview more people. For instance, when war breaks out in a foreign country, it is not enough to see images of fighting; people who really want to understand the conflict need to turn to written news to absorb the complexity of the situation. The same is true of conflicts involving local school boards or city councils. Conflicting views are often most clearly explained in a written form.

Whether broadcast or print, every source of news has a bias because the reporter in charge of the story has made certain decisions about what to include and how to express it. One reporter covering a tsunami might focus on victims who are blaming their governments for not warning them. Another reporter covering the same tsunami may ignore those complaints and focus on explaining causes of tsunamis. Either way, there is always a particular viewpoint. Ultimately, this bias explains why no single source of news or type of media can keep a person completely informed.

# Independent Writing Task II

## Prompt

Do you believe that a wealthy person can have a meaningful friendship with a poor person?
Use specific examples and reasons to support your opinion.

### Brainstorm

# Model Answer

**Prompt**

Do you believe that a wealthy person can have a meaningful friendship with a poor person?
Use specific examples and reasons to support your opinion.

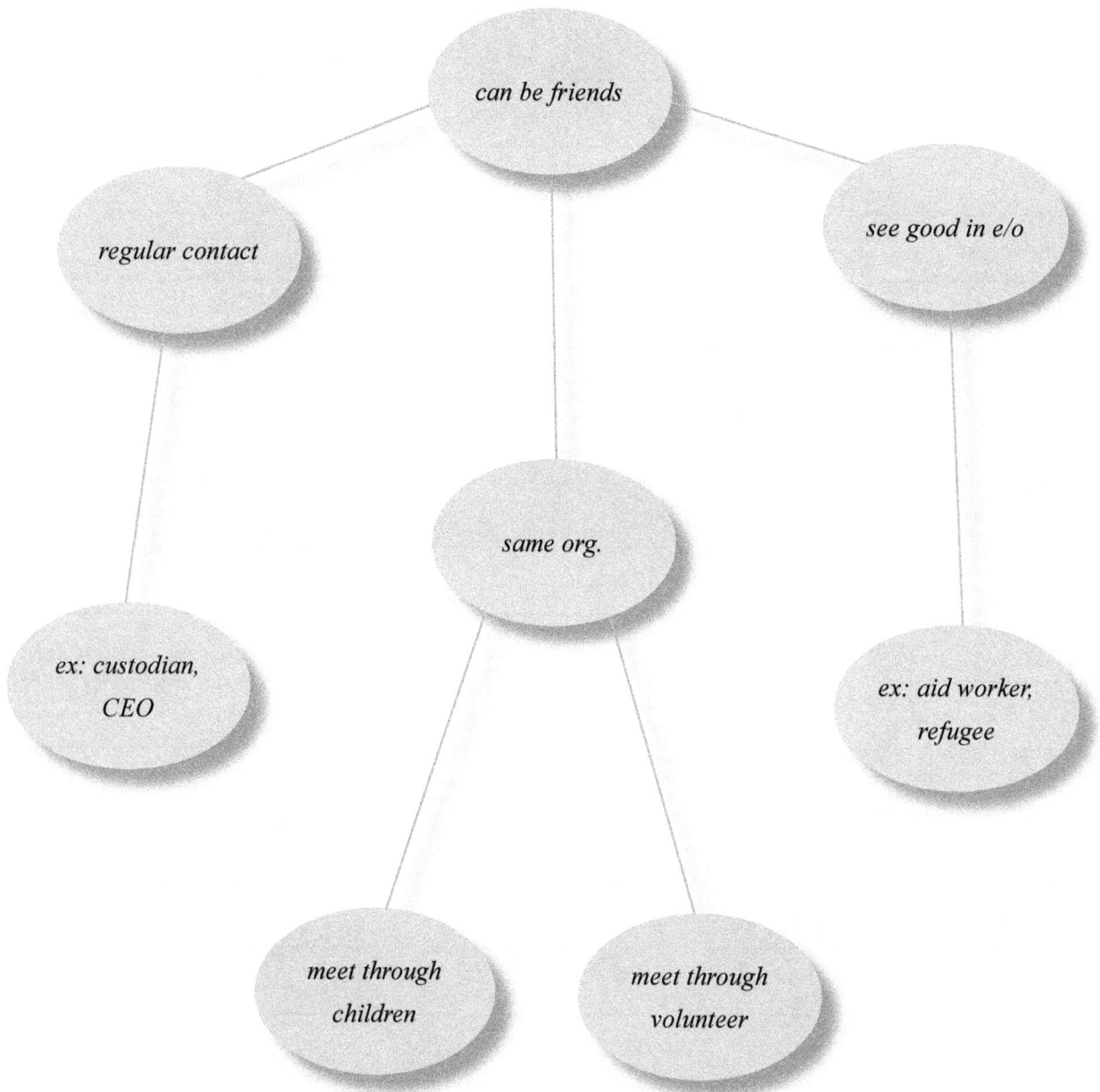

Brainstorm

can be friends

regular contact

see good in e/o

same org.

ex: custodian, CEO

ex: aid worker, refugee

meet through children

meet through volunteer

It is difficult for people to avoid judging others, including those who have a different economic status. **However, there are many examples of people forming close relationships in spite of great differences in wealth. Wealthy and poor people can form meaningful friendships through a variety of circumstances.**

<u>One factor in building any friendship is getting to know each other through regular contact.</u> Normally, those with higher incomes and those with lower incomes do not cross paths socially. Yet when they do, it is not unusual for a friendship to form. For example, one man I know worked as a head custodian at a large library. He became friends with the library's director because they chatted when he cleaned her office, and because they had to meet to make practical decisions about the library buildings. After the director retired, they remained friends, even though they had such a different status in the workplace.

<u>Two people from very different income levels may share a common project or belong to the same organization, leading them to feel a sense of closeness.</u> One way that people from different backgrounds meet is through their children. For example, if a child from a wealthy family and a child from a poor family go to the same school, their parents may see each other when the children get together at birthday parties or sports activities, or the parents may volunteer at a school festival. Having such experiences in common often binds people together.

Finally, <u>a person may simply recognize the good qualities in another person and be willing to cross social boundaries.</u> For example, one of my friends volunteered in a foreign refugee camp in a war-torn region of the world. As a middle-class American, she was extremely rich compared to the refugees, who had no money at all. Still, she and one of the young men in the camp became good friends. They communicated regularly for many years in spite of living on different continents in such different circumstances.

In summation, people can have many qualities in common with each other, even if they come from different economic backgrounds. I believe that relationships between people with great differences in income can happen, and can flourish as well.

# Integrated Writing Task 5

Infomercials are long-format commercials. In the United States, they typically run from 5 to 30 minutes and are shown on local television stations late at night or early in the morning. They usually offer a phone number and urge viewers to buy the product immediately and directly. Some popular infomercial products include exercise equipment, cleaning products, and self-help books. For an entrepreneur with a new product, infomercials may be a useful tool for getting started.

Infomercials provide businesses with more time to talk about their products to consumers. Not only does this create an opportunity to bond with the viewers but also to demonstrate and explain an unusual or unique product. If a product is also available in some retail stores, an infomercial can persuade viewers of its value.

Another benefit of infomercials for businesses is that they are inexpensive. Regional airtime in the middle of the night will cost several hundreds of dollars, unlike the hundreds of thousands of dollars for primetime. Also, it is much less expensive to make an infomercial than a primetime 30-second commercial. Infomercials usually rely on one or two people talking on a plain set, and maybe a few film clips of the product at work. As a result, these cost a fraction of what it costs to produce primetime commercials.

Finally, infomercials are good for companies because they can be successful. It has been estimated that they result in about $200 billion in sales each year, and that amount is growing. True, most viewers ridicule infomercials, but that does not stop some from watching. Of those who do, about one percent call up right away—still creating substantial profit margins—and up to 15 percent will buy the product if they see it in a store.

Overall, infomercials are a low-risk method for promoting a product.

🔊 Now listen to part of a lecture on the topic you just read about.

## Notes

| P: | L: |
|---|---|
| | |
| | |
| | |

**Prompt**

Summarize the points made in the lecture, being sure to explain how they oppose specific points made in the reading passage.

_____

_____

_____

_____

_____

_____

_____

_____

_____

_____

_____

_____

_____

_____

_____

_____

_____

_____

_____

_____

_____

# Model Answer

Infomercials are long-format commercials. In the United States, they typically run from 5 to 30 minutes and are shown on local television stations late at night or early in the morning. They usually offer a phone number and urge viewers to buy the product immediately and directly. Some popular infomercial products include exercise equipment, cleaning products, and self-help books. For an entrepreneur with a new product, infomercials may be a useful tool for getting started.

Infomercials provide businesses with more time to talk about their products to consumers. Not only does this create an opportunity to bond with the viewers but also to demonstrate and explain an unusual or unique product. If a product is also available in some retail stores, an infomercial can persuade viewers of its value.

Another benefit of infomercials for businesses is that they are inexpensive. Regional airtime in the middle of the night will cost several hundreds of dollars, unlike the hundreds of thousands of dollars for primetime. Also, it is much less expensive to make an infomercial than a primetime 30-second commercial. Infomercials usually rely on one or two people talking on a plain set, and maybe a few film clips of the product at work. As a result, these cost a fraction of what it costs to produce primetime commercials.

Finally, infomercials are good for companies because they can be successful. It has been estimated that they result in about $200 billion in sales each year, and that amount is growing. True, most viewers ridicule infomercials, but that does not stop some from watching. Of those who do, about one percent call up right away—still creating substantial profit margins—and up to 15 percent will buy the product if they see it in a store.

Overall, infomercials are a low-risk method for promoting a product.

## LECTURE

*Infomercials are probably quite familiar to people who watch television late at night or early in the morning. Business entrepreneurs may think that investing in an infomercial to reach these viewers is a good idea. But they should know about the disadvantages of infomercials.*

*First, the reading passage says that infomercials are effective because they allow businesses large blocks of time to present information about products. But is this really a good thing? Researchers claim that about 75 percent of all consumers react negatively to infomercials the longer they watch them. This is because the speakers seem less trustworthy the more they praise their products.*

*Second, the reading states that infomercials are a worthy investment for businesses because they're less costly to make and to air than prime time ads. However, the infomercials also reach a much more limited audience. For television stations, the time from about 1 am to 6 am is known as the "graveyard" slot—in other words, a time when there's practically no live audience. That, of course, is why the airtime is so inexpensive. Infomercials also tend to air only on local stations, reaching only a particular region.*

*The strongest claim for infomercials is that they've made a lot of money for businesses. But these might be one-time profits. An infomercial may create a permanent negative association in the public's mind, so that while it may attract impulse buyers at first, in the long run, it'll seem tacky. I myself would be less likely to buy an onion-chopper or a "miracle" sponge in a store if I had seen it on a cheap infomercial.*

*So overall, entrepreneurs who want not only to enter the market but also to build a solid base for the future should avoid infomercials.*

## Notes

| **P:** infomercial = good for business | **L:** infomercial = bad for business |
|---|---|
| provides more time to sell the product | longer time → extra sales time → sales ppl. seem untrustworthy |
| inexpensive comp. to regular commercial | very limited audience |
| can make $; $200 billion market | most $ from one-time profits |

The lecture challenges the idea that infomercials bring any lasting benefits to businesses. According to the lecture, the benefits of infomercials are short-lived, and the downsides can harm businesses forever.

To start, the lecture points out that having a long time to advertise a product may not actually benefit a business. The reading claims that the long format allows companies to describe a product in more detail, which causes the consumer to see its worth and buy it. However, the lecture refers to research claiming that such lengthy explanations make customers suspicious. The more claims a speaker makes about a product, the less trust the audience feels.

Next, the lecture does not dispute that infomercials may be relatively inexpensive, both to produce and to air on local stations during the middle of the night. However, in context of the very small, local audience that they will reach, they may not be worth even the small amounts spent on them.

Finally, using infomercials to advertise a product could ruin the product's image. It could create a perception in the viewers' minds that the product is of low quality. The product may sell at first, when viewers are caught up in the moment, but its reputation will suffer in the long run. If a company wants to sell a product continuously, it may be better to find other ways to market the product.

# Independent Writing Task I

**Prompt**

Do you agree or disagree with the following statement? People nowadays spend too much money on their pets. Use specific details and examples to support your opinion.

**Brainstorm**

_____

_____

_____

_____

_____

_____

_____

_____

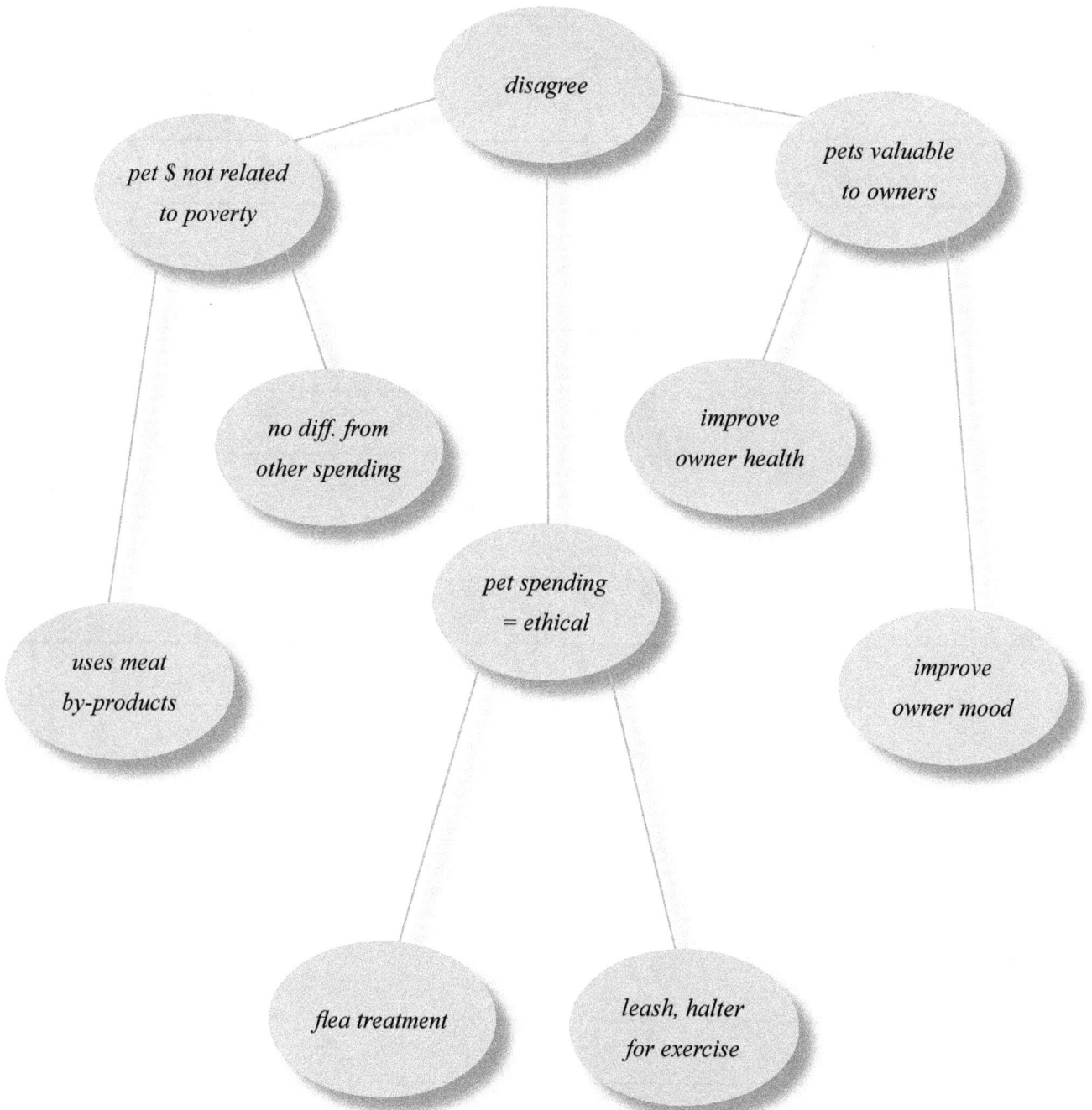

**Prompt**

Do you agree or disagree with the following statement? People nowadays spend too much money on their pets. Use specific details and examples to support your opinion.

**Brainstorm**

- disagree
  - pet $ not related to poverty
    - no diff. from other spending
    - uses meat by-products
  - pet spending = ethical
    - flea treatment
    - leash, halter for exercise
  - pets valuable to owners
    - improve owner health
    - improve owner mood

Many people in the world go hungry and lack basic health care. Thus, it is reasonable to question the amount of resources some people spend on pets. **However, spending money on pet food and veterinary care is a small part of a complicated world economy. Such spending is justified because it does not necessarily affect world hunger and because it is responsible and fair.**

First, <u>spending money on pets and pet food does not take money away from poor countries.</u> There is no logical direct relationship between extreme poverty in some regions of the world and the money that people in affluent countries spend on their pets. Most pet food comes from meat industry byproducts that are not fit for humans to eat. Products for one's pets do not use resources that would otherwise be used in food donations.

Meanwhile, <u>spending money on pets to keep them healthy and comfortable is the ethical thing to do. People who keep animals are responsible for them.</u> For example, dogs depend on their owners to keep them clean and free of fleas. The veterinary field has developed excellent flea treatments, which are expensive, but which vastly improve a dog's quality of life. Likewise, dogs are also more relaxed if they get enough exercise, which may require buying a leash and halter for walks. Dogs and other pets have a basic right to physical care.

Finally, <u>pets provide benefits to their owners and society. Whatever pet owners spend on pets, it is likely that they gain more in return.</u> Studies have shown that pets lower their owners' levels of stress, possibly because of the unconditional love they offer. People with pets have reduced chances of heart attack or stroke. Moreover, pets can improve people's moods, which is why pets are sometimes used to comfort and cheer people in hospitals.

Overall, pet owners should not feel guilty about how much they spend on their pets. After all, spending money on pets contributes to the health of not only the animals, but their owners as well.

# Independent Writing Task II

## Prompt

Do you agree or disagree with the following statement? Professional athletes do not deserve the large salaries that they are routinely paid. Use specific reasons and examples to support your position.

**Brainstorm**

_____

_____

_____

_____

_____

_____

_____

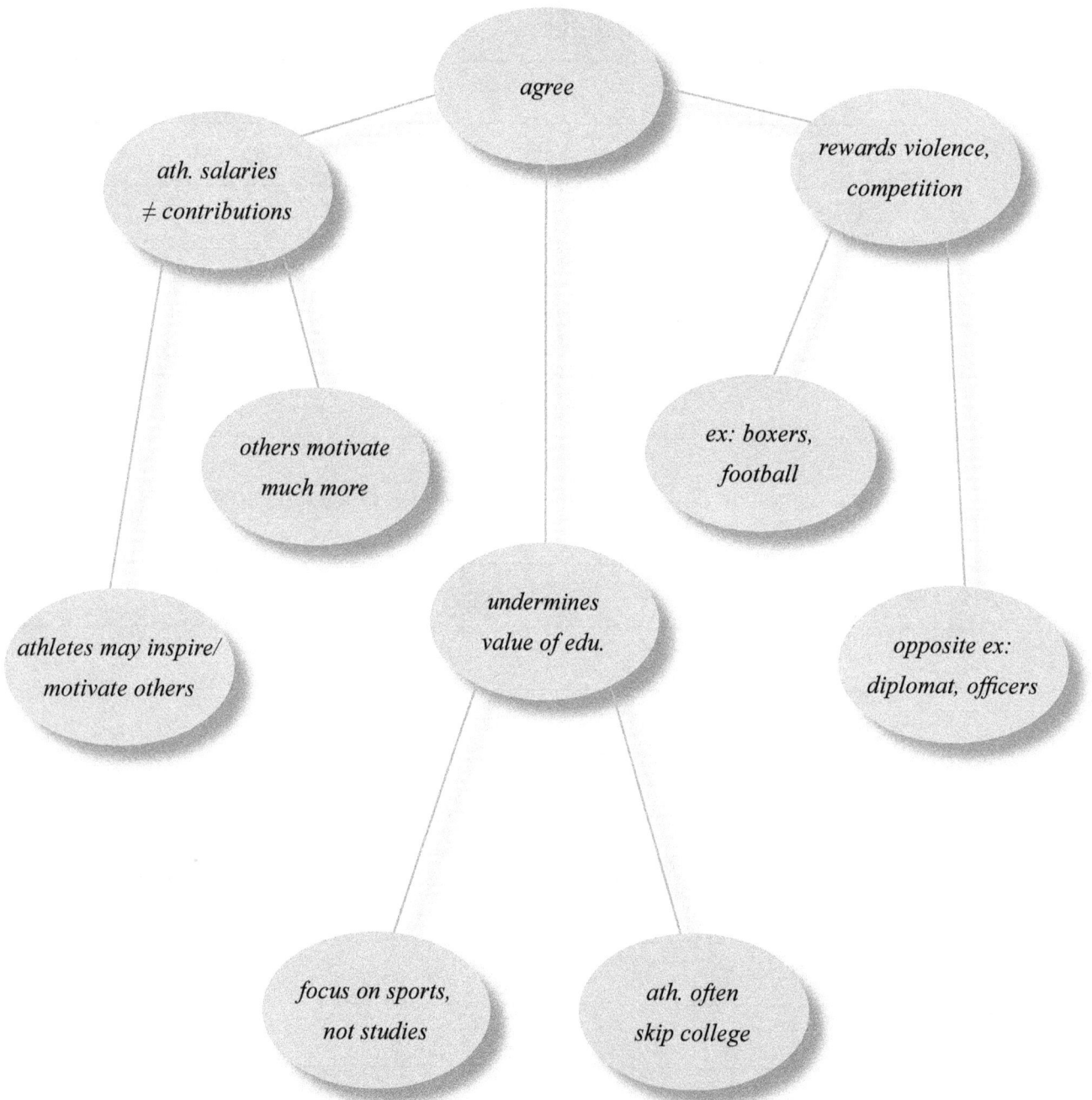

**Prompt**

Do you agree or disagree with the following statement? Professional athletes do not deserve the large salaries that they are routinely paid. Use specific reasons and examples to support your position.

## Brainstorm

agree

ath. salaries ≠ contributions

rewards violence, competition

others motivate much more

ex: boxers, football

athletes may inspire/ motivate others

undermines value of edu.

opposite ex: diplomat, officers

focus on sports, not studies

ath. often skip college

Whether through sponsorship or contract, many athletes make millions of dollars each year. Meanwhile, teachers who educate future generations and construction workers who build our cities receive tiny salaries by comparison. **Therefore, professional athletes do not deserve their current salaries for a number of reasons.**

One reason is that athletes' salaries do not represent the activities that should be rewarded in society. Although athletes must work hard to become the best in their chosen sport, they are ultimately working hard to master a game. Athletes might inspire some people to exercise more or work harder for a goal, but their contribution to society is vastly disproportionate to their huge earnings. The most competent and inspiring teachers receive an average salary for personally devoting themselves to hundreds or even thousands of students, so an athlete should not receive millions of dollars for simply being a public role model.

Furthermore, offering contracts worth millions of dollars to professional athletes undermines the message that education matters. Many parents push their children to succeed at sports with the hopes that the children will one day earn a scholarship, and perhaps even become professional and earn recognition and wealth. In the process, their children learn to put more emphasis on sports than education. They may also become aware of professional athletes who are drafted from high school and college teams, essentially giving up their education to become professional athletes. Paying huge salaries to superstar athletes misleads children about the surest way to success.

Finally, many sports, such as boxing and American football, promote excessive violence and competition as the path to wealth. Those who work at keeping peace, such as diplomats and parole officers, are paid nearly nothing compared to the colossal salaries of professional boxers, who are literally paid to knock their opponents unconscious. All societies should promote communication and cooperation, not brutality and needless competition.

While athletes themselves are not to blame for their excessive salaries, they should not be among the wealthiest people in society simply because they have mastered a game. The money spent toward promoting rivalry and violence should instead go toward promoting peace and education.

# Integrated Writing Task 6

## PASSAGE

When people imagine a future in which humans set up colonies on other planets, they usually think of Mars. However, there are several reasons that Venus would be a more viable option for human communities than any other known planet.

Venus is the closest planet to Earth. When Venus and Earth orbit nearest each other, about once every 19 months or so, they are only 40-million kilometers apart; the closest Earth gets to Mars is 56-million kilometers, and Earth cycles this close only about once every 24 months. As a result, transporting people and resources to Venus would be quicker and more efficient than elsewhere.

Another huge advantage of inhabiting Venus is that its mass is similar to Earth's, so it has a similar gravitational pull. Other planets may have too little or too much gravity for humans to maintain healthy bones. Mars, for example, has a surface gravity that is 38 percent of Earth's. Scientists do not yet know how long humans could survive without the Earth's gravitational pull, but they do know that gravity plays a large role in maintaining the human skeleton.

Lastly, Venus' upper atmosphere is the most habitable place of any known planet outside of Earth. There, at an altitude of 50 kilometers, the pressure, gravity and temperature (0 to 50 degrees Centigrade) are almost identical to those environmental factors on Earth. Thus, some scientists suggest that humans could colonize Venus' atmosphere. The idea is that inhabitants could live in huge bubbles that would float at just the right elevation, carried by the wind currents around Venus. Such bubbles could support life for large outposts of humans.

Now listen to part of a lecture on the topic you just read about.

Notes

| P: | L: |
|---|---|
|  |  |
|  |  |
|  |  |

**Prompt**

Summarize the points made in the lecture, being sure to explain how they oppose specific points made in the reading passage.

_____

_____

_____

_____

_____

_____

_____

_____

_____

_____

_____

_____

_____

_____

_____

_____

_____

_____

_____

_____

_____

# Model Answer

When people imagine a future in which humans set up colonies on other planets, they usually think of Mars. However, there are several reasons that Venus would be a more viable option for human communities than any other known planet.

Venus is the closest planet to Earth. When Venus and Earth orbit nearest each other, about once every 19 months or so, they are only 40-million kilometers apart; the closest Earth gets to Mars is 56-million kilometers, and Earth cycles this close only about once every 24 months. As a result, transporting people and resources to Venus would be quicker and more efficient than elsewhere.

Another huge advantage of inhabiting Venus is that its mass is similar to Earth's, so it has a similar gravitational pull. Other planets may have too little or too much gravity for humans to maintain healthy bones. Mars, for example, has a surface gravity that is 38 percent of Earth's. Scientists do not yet know how long humans could survive without the Earth's gravitational pull, but they do know that gravity plays a large role in maintaining the human skeleton.

Lastly, Venus' upper atmosphere is the most habitable place of any known planet outside of Earth. There, at an altitude of 50 kilometers, the pressure, gravity and temperature (0 to 50 degrees Centigrade) are almost identical to those environmental factors on Earth. Thus, some scientists suggest that humans could colonize Venus' atmosphere. The idea is that inhabitants could live in huge bubbles that would float at just the right elevation, carried by the wind currents around Venus. Such bubbles could support life for large outposts of humans.

LECTURE

*Many science fiction writers have predicted that humans will eventually colonize Mars, and that day may indeed arrive. However, the article you just read proposes that Venus is a better candidate. But when we examine the reasons closely, we learn that Venus may be no more inhabitable than other planets.*

*First, the reading claims that Venus' physical closeness to Earth makes it easier to reach than any other planet. That's true, but it's still a long, long trip, requiring around six months, depending on how close the planets are orbiting and how fast a ship is moving. Because of the distance and expense of travel, a colony on Venus would have to be completely self-sufficient, as it couldn't depend on any meaningful amount of regular supplies from Earth.*

*Now while it's true that Venus and Earth share a similar level of gravity, I'm sorry to say that the similarity is outweighed by many differences. The atmosphere is mostly dense carbon dioxide, with toxic sulfuric clouds. There's no oxygen. At the surface of Venus, the pressure and heat are so great that even unmanned spacecraft that have landed there were quickly compressed and melted. At this point, no foreseeable technologies will allow humans to live in such conditions.*

*As to the idea of colonizing the upper atmosphere with floating bubbles, in spite of the relatively comfortable temperatures and air pressure, the technical problems still appear to be insurmountable. Scientists would have to invent a bubble wall that'd hold a colony, protect it from toxic gases, and stand up to the fierce winds around the planet. Most importantly, they'd have to figure out a way to create oxygen and to extract the trace amounts of water that can be found in the atmosphere of the otherwise dry planet.*

*So unfortunately, due to its distance, surface pressure, heat, and atmosphere, Venus is simply too hostile an environment for humans.*

**Notes**

| P: benefits of colonizing Venus | L: problems with colonizing Venus |
|---|---|
| closest planet to Earth | still very far; colony must be self-sufficient |
| similar size/gravity; ok for human bones | toxic atm.; high surface pressure |
| upper atm. similar to Earth conditions | no tech. for living bubbles; planet too harsh |

The lecture questions the reading's claims that Venus is a desirable location for a human colony. Although the lecture does not dispute the positive qualities that Venus has, it claims that they are overshadowed by challenges.

First, although Venus is Earth's closest planetary neighbor, the complexities of planetary orbits and vast, interplanetary distances make it inaccessible. About every year and a half, Venus orbits close to Earth, but it is still about 40-million kilometers away, requiring months of travel by rocket. According to the lecture, any colony there would not be able to depend upon deliveries from Earth.

Second, the conditions on the surface of Venus are so hostile that they make the planet's desirable gravity less relevant. The atmospheric pressure at the plant's surface crushes any probes sent there, and the heat liquefies them. Humanity has not developed the technology to counter such effects. Moreover, the atmosphere is mostly carbon dioxide and toxic sulfur dioxide, and there is no oxygen at all.

Finally, floating cities may not ever be practical, and certainly are not possible in the foreseeable future. While the lecturer agrees that Venus' upper atmosphere shares some of Earth's conditions, it still lacks water and oxygen. In addition to solving that problem, scientists would have to invent a bubble that was strong enough to hold up the people, keep out toxic gases, and resist the strong winds that circle Venus.

Overall, the harsh conditions on and around Venus and its lack of water and oxygen override its few advantages.

# Independent Writing Task I

**Prompt**

Do you agree or disagree with the following statement? The ideal way to learn about other countries is to read articles in newspapers and magazines. Explain your answer using specific details and reasons.

## Brainstorm

**Prompt**

Do you agree or disagree with the following statement? The ideal way to learn about other countries is to read articles in newspapers and magazines. Explain your answer using specific details and reasons.

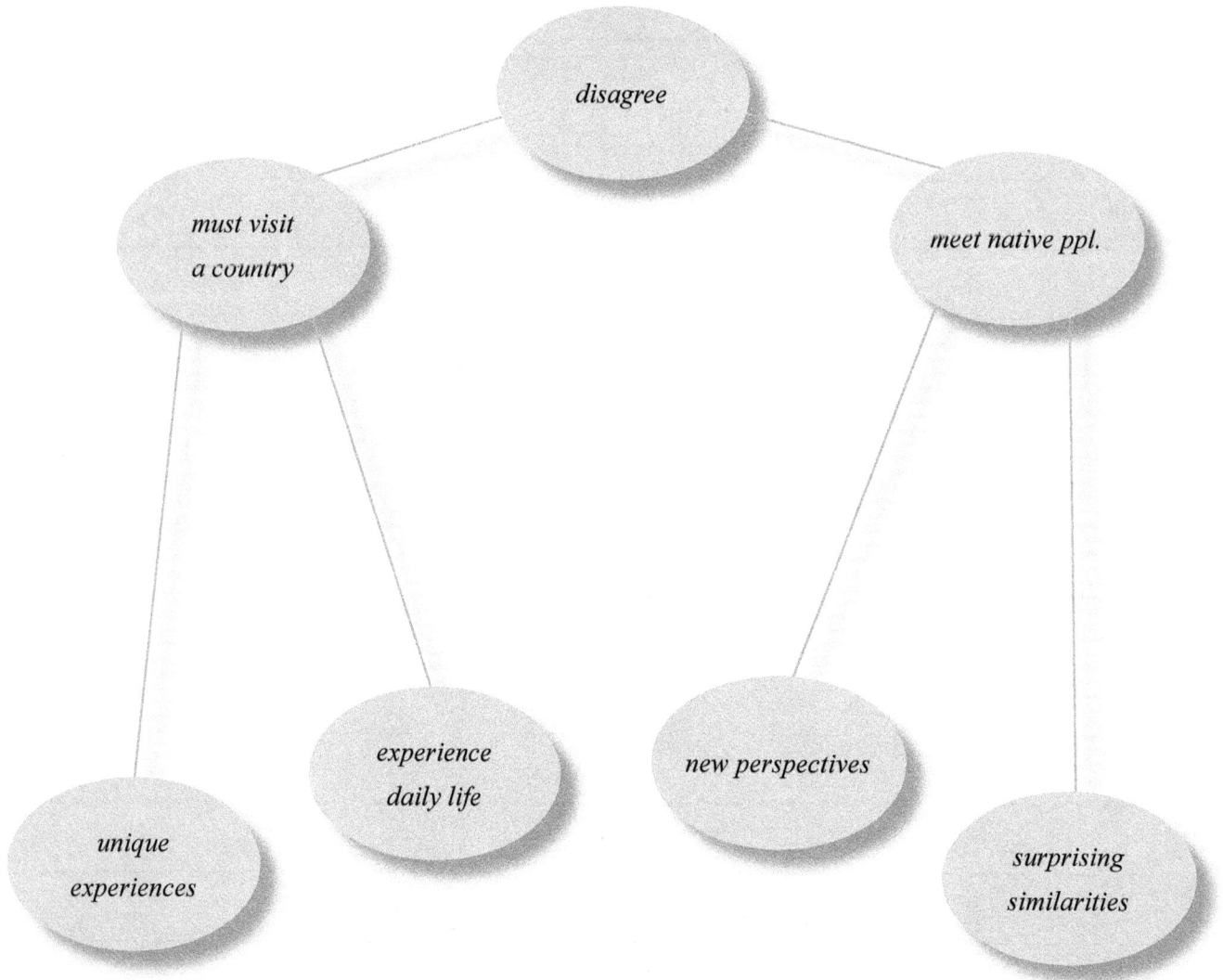

Magazines and newspapers can describe many aspects of a foreign country. A reader can get an idea of its geography, culture, and politics. **Yet reading about a country cannot compare to traveling there. Indeed, visiting a country provides one with unique experiences and personal encounters.**

<u>There is no substitute for experiencing the sights, sounds, smells, and tastes of a place in person.</u> Many experiences cannot be conveyed in printed word or even in images. For example, looking at a picture of Paris' Eiffel Tower in a magazine cannot match the grandeur of standing at the base of the massive structure, and all the descriptions in the world cannot convey the experience of bathing and dining at a Japanese hot spring resort. The same is also true for experiencing elements of daily life in an unfamiliar place, such as crowding onto a subway or buying a snack from a food cart. Someone writing about a location must limit descriptions, but first-hand experience allows for endless new discoveries.

<u>Traveling to a foreign country is especially eye opening when one has a chance to meet with and talk to some of its inhabitants.</u> It is intriguing to communicate with people directly and gain a sense of their daily lives and their beliefs. They may offer an unexpected perspective on their own culture, or on yours. In some cases, conversations may be a window into differences. For example, my mother was shocked when, in the course of a conversation, she found that a woman her age from another country did not know who the Beatles were. She had assumed that knowledge of the British rock group was universal, and came to realize that Western culture does not reach every corner of the world. At other times, a traveler may be struck by similarities between all people, such as how children everywhere seem to like chewing gum.

Ultimately, one must become immersed in a foreign culture to appreciate all that it has to offer. While a picture in a magazine may be worth a thousand words, it cannot convey even a fraction of what a first-hand experience can.

# Independent Writing Task II

▶ Prompt ◀

Some people believe that governments should support scientific research, even if the research does not appear to have any practical purpose. Others feel that governments are obligated to spend as much money as possible on basic social needs. Which of these two opinions do you agree with? Use examples and specific reasons to develop your response.

**Brainstorm**

# Model Answer

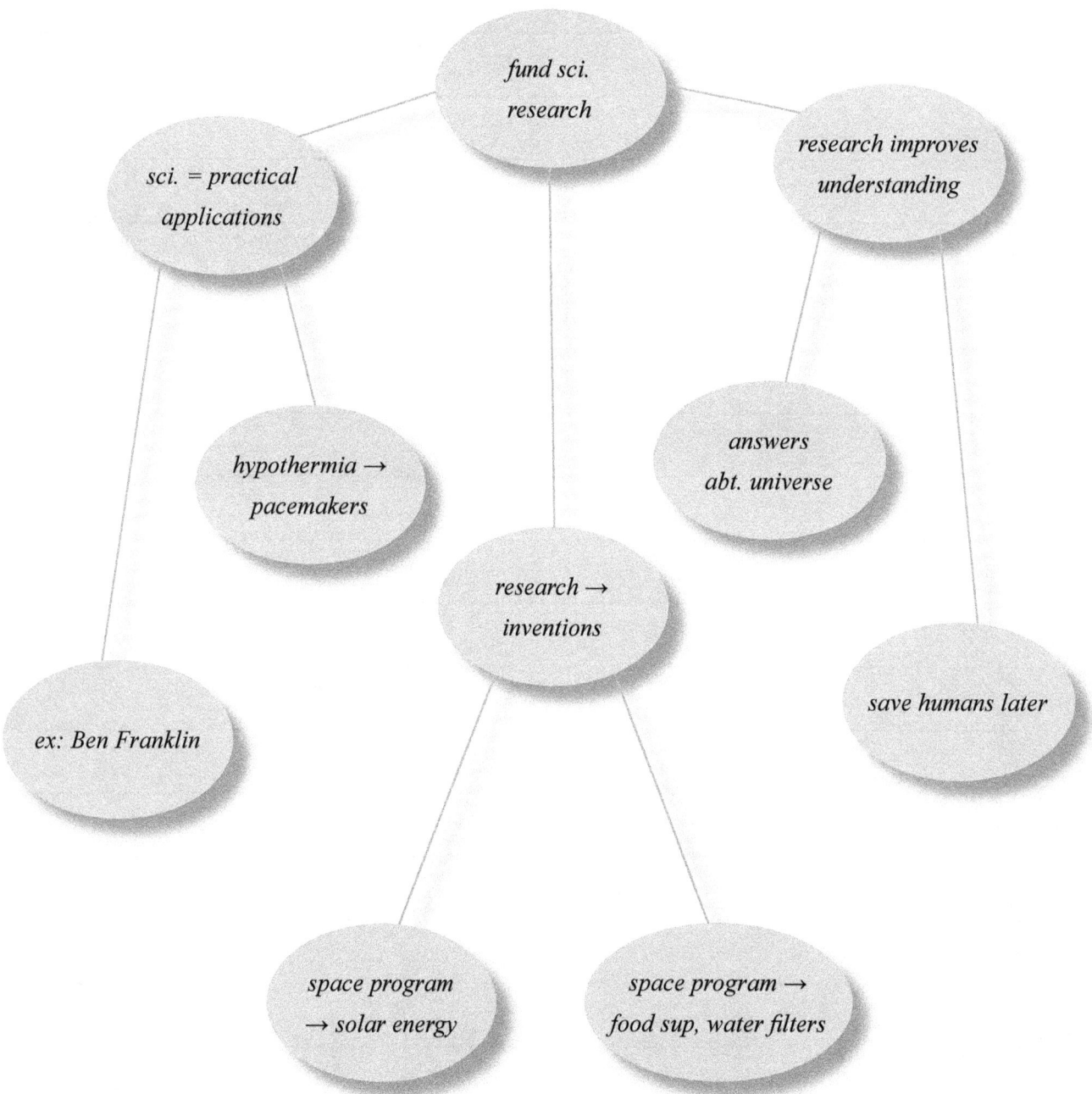

**Prompt**

Some people believe that governments should support scientific research, even if the research does not appear to have any practical purpose. Others feel that governments are obligated to spend as much money as possible on basic social needs. Which of these two opinions do you agree with? Use examples and specific reasons to develop your response.

### Brainstorm

*fund sci. research*

*sci. = practical applications*

*research improves understanding*

*hypothermia → pacemakers*

*answers abt. universe*

*research → inventions*

*ex: Ben Franklin*

*save humans later*

*space program → solar energy*

*space program → food sup, water filters*

Many great inventions were created accidentally, often while scientists were trying to solve another scientific problem. Critics sometimes dismiss scientific research as "counting the spots on ladybugs' backs." These critics believe that governments should meet basic social needs instead. **Nevertheless, governments should support scientific research as much as possible because it may lead to valuable, practical discoveries.**

One major benefit of seemingly impractical scientific research is that it always has potential for surprising applications. For instance, when inventor Benjamin Franklin investigated electricity, he was pursuing his curiosity about physics. Yet his investigations established the foundations for the electricity that permeates daily life, from electric toothbrushes to entire power grids. Another example is that pacemakers came into existence through an engineer's investigations into hypothermia, not through research into the workings of the heart.

Scientists often create useful tools while conducting seemingly unnecessary scientific research. Investigations into different forms of space travel involve gathering obscure information about the solar system and the universe. However, making space travel possible has spurred scientists to invent invaluable technologies and materials along the way. For example, in the 1950s, scientists looking for a way to power the first space satellites invented solar batteries. Thus, the solar energy industry was born. Figuring out how to provide food and water to astronauts in space has resulted in new food supplements and water filtration systems that are now widely used on Earth.

Furthermore, scientific research regarding the nature of the universe may save lives in the future. Researching matter-consuming black holes in far-flung galaxies may not seem useful to people now, but it will help scientists understand the extent and formation of our universe. It is likely that such knowledge will eventually lead to countless practical benefits.

Societies should not see seemingly impractical scientific research as being in competition with social programs. Rather, funding scientific research is a way of creating better conditions for people now and in the future.

# Integrated Writing Task 7

When a natural disaster occurs, dozens of private charities seem to appear ready to provide help. The public often responds by flooding them with monetary contributions. But when giving to charity, it is rarely a good idea to rush, even in urgent situations.

First, one needs time to research the reputation of a charity before donating. Although donors hate to think of people suffering from cold or hunger, rushing to give money in the wake of a political crisis or a natural disaster is never a good idea. Regrettably, disreputable groups sometimes take advantage of the crisis to persuade the public to part with its money. It is impossible for donors to verify that their money goes to the people it is supposed to help, so one should always make sure to donate to charities with sterling reputations.

Unfortunately, even well-known, long-established charities may use donors' money for their own private expenses. In some cases, people might donate to help an impoverished child pictured on a brochure without realizing that part of each dollar they give goes into million-dollar salaries for the charity's executives. Charity groups also have expenses including regular staff, offices, advertising, fundraising, travel, and so on. Ultimately, many donations fund the charity more than they fund the people the charity claims to help.

Moreover, most charitable groups have no system of evaluating their own effectiveness. They do not collect data to get feedback. For example, a charity might distribute thousands of tents after a disaster, but the tents may not work or be too small for the typical family in the region. Or a charity might give away grains that cannot be cooked because there is no firewood. Or a charity might provide vaccinations that people already had. In short, there is no way for donors to find out whether a private charitable organization sets productive goals or accomplishes its goals successfully.

🔊 Now listen to part of a lecture on the topic you just read about.

Notes

| P: | L: |
|---|---|
|  |  |

**Prompt**

Summarize the points made in the lecture, being sure to explain how they oppose specific points made in the reading passage.

_____

_____

_____

_____

_____

_____

_____

_____

_____

_____

_____

_____

_____

_____

_____

_____

_____

_____

_____

### PASSAGE

When a natural disaster occurs, dozens of private charities seem to appear ready to provide help. The public often responds by flooding them with monetary contributions. But when giving to charity, it is rarely a good idea to rush, even in urgent situations.

First, one needs time to research the reputation of a charity before donating. Although donors hate to think of people suffering from cold or hunger, rushing to give money in the wake of a political crisis or a natural disaster is never a good idea. Regrettably, disreputable groups sometimes take advantage of the crisis to persuade the public to part with its money. It is impossible for donors to verify that their money goes to the people it is supposed to help, so one should always make sure to donate to charities with sterling reputations.

Unfortunately, even well-known, long-established charities may use donors' money for their own private expenses. In some cases, people might donate to help an impoverished child pictured on a brochure without realizing that part of each dollar they give goes into million-dollar salaries for the charity's executives. Charity groups also have expenses including regular staff, offices, advertising, fundraising, travel, and so on. Ultimately, many donations fund the charity more than they fund the people the charity claims to help.

Moreover, most charitable groups have no system of evaluating their own effectiveness. They do not collect data to get feedback. For example, a charity might distribute thousands of tents after a disaster, but the tents may not work or be too small for the typical family in the region. Or a charity might give away grains that cannot be cooked because there is no firewood. Or a charity might provide vaccinations that people already had. In short, there is no way for donors to find out whether a private charitable organization sets productive goals or accomplishes its goals successfully.

### LECTURE

*You just read a passage that advises using caution when donating to a charity during times of crisis or disaster. While people should be cautious about giving to charities, they shouldn't accept the reading's cynical conclusions about all private charities.*

*The reading begins by warning against giving to charities in haste, even if one is responding emotionally to the needs of others. That's good advice, as scam artists frequently pressure people into hurried decisions. But contrary to claims made in the reading, it's easy to research the legitimacy of a charity via the Internet. For example, the Better Business Bureau, or BBB for short, lists private organizations that have registered nonprofit tax status. Donors can also type the organization's name into a search engine with the word "scam" or "complaint," and see if anything comes up. Even better, donors can decide which groups to give to, look up their websites or phone numbers, and contact their offices themselves.*

*The reading makes much of the fact that some established charities spend too much on executive salaries and operating expenses. Again, one way to research organizations is to use the Internet, where it's possible to find a number of independent charity-rating services. The services investigate and report on the ratio of operating costs to project spending. For example, one service awards charities a letter grade, "A" through "F." In order to earn an "A," a charity must not spend more than 25 percent of its income on its own salaries and operations.*

*Now I think the reading makes a very astute criticism by pointing out that charities have often just assumed they helped the people, without taking the trouble to collect evidence, documentation, or feedback. That's why these days the ratings services mentioned above are beginning to request such records. Since many donors check the ratings before donating, charities are now highly motivated to collect such data in order to maintain good ratings.*

## Notes

| P: charities can be bad | L: charities not bad |
|---|---|
| no way to verify charity honesty | check BBB/Internet research → verify charity honesty |
| donations → pay for salaries | internet rating services show $ spent on salaries |
| no feedback, may not be helping | rating services requesting records of effectiveness/feedback |

The lecture challenges the cynical view that the reading expresses toward charities. The lecture provides information about how to select decent charitable organizations, and encourages people not to give up on all charities.

First, there are simple ways to distinguish productive charities from fraudulent ones, as long as one has access to the internet. The Better Business Bureau lists all registered, private, non-profit organizations on its website. One can also research a charity by typing its name into a search engine along with words such as "scam." The easiest way to avoid giving to fake charities is to use the internet or phone book and contact established charities personally.

The internet also provides access to rating services that keep track of how charities spend donations. Would-be donors can use the rating services to predict how much of each dollar they give will go toward the charitable cause rather than salaries or operating expenses.

Finally, the lecture agrees with the reading's claim that it is hard to determine whether a charity is effective. For example, if a charity administers tents to people in need, the charity must ensure that the tents are functional. But the lecture adds to the reading by explaining that a major shift is currently taking place. Rating services are starting to hold charities more accountable in terms of meeting their goals. Charitable organizations that want good ratings from the rating services are starting to look for ways to evaluate how well they are meeting the needs of those who receive their charity.

In all, the lecture insists that there is plenty of information available to help people feel confident when giving to others.

# Independent Writing Task I

**Prompt**

Do you agree or disagree with the following statement? Although many people are practicing environmental conservation, the ecological outlook for the Earth will not improve in the future. Use specific examples and reasons to support your view.

**Brainstorm**

_____

_____

_____

_____

_____

_____

_____

# Model Answer

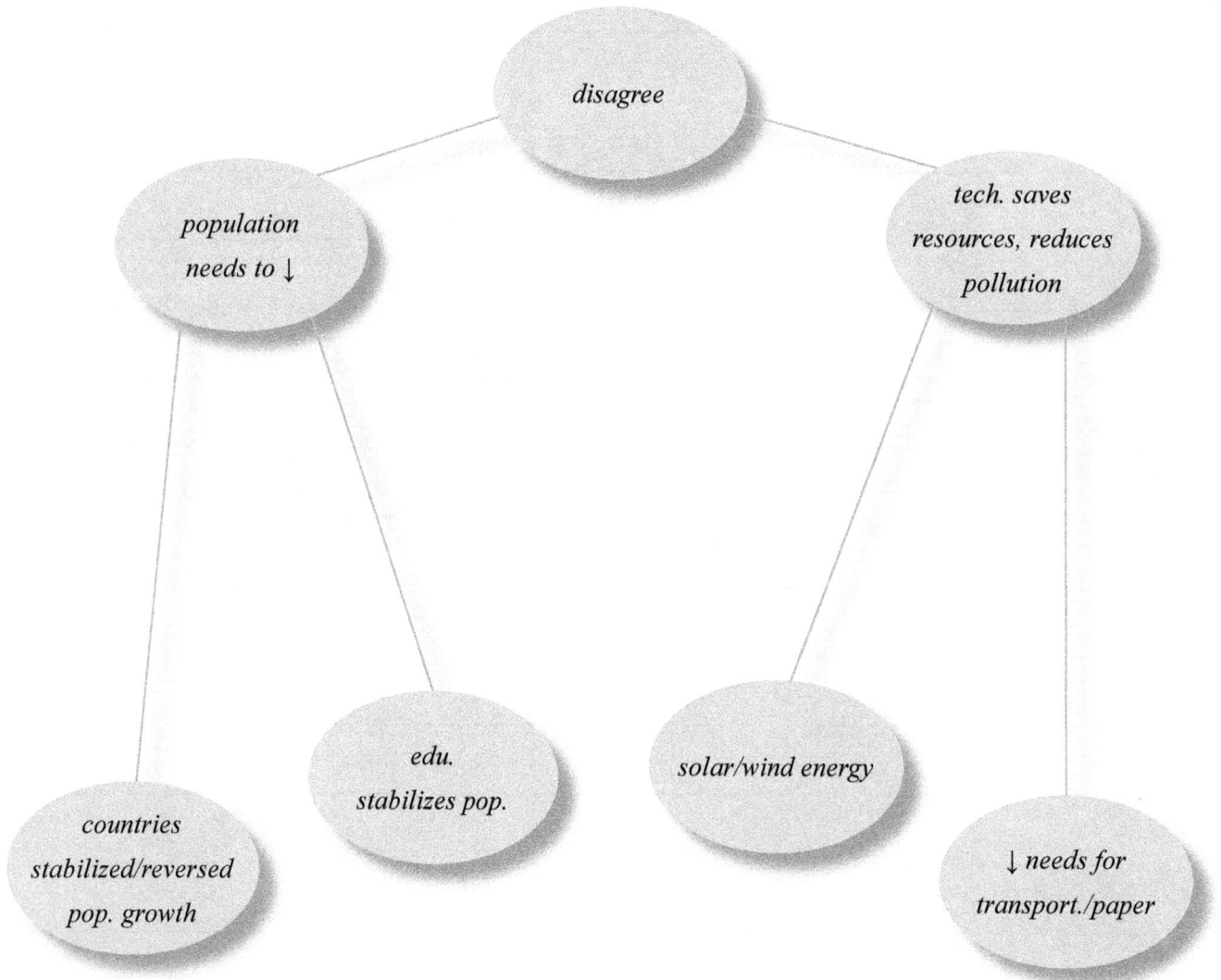

Because of the effects of global warming, clean water shortages, and loss of wilderness, many people today feel hopelessness when they consider the coming years. Yet humans have met many other challenges, and there is no reason to conclude that we cannot meet these challenges as well. **The ecological outlook for Earth will improve as humans increase their environmental awareness and technological capabilities.**

First, <u>there is a growing understanding that slowing and reversing population growth will put less strain on the planet's resources.</u> In a few regions of the world, population levels have stabilized or even begun to decrease. Based on data from these regions, the most effective way to ensure that a population stabilizes is to provide opportunities for education. In general, people who are able to complete school tend to have fewer children. As education has many other benefits, governments and private donors will likely see the wisdom of making schools a top priority around the globe.

Second, <u>new technology is constantly improving the chances that we can halt global warming and pollution from the burning of fossil fuels.</u> Inventors and innovators all over the world are constantly improving and creating technology with the goal of meeting demands for sustainability. For example, not only are the solar- and wind-energy industries growing, but people are also investigating other sources of clean energy, such as harvesting kinetic energy from ocean waves. Another example is the spread of the smart phone, a relatively inexpensive computer that fits in the palm of one's hand. Widespread access to the internet via such phones has the potential to reduce the need for transportation of goods and people, and to halt the destruction of forests for paper, among other benefits.

It is not too late to reverse the ecologically harmful practices that presently prevail among humans, as long as people are willing to consider adapting to change. More schools and new technologies are two of the keys to a better life on Earth.

# Independent Writing Task II

---

**Prompt**

Many current movies and television shows glamorize crime and criminals. Do you think that movies and TV programs should focus primarily on good people being rewarded and bad people being punished? Use specific reasons and examples in your discussion.

---

## Brainstorm

---

**Prompt**
Many current movies and television shows glamorize crime and criminals. Do you think that movies and TV programs should focus primarily on good people being rewarded and bad people being punished? Use specific reasons and examples in your discussion.

**Brainstorm**

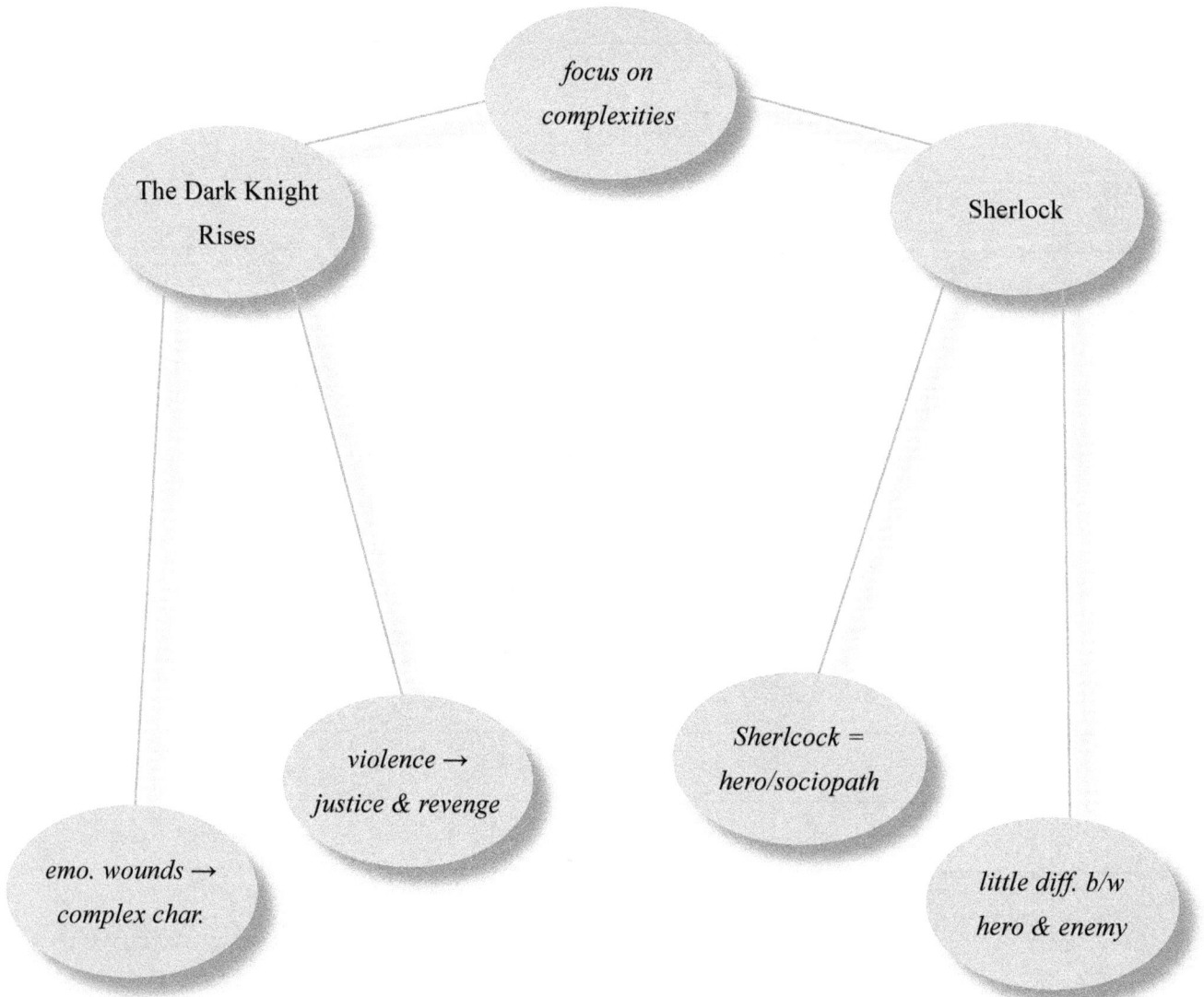

focus on complexities

The Dark Knight Rises

Sherlock

violence → justice & revenge

Sherlcock = hero/sociopath

emo. wounds → complex char.

little diff. b/w hero & enemy

Audiences are interested in stories about good and evil. Many successful movies and shows have characters that are entirely good or completely bad. Movies such as *The Lord of the Rings* and the *Harry Potter* series show good characters rewarded and bad characters permanently punished. These movies, along with animated features such as *Toy Story* and *Monster's Inc.*, are very popular. However, many viewers enjoy a more complicated version of good and evil. **Therefore, television shows and movies should have characters that are morally complex, and not always completely good or completely bad. In this way, the stories will look more like real life.**

An excellent example of a film with a complex depiction of good and evil is the most recent Batman film, *The Dark Knight Rises.* In this film, the Bruce Wayne character once again shows himself to be emotionally wounded and morally complex. Furthermore, because of his wounds, the audience forgives his violent actions. In fact, the combination of these two elements makes his character more interesting. Although the legal system in Gotham is horribly corrupt, Wayne acts completely outside of the boundaries of any moral system. He commits acts of violence both to establish a system of human justice and to seek vengeance.

A current television series with a complex perspective on good and evil is the BBC's *Sherlock.* Although Dr. Watson maintains that Sherlock is a high functioning autistic, Sherlock Holmes describes himself as a "high-functioning sociopath" who lacks a sense of empathy and the other emotional controls that keep 'normal' people from committing violent crimes. We know that it is wrong to injure or kill someone to achieve our own selfish ends. Sherlock does not. The reason he does not act on his most sociopathic impulses is that he is worried about getting caught. That is the difference between Sherlock and the character of his arch-enemy, Moriarty. Furthermore, Sherlock knows that he can always get his sociopathic thrill by chasing down the 'real' sociopaths.

The tension between good and evil is what makes these stories so compelling. Characters know what is right and what is wrong, but circumstances often pull them in both directions. The audience wants to know what these characters will do. This is why movies and television shows should not focus solely on rewarding good characters and punishing bad ones. Audiences know that the world is more complicated.

# Integrated Writing Task 8

## PASSAGE

Every time a person uses a credit card, that person is borrowing money from the company that issued the card; the cardholder then pays the money back with interest over a period of months or years. Today, it seems that everyone has a credit card. In the past, banks and companies only issued credit cards to people who had proven that they were responsible and possessed "good credit." Now, even a college student without a steady income may be issued a card. For many reasons, using a credit card is a risky idea.

For one, credit card use encourages impulse shopping, overspending, and inevitably, great debt. This debt is not something that people can pay off quickly. It may remain with them for years, or possibly a lifetime. Emotionally and financially, this is a heavy burden. Those who acquire credit card debt may even end up paying double or triple the cost of an item just in credit card interest.

Furthermore, the companies that issue credit cards are infamous for applying hidden fees and raising interest rates once people are in debt. This is a common strategy used by banks and companies today. Initially, they issue the credit cards at low interest rates, and once the customer is "hooked," the financial institutions change their payment policies. Raising interest rates and adding hidden fees allow banks and companies to charge their customers more money, further increasing card-holder debt.

A final reason that credit cards are tricky to manage is that they can eventually leave people with bad credit ratings. These credit ratings occur when people are unable to meet their payment obligations over time. Once a person has developed a bad credit score, he or she will have trouble regaining the trust of the financial industry. This is especially damaging to young people, who may need to acquire loans to purchase cars or homes in the future.

🔊 Now listen to part of a lecture on the topic you just read about.

## Notes

| P: | L: |
|----|----|
|    |    |

> **Prompt**
> Summarize the points made in the lecture, being sure to explain how they oppose specific points made in the reading passage.

_____

_____

_____

_____

_____

_____

_____

_____

_____

_____

_____

_____

_____

_____

_____

_____

_____

_____

## Model Answer

**PASSAGE**

Every time a person uses a credit card, that person is borrowing money from the company that issued the card; the cardholder then pays the money back with interest over a period of months or years. Today, it seems that everyone has a credit card. In the past, banks and companies only issued credit cards to people who had proven that they were responsible and possessed "good credit." Now, even a college student without a steady income may be issued a card. For many reasons, using a credit card is a risky idea.

For one, credit card use encourages impulse shopping, overspending, and inevitably, great debt. This debt is not something that people can pay off quickly. It may remain with them for years, or possibly a lifetime. Emotionally and financially, this is a heavy burden. Those who acquire credit card debt may even end up paying double or triple the cost of an item just in credit card interest.

Furthermore, the companies that issue credit cards are infamous for applying hidden fees and raising interest rates once people are in debt. This is a common strategy used by banks and companies today. Initially, they issue the credit cards at low interest rates, and once the customer is "hooked," the financial institutions change their payment policies. Raising interest rates and adding hidden fees allow banks and companies to charge their customers more money, further increasing card-holder debt.

A final reason that credit cards are tricky to manage is that they can eventually leave people with bad credit ratings. These credit ratings occur when people are unable to meet their payment obligations over time. Once a person has developed a bad credit score, he or she will have trouble regaining the trust of the financial industry. This is especially damaging to young people, who may need to acquire loans to purchase cars or homes in the future.

**LECTURE**

As the reading passage acknowledges, credit cards are more prevalent today than ever before. One reason for this may be the convenience of online banking and shopping, which makes managing and using a credit card easier than ever before. But contrary to what the reading implies, this shift is not necessarily bad. It's actually a positive change for several reasons.

To start, the reading claims that credit cards encourage overspending, which leads to debt. Indeed, this is a sad truth for a minority of irresponsible credit card holders. But for the vast majority, credit cards result in temporary rather than permanent debt. When people pay off their credit card balances, they actually raise their credit scores. And for young people, credit cards provide opportunities to build strong credit ratings by making many small purchases, such as groceries and textbooks.

Next, the passage states that credit card companies add hidden fees and raise interest rates on customers once they're in debt. This may be true for some of the organizations that issue credit cards, but there's a great deal of competition in the credit business. Credit issuers know that raising interest rates unexpectedly or adding fees may convince customers to refinance their debt using another company. Their motivation is to retain customers and keep them paying their monthly interest.

Last, the reading argues that credit cards inevitably result in bad credit ratings for users, which may disqualify them from future loans for cars and houses. But this statement is not true either. Most credit card companies are willing to make "deals" for the repayment of debt at mutually acceptable rates for people who are overburdened with debt. The credit card companies do not profit when their customers are unable to pay anything at all.

## Notes

| P: credit cards bad | L: refutes reading |
|---|---|
| encourage overspending → lifelong debt | most ppl. = small debt that ↑ credit score |
| credit co. applies hidden fees once user in debt | hidden fees uncommon; co. wants to keep customers |
| bad credit → can't buy home, car | co. works w/ bad credit customer to help pay off debt |

The lecture contradicts the negative attitude toward credit cards presented in the reading. Credit cards are quite useful and not as dangerous as the reading depicts them, according to the lecture.

First, the lecture explains that credit card users usually accumulate small debts. The reading indicates credit cards encourage overspending and put people into permanent debt. However, the lecture points out that credit card use results in temporary and minor debt for most people. And when paid off on time, credit card use is actually a great way to build a strong credit rating, especially for young people.

Second, most credit card companies compete for customers. The reading claims that credit card companies offer low interest rates at first, but then raise them later or add secret fees. However, the lecture points out that if creditors act in this manner, they risk losing customers. Most credit card issuers are interested in upholding their reputation because they know that it is the best way to maintain customer loyalty.

Finally, credit card companies try to help those in debt. The reading says that credit cards ruin people's futures by ensuring bad credit ratings, but the lecture claims that this rarely happens. In fact, the lecture contends that most credit card companies negotiate payment terms for burdened customers, so the customers are able to avoid bad credit ratings. Most credit card companies do this because they realize that bad credit ratings hurt their chances of receiving customer payments.

# Independent Writing Task I

### Prompt

Do you agree or disagree with the following statement? Countries develop most successfully when governments invest more money in grade school children than in college students. Use specific examples and reasons to support your answer.

## Brainstorm

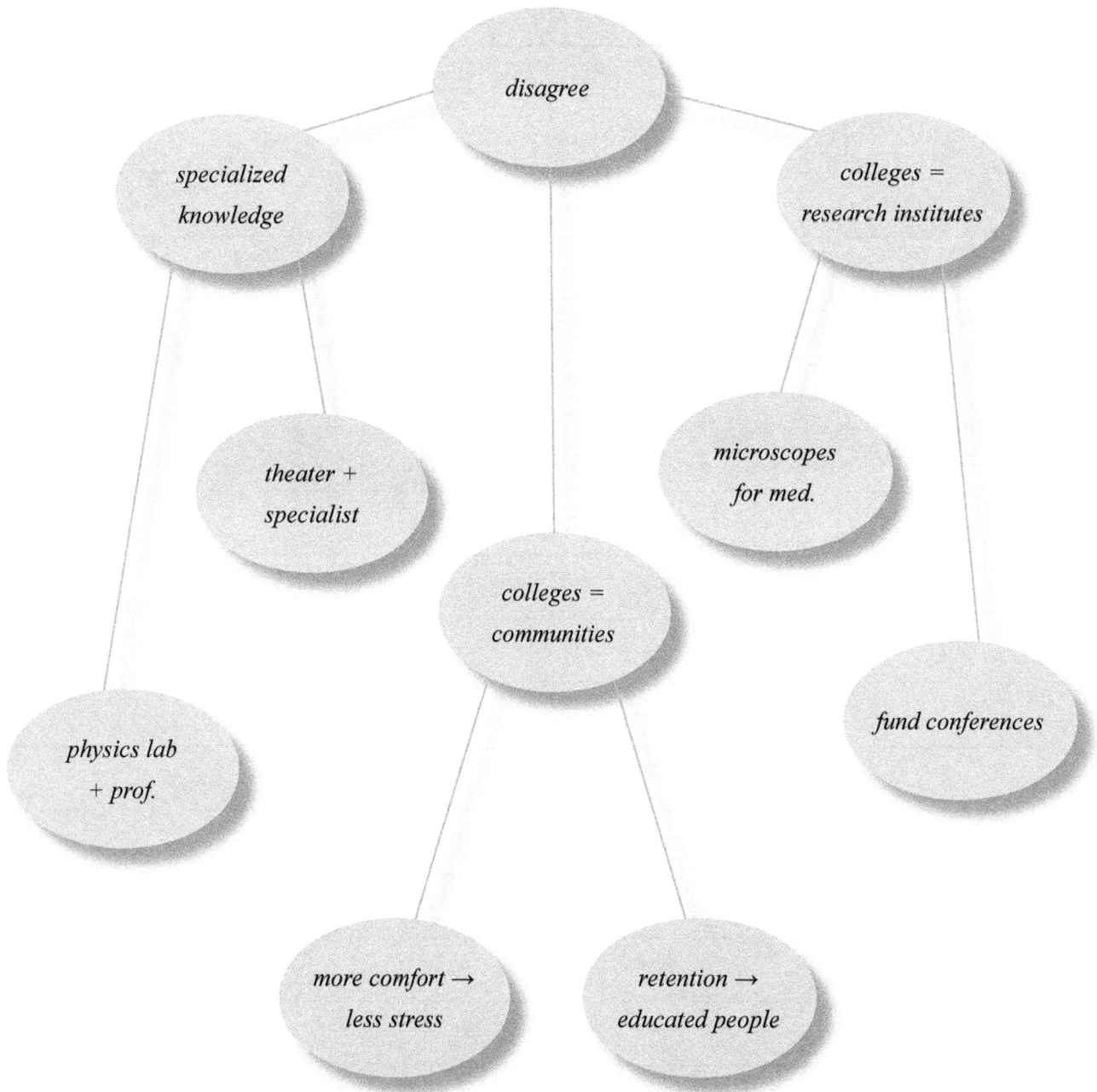

**Prompt**

Do you agree or disagree with the following statement? Countries develop most successfully when governments invest more money in grade school children than in college students. Use specific examples and reasons to support your answer.

## Brainstorm

*disagree*

*specialized knowledge*

*colleges = research institutes*

*theater + specialist*

*microscopes for med.*

*colleges = communities*

*physics lab + prof.*

*fund conferences*

*more comfort → less stress*

*retention → educated people*

Ideally, governments should provide a sufficient amount of money for all levels of education, from grade school through college. Each phase of schooling prepares a student for a different stage in his or her life. **On a per-pupil basis, however, colleges should receive more funding than grade schools, as it costs more to provide a college education, and better-funded colleges help countries and societies develop successfully.**

While the first years of schooling introduce general knowledge and broad concepts, college-level education promises students in-depth knowledge into a specific field of study. As a result, students majoring in physics will need a laboratory and an expert in the field as a teacher. A theater student will need a theater and professional acting instructors. Because higher education must provide specialized learning facilities and instructors, college education is more costly per student than lower-level education.

Furthermore, while elementary schools serve a neighborhood, bigger colleges often enroll students from around the nation or from other countries, meaning the college itself must function as an entire community. It must provide housing, food, libraries, health clinics, and recreational facilities. If the college is financially able to provide comfortable living arrangements, its students will experience less stress and be successful in their studies. Society benefits from students completing their college education and entering the work force with higher-level skills.

Lastly, colleges are expected to provide research and insight in academic fields as well as an education. Hence, colleges need more money to conduct up-to-date research than do grade schools. For instance, if a college cannot afford to replace its outdated microscopes, then it will not be able to perform cutting-edge medical research. If a college cannot afford to host visiting scholars and conferences, its researchers may not be able to stay as up-to-date as others in their fields.

To conclude, while each year of schooling is crucial to a student's success, some stages of education inevitably require more money than others. Colleges and universities need higher levels of funding in order to provide the services that we expect from them.

# Independent Writing Task II

Prompt

**Prompt**

Do you think that university professors should spend more time teaching classes or conducting research? Use specific reasons and examples to explain your opinion.

## Brainstorm

# Model Answer

**Prompt**

Do you think that university professors should spend more time teaching classes or conducting research? Use specific reasons and examples to explain your opinion.

**Brainstorm**

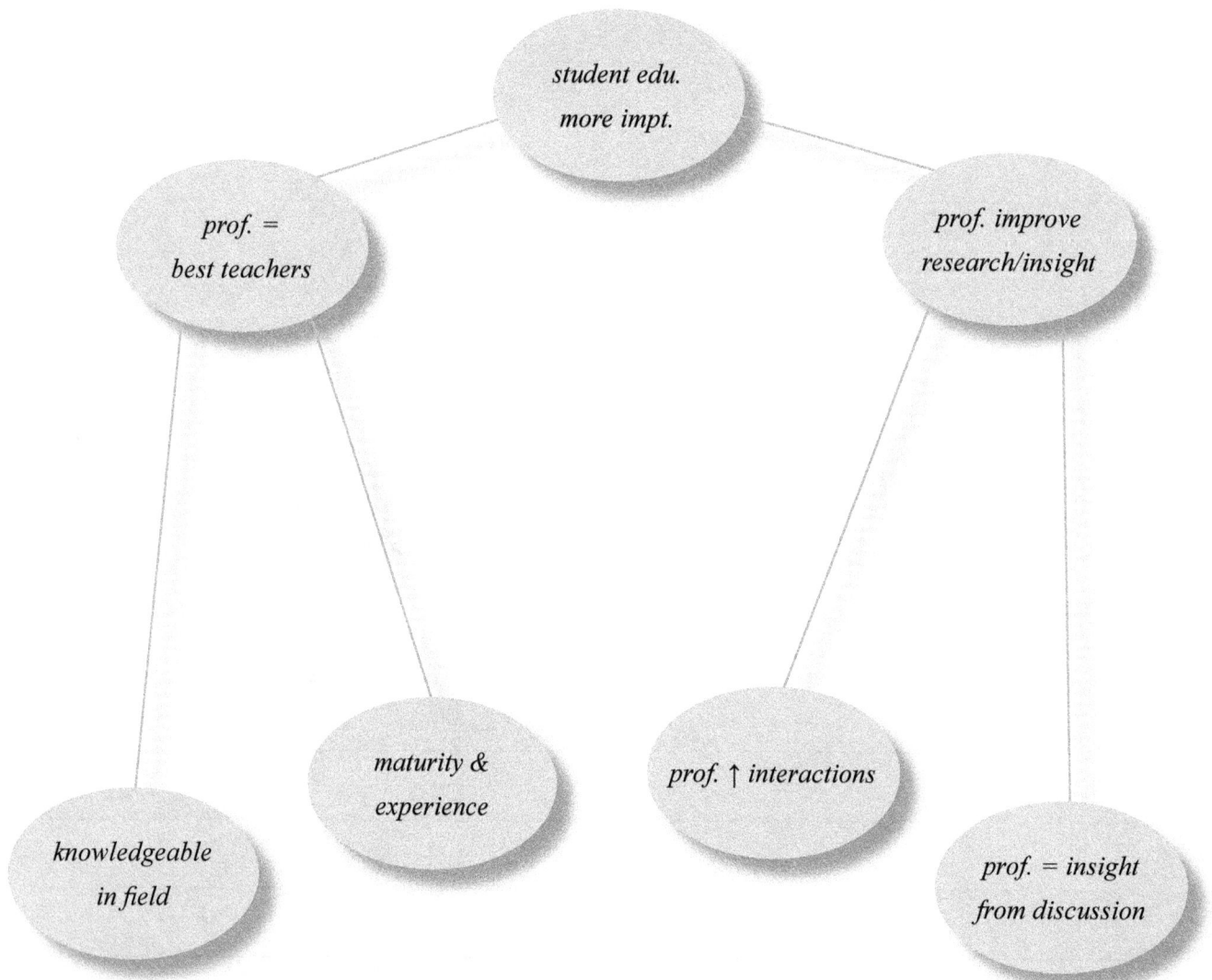

The public expects a great deal from college and university professors. The perfect professor would be zealous about contributing to his or her field and equally zealous about educating undergraduate students. **While both tasks are important, teaching should be the top priority of professors because it will intellectually benefit both the students and the professor.**

First, <u>students will benefit if professors present lectures, lead discussions, and grade papers instead of having graduate students fulfill these tasks.</u> It is inevitable that graduate students will teach some introductory courses because of tight college budgets, but students should primarily learn from professors who are experts in their respective fields. For example, a 60-year-old professor of history is likely to have a better understanding of past events than a 23-year-old graduate student. Moreover, professors are likely to have more maturity and experience when helping students make important discoveries of their own. For instance, during my first year of college, I was fortunate enough to have an experienced professor who asked me thought-provoking questions that challenged my perceptions of the world.

Furthermore, <u>interacting with students can benefit professors.</u> If a professor is always busy conducting research and communicating mainly with peers in the same field, then he or she might become isolated. Teaching about a topic forces one to think about how to articulate ideas simply, generating creativity in the process. Additionally, fresh perspectives and new questions that come up in the classroom may stimulate new paths of inquiry or insight for the professor. For example, a student in a computer programming class might ask a particularly challenging question that causes the professor to reassess his position on the topic.

Professors should not have to give up research for teaching, but education should be their top priority. After all, the students of today will be the professors of tomorrow. Meanwhile, professors themselves are likely to experience personal and academic gains from classroom discussions.

# Integrated Writing Task 9

*Cloud seeding* is an attempt at weather modification in which chemicals, such as silver and potassium iodide crystals, are sprayed into clouds to encourage precipitation. Theoretically, water molecules in the cloud condense around the crystals and fall to the ground. The technique is still in its infancy, even though it has been used for more than 60 years. In a world facing shortages of fresh water for an ever-growing population, cloud seeding may become a crucial tool for generating rain and snow.

One reason to pursue cloud seeding is that it has the potential to mitigate drought. That is, when people are desperate for clean, fresh water, cloud seeding could help meet the need in the quickest and most cost-effective way. It is less expensive and quicker than building canals or desalinization plants. Moreover, researchers suspect that air pollution inhibits rainfall; cloud seeding may be able to stimulate rainfall, which would negate some of the environmental harm caused by air pollution.

Cloud seeding may also benefit agriculture. If researchers are able to perfect the science, it could be used to bring rain to crops, helping feed the people of that region. Cloud seeding has the potential to avert hailstorms and hurricanes, which would also prevent crop damage. Anything that could prevent famine is worth investigation, including cloud seeding.

There are many ways that cloud seeding could benefit a region's economic and social stability. Many regions generate electric power with water turbines in dams; these areas must receive adequate snow and rain in order to avoid power shortages. Ski resorts and tourist spots also rely on regular precipitation. China even used cloud seeding to try to ensure that there would not be rain during the Beijing Olympics. People in areas where there is threat of wildfire dream of being able to douse fires with rain. In fact, people have dreamed of many benefits of being able to control rain.

🔊 Now listen to part of a lecture on the topic you just read about.

| Notes |
| :---: |

| P: | L: |
| --- | --- |
|  |  |
|  |  |
|  |  |
|  |  |

**Prompt**

Summarize the points made in the lecture, being sure to explain how they oppose specific points made in the reading passage.

_____

_____

_____

_____

_____

_____

_____

_____

_____

_____

_____

_____

_____

_____

_____

_____

_____

_____

_____

_____

# Model Answer

*Cloud seeding* is an attempt at weather modification in which chemicals, such as silver and potassium iodide crystals, are sprayed into clouds to encourage precipitation. Theoretically, water molecules in the cloud condense around the crystals and fall to the ground. The technique is still in its infancy, even though it has been used for more than 60 years. In a world facing shortages of fresh water for an ever-growing population, cloud seeding may become a crucial tool for generating rain and snow.

One reason to pursue cloud seeding is that it has the potential to mitigate drought. That is, when people are desperate for clean, fresh water, cloud seeding could help meet the need in the quickest and most cost-effective way. It is less expensive and quicker than building canals or desalinization plants. Moreover, researchers suspect that air pollution inhibits rainfall; cloud seeding may be able to stimulate rainfall, which would negate some of the environmental harm caused by air pollution.

Cloud seeding may also benefit agriculture. If researchers are able to perfect the science, it could be used to bring rain to crops, helping feed the people of that region. Cloud seeding has the potential to avert hailstorms and hurricanes, which would also prevent crop damage. Anything that could prevent famine is worth investigation, including cloud seeding.

There are many ways that cloud seeding could benefit a region's economic and social stability. Many regions generate electric power with water turbines in dams; these areas must receive adequate snow and rain in order to avoid power shortages. Ski resorts and tourist spots also rely on regular precipitation. China even used cloud seeding to try to ensure that there would not be rain during the Beijing Olympics. People in areas where there is threat of wildfire dream of being able to douse fires with rain. In fact, people have dreamed of many benefits of being able to control rain.

## LECTURE

*As the reading points out, our world is definitely facing a fresh water crisis, so controlling rainfall and snowfall would be ideal. But cloud seeding is not worth pursuing for several reasons.*

*For one, we shouldn't consider cloud seeding as a way to prevent drought for the simple reason that we have no idea whether the method really works. There's no way to test its effectiveness. When cloud seeding seems to induce rain, scientists can't prove that seeding caused the rain. Even if we could predict exactly where the rain produced by cloud seeding would fall, cloud seeding would only work when there are clouds. It's overly optimistic to think that we could relieve water shortages by controlling weather.*

*Secondly, the reading says that cloud seeding might prevent hunger, as it could help bring regular water to farms and protect crops from storm damage. While this is a noble goal, it doesn't make cloud seeding a worthy investment. Cloud seeding adds chemicals to the environment, and we simply don't know the effects of repeated doses of silver iodide on our soil or in our oceans. The chemicals could potentially damage crops or disrupt the equilibrium of an ecosystem.*

*Finally, the reading says that cloud seeding could stabilize the economies and safety of some regions, such as regions that depend on water for electric power. But even this proposition has its issues: if rain and snow can be controlled, then they can be misused as well. Terrorists could use cloud seeding as an environmental weapon by flooding entire regions. Moreover, military conflict could ensue if one region accuses its neighbor of draining its water by moving clouds.*

*We need to admit that controlling rain probably does not work, and even if it does, it could cause more harm than good.*

**Notes**

| P: cloud seeding could be effective | L: cloud seeding unrealistic |
|---|---|
| prevent droughts | has not been proven effective |
| spur/protect agriculture | add chemicals to env. |
| benefit econ. | could be misused (terrorists, war) |

The reading presents the potential benefits of cloud seeding, which involves adding chemicals to clouds to produce rain or snow. The lecturer does not believe that cloud seeding can solve water shortages or otherwise control the weather. The lecture clarifies that cloud seeding may be little more than a dream, and that it may cause more problems than it solves.

According to the lecture, the most basic problem with cloud seeding is that it may not work, as scientists have no way of measuring its success. If the clouds are seeded and then it rains, researchers do not know whether cloud seeding or nature produced the rain. Moreover, even if cloud seeding does work, we cannot control exactly where rain will fall. Additionally, cloud seeding requires clouds, so it is not really a practical solution to drought, which is usually accompanied by clear skies.

Second, the lecture states that cloud seeding adds chemicals to the atmosphere that may not be environmentally safe. When these chemicals permeate soil, they may end up harming the crops or livestock that provide our food. Thus, cloud seeding may not be helpful to agriculture, as the reading claims. Rather, it may prove to be a danger in the long term.

Finally, the lecture claims that artificially produced rain and snow might have just as many negative effects as positive ones on a region's economy. For example, criminal forces could take control of a region's weather. Another danger is that cloud seeding could trigger conflicts over who should get the rain from moving clouds.

# Independent Writing Task I

**Prompt**

Some parents help their children with schoolwork while others offer only encouragement. Which approach more effectively inspires independence in children? Use specific examples and reasons to support your answer.

**Brainstorm**

_____

_____

_____

_____

_____

_____

_____

_____

# Model Answer

> **Prompt**
>
> Some parents help their children with schoolwork while others offer only encouragement. Which approach more effectively inspires independence in children? Use specific examples and reasons to support your answer.

**Brainstorm**

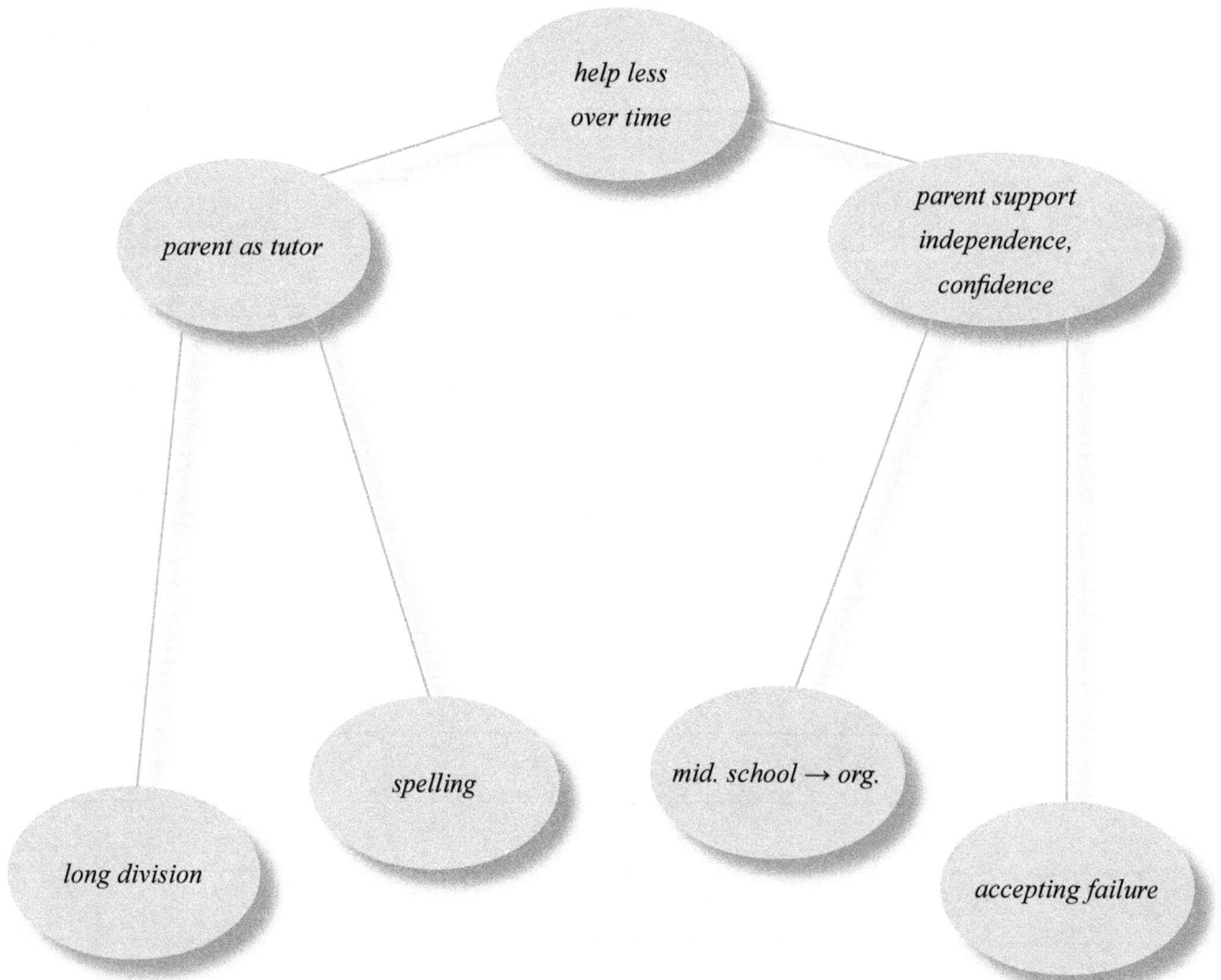

A parent often views his or her child's academic success as crucial to the child's future happiness. Thus, some parents help their children complete schoolwork, hoping that their child's success on each assignment will ensure his or her eventual career success. A different parenting philosophy is to simply offer encouragement from the sidelines. **I believe that, for most children, providing a mix of both hands-on help and a push toward independence is the best approach.**

On the one hand, <u>parents can be great tutors by supplementing classroom teaching, as classroom teachers cannot meet each student's learning needs.</u> I remember how difficult it was for me to learn long division when I was a child. I became nervous when the teacher explained it carefully to the class, so I could not concentrate. It was only later when my mother patiently re-taught me the process at the kitchen table that I understood. Besides re-teaching, parents can also help children practice skills and memorize information. For example, parents can listen to their children read or quiz them on spelling words. Parents can give the personal attention that a child may need.

On the other hand, <u>parents should be careful not to do too much of their children's work for them.</u> Parents should gradually step back and require their children to become more self-sufficient as they grow. For example, by the time a child is in middle school, he or she should keep track of when assignments are due and should practice organizing his or her notes and homework independently. Parents should accept that children might fail at first as they learn these skills, but in the long run they will feel more confident, and will be much more psychologically prepared for academic challenges.

Parents can help children succeed academically, but not by taking over all of a child's academic duties. The best way to help a child succeed is to provide less and less support as the child matures. By doing so, a child can feel a sense of accomplishment and independence.

# Independent Writing Task II

**Prompt**

Do you agree or disagree with the following statement? The quality of an education is determined by the amount of money that the university spends on professors' salaries. Explain your position using reasons and details.

**Brainstorm**

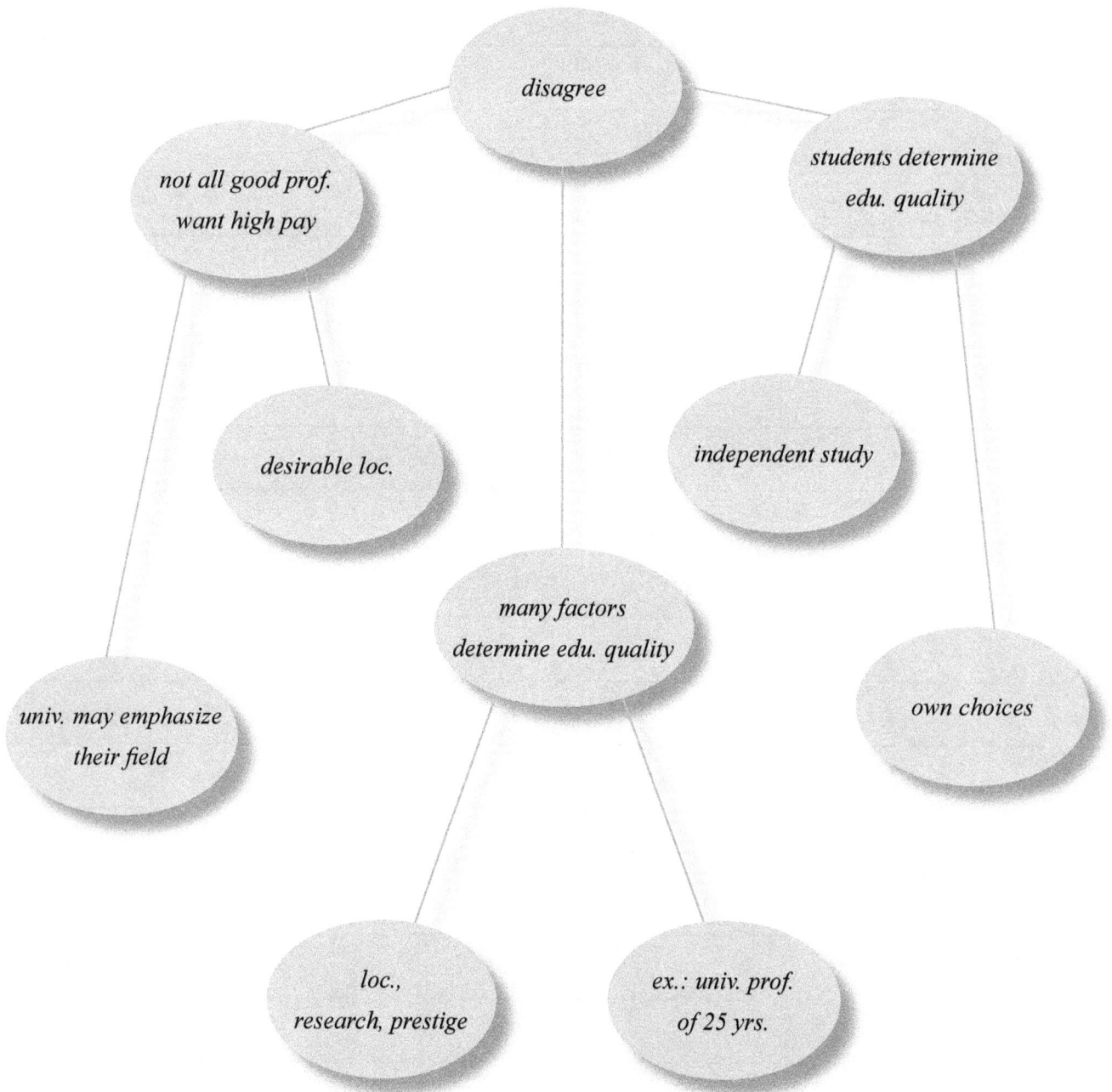

**Prompt**

Do you agree or disagree with the following statement? The quality of an education is determined by the amount of money that the university spends on professors' salaries. Explain your position using reasons and details.

## Brainstorm

- *disagree*
  - *not all good prof. want high pay*
    - *desirable loc.*
    - *univ. may emphasize their field*
  - *many factors determine edu. quality*
    - *loc., research, prestige*
    - *ex.: univ. prof. of 25 yrs.*
  - *students determine edu. quality*
    - *independent study*
    - *own choices*

College experiences are not standardized. Some college students will learn more than others will, and it is difficult for students and parents to predict where they can gain the highest quality education. **A university that pays high salaries in an effort to attract the most renowned scholars may not necessarily be the best university for a number of reasons.**

First, <u>many professors are attracted to a particular university because it offers more than simply a high salary.</u> Professors may be drawn to a university's location, research facilities, or historical prestige. For example, one of my undergraduate professors had been teaching at my university for over 25 years by the time I took one of his classes. He is a world-renown linguist, and had been offered positions at more prestigious universities, but he remained at my school because of its location. My university is located near a well-known surf spot, and my professor is an avid surfer. Thus, he turned down higher salaries so he could continue his hobby.

<u>Even if a university attracts the best faculty in the world, many other factors have equal or greater effects on learning.</u> Universities that hire more professors, offer smaller classes, provide more tutors, and avoid putting too much pressure on their faculties may support learning in the best way. Additionally, universities that meet the practical needs of their student population, whether it is a quiet study area or online classes, may provide the best education for a particular student.

Finally, <u>students themselves play the biggest role in how much they learn.</u> Because students are expected to read, discuss, write, and research on their own, most learning in college takes place outside of the classroom. Additionally, students are largely responsible for choosing their own classes and following their own passions, so they control many factors that determine the quality of their own education.

A professor's salary is a minor factor when determining the quality of a university's education. Great professors may be found even where the pay is lower. Ultimately, there is no one indicator of whether a student will learn more or less at college, as many complex factors play a part.

# Integrated Writing Task 10

In 1996, scientists made a startling announcement: they may have found evidence of primitive life inside a 4-billion year old Martian rock that fell to Earth 13,000 years ago. The potato-sized meteorite contained what appeared to be fossilized microbes from a time when Mars' surface contained liquid water. The news made headlines around the world, and United States President Bill Clinton held a news conference to discuss the discovery. However, since then, many in the scientific community have dismissed the findings.

One reason that the Martian meteorite probably does not contain evidence of life is due to the type of material found on it. The chain structures revealed under an electron microscope resemble bacteria-like life forms. However, these life forms are smaller than any form of life, or fossilized life, in Earth's known history. At their size, 20 to 100 nanometers, they are too small to possess DNA or RNA chains, considered the building blocks of life on Earth.

Another reason that the Martian meteorite probably does not offer proof of life on Mars is that there is no way to determine whether it was contaminated with organisms after it fell to Earth. In other words, the meteorite has been on Earth for so long that some type of Earth bacteria might have inhabited the rock. Terrestrial "contamination" is commonly found on most meteorite specimens on Earth.

Finally, the Martian meteorite was in outer space for too long to possibly hold any evidence of life. According to scientists, the meteorite was in space for 16 million years before it crashed to Earth. Any life, or evidence of life, would have been destroyed by the conditions in space, since outer space is filled with radiation and temperatures averaging -270 degrees Celsius.

🔊)) Now listen to part of a lecture on the topic you just read about.

Notes

| P: | L: |
|----|----|
|    |    |

> **Prompt**
> Summarize the points made in the lecture, being sure to explain how they oppose specific points made in the reading passage.

_____

_____

_____

_____

_____

_____

_____

_____

_____

_____

_____

_____

_____

_____

_____

_____

_____

_____

_____

_____

# Model Answer

In 1996, scientists made a startling announcement: they may have found evidence of primitive life inside a 4-billion year old Martian rock that fell to Earth 13,000 years ago. The potato-sized meteorite contained what appeared to be fossilized microbes from a time when Mars' surface contained liquid water. The news made headlines around the world, and United States President Bill Clinton held a news conference to discuss the discovery. However, since then, many in the scientific community have dismissed the findings.

One reason that the Martian meteorite probably does not contain evidence of life is due to the type of material found on it. The chain structures revealed under an electron microscope resemble bacteria-like life forms. However, these life forms are smaller than any form of life, or fossilized life, in Earth's known history. At their size, 20 to 100 nanometers, they are too small to possess DNA or RNA chains, considered the building blocks of life on Earth.

Another reason that the Martian meteorite probably does not offer proof of life on Mars is that there is no way to determine whether it was contaminated with organisms after it fell to Earth. In other words, the meteorite has been on Earth for so long that some type of Earth bacteria might have inhabited the rock. Terrestrial "contamination" is commonly found on most meteorite specimens on Earth.

Finally, the Martian meteorite was in outer space for too long to possibly hold any evidence of life. According to scientists, the meteorite was in space for 16 million years before it crashed to Earth. Any life, or evidence of life, would have been destroyed by the conditions in space, since outer space is filled with radiation and temperatures averaging -270 degrees Celsius.

## LECTURE

*You just read about some of the scientific criticisms of the 1996 study that found evidence of ancient Martian life. The passage provides some convincing arguments. Nevertheless, while the information is persuasive, it doesn't disprove the possibility that the Martian meteorite contains evidence of life on Mars.*

*To begin, the reading states that the Martian meteorite contains fossil-like structures smaller than any known life form on Earth. At the time of its discovery, that was true. But since 1996, biologists on Earth have cultivated nanobacteria of similar size in the laboratory, proving that such minute life can exist. Also, it doesn't make sense to say that because something doesn't exist on Earth, it couldn't have ever existed on Mars. The whole point of astrobiology is to recognize life in different forms.*

*Next, the reading theorizes that the evidence of life found on the Martian meteorite may have taken up residence on the rock once it was on Earth. One problem with this theory is that the bacteria-like structures are deeply embedded in the meteorite, and increase in density closer to the center. A meteorite that became contaminated by terrestrial life would leave evidence mainly on the surface layer.*

*Finally, the reading states that the Martian meteorite can't provide evidence of life because of the millions of years it spent in outer space. According to the reading, the conditions in outer space would have eradicated any life form or fossil very quickly. However, this claim is completely inapplicable to the Martian meteorite. When the rock left Mars, the life forms could've been long dead and their imprints fossilized deep within the rock. Since the 1996 finding, the scientists have identified similar shapes within other Martian rocks. It's certainly conceivable that the fossils could've remained intact even as they journeyed through space.*

**Notes**

| P: Martian rock doesn't contain life | L: Martian rock may contain life |
| --- | --- |
| structures too small to be life | nanobacteria created since meteorite's discovery |
| may have been contaminated by Earth life | evidence found in rock, no contamination possible |
| in space for 16 mil. yrs. | fossil imprints in the rock wouldn't wear away in space |

The reading discusses the discovery of a Martian meteorite, claiming that this meteorite does not contain evidence of extraterrestrial life. The lecture refutes the reading by claiming that the meteorite may contain evidence of life on Mars. The lecture provides logical arguments that oppose those presented in the reading.

First, the lecture maintains that living organisms could have left the fossils within the meteorite, even though they are smaller than any naturally occurring terrestrial life form yet discovered. According to the lecture, these fossils could have been left by life forms with which people are not yet familiar. The lecture adds that nanobacteria the size of those life forms found within the meteorite have since been grown in laboratory conditions on Earth.

Second, the lecture presents logical counter arguments to the reading's claims that the fossils were made by organisms from Earth. The lecture points out that the fossils and other evidence were found deep inside the meteorite, and that they increase in density deeper in the rock. If the rock were colonized by life forms after it landed on Earth, it would make more sense for that evidence to be found on the meteorite's exterior.

Finally, the fossils could have survived their time in space. The lecture agrees with the reading's claim that the meteorite spent millions of years in harsh space conditions, but points out that the fossils are deeply embedded in the meteorite and are merely an imprint, not a living organism. It is quite likely that the fossilized imprints remained intact within the Martian meteorite, according to the lecture.

# Independent Writing Task I

## Prompt

Do you agree or disagree with the following statement? It is easier to become an educated person now than it was in the past. Use specific details and reasons in your discussion.

## Brainstorm

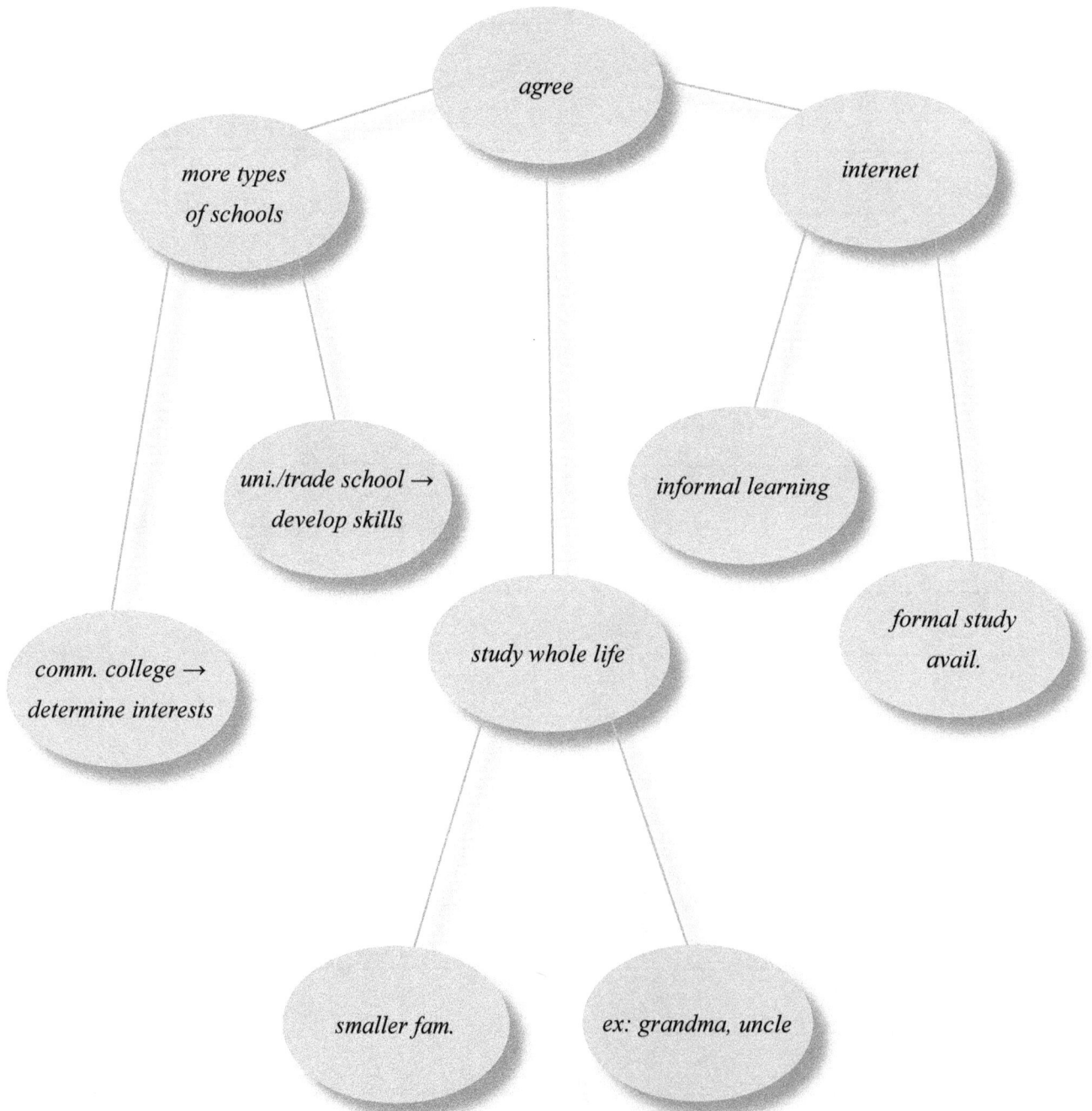

**Prompt**

Do you agree or disagree with the following statement? It is easier to become an educated person now than it was in the past. Use specific details and reasons in your discussion.

## Brainstorm

**agree**

**more types of schools**

**internet**

**uni./trade school →
develop skills**

**informal learning**

**comm. college →
determine interests**

**study whole life**

**formal study
avail.**

**smaller fam.**

**ex: grandma, uncle**

Many past cultures viewed education as the ultimate privilege. Knowledge that is commonplace today was once only available to an elite few. **Societal and technological changes have made education less expensive and more accessible, so it is easier to become an educated person today than at any other time in history.**

First, <u>it is easier to become educated nowadays because more types of schools exist than ever before.</u> Students looking for a general education before deciding on a specific field of study can get an affordable education at a community college. Many four-year universities offer hundreds of majors as well as masters and doctoral programs for the most committed students. And trade schools offer students opportunities to develop the skills for a particular profession, such as that of a mechanic or an electrician. Clearly, there are educational opportunities to fit the learning needs of every individual.

Second, <u>it is now more widely accepted for education to continue beyond the traditional college age.</u> Part of this may be because people in many regions tend to have fewer children than previous generations. With smaller families to support and care for, more people are able to pursue education at any age. For example, my grandmother had only two children, and when they were grown, she went back to school and earned a special counseling certificate. My uncle also had only two children, and he was able to earn a master's degree in his field when his children started elementary school. Social changes have made it easier for people today to pursue academic achievement throughout their lives.

Third, <u>internet-based learning is possible for anyone with access to a computer and an internet connection.</u> Whether a person wants to learn the correct way to conjugate a verb or the proper way to repair a car, the information is as close as the nearest computer. The internet provides the most flexible manner of formal education, as well. A student can log in to most internet classes at any time. Thus, people can continue their educations even when they cannot get to a campus because of work schedules, distance, health, or weather concerns.

Many societies still have a long way to go to open up educational opportunities to everyone, but the path toward learning is definitely more diverse and accessible today than it was in the past.

# Independent Writing Task II

---

**Prompt**

Do you agree or disagree with the following statement? Parents should set strict limits on how much time their children spend watching television. Use specific reasons and examples to develop your response.

**Brainstorm**

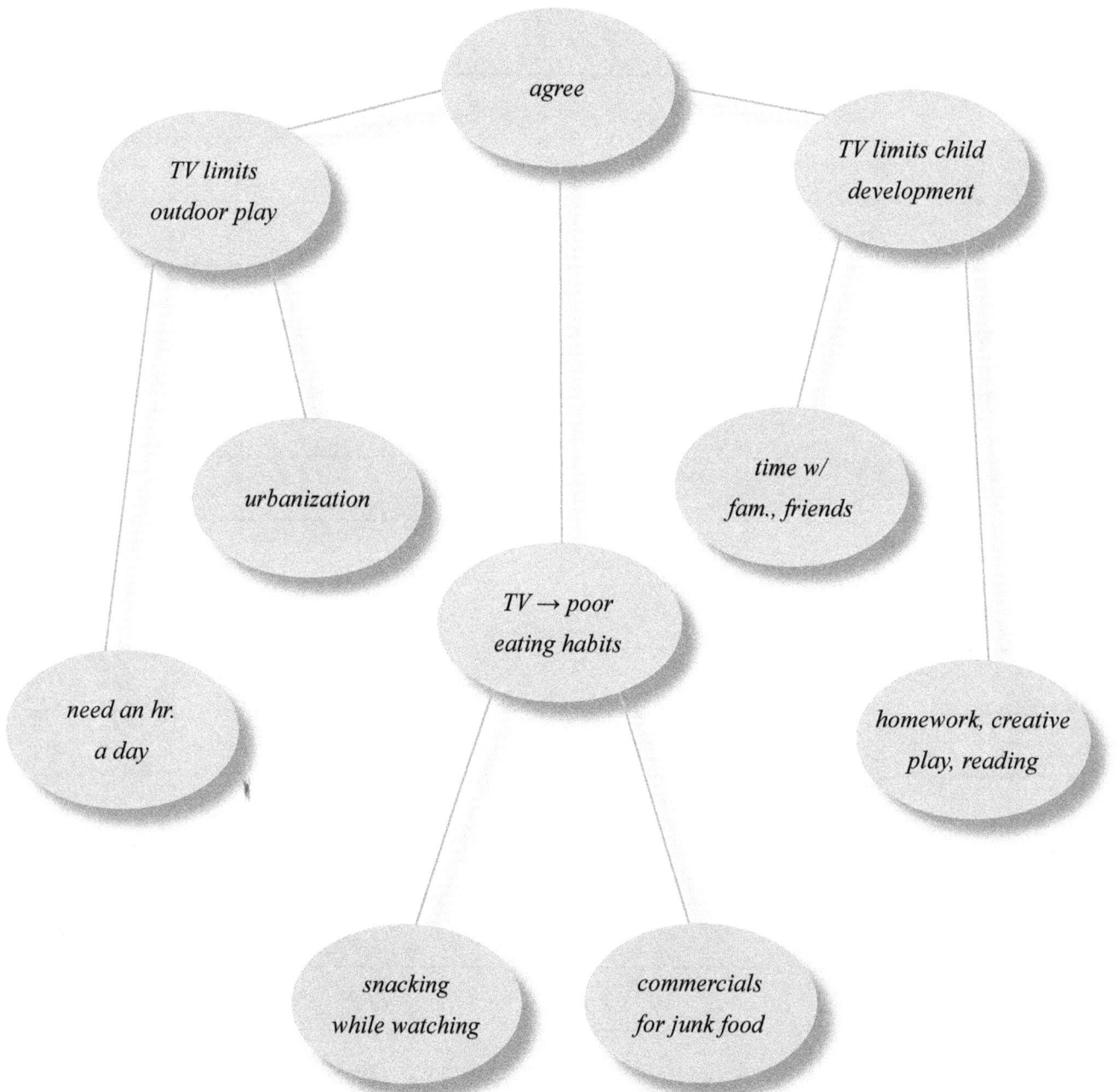

# Model Answer

**▶ Prompt ◀**

Do you agree or disagree with the following statement? Parents should set strict limits on how much time their children spend watching television. Use specific reasons and examples to develop your response.

**Brainstorm**

agree

TV limits outdoor play

TV limits child development

urbanization

time w/ fam., friends

TV → poor eating habits

need an hr. a day

homework, creative play, reading

snacking while watching

commercials for junk food

In the past, most children spent hours playing outside each day or helping with chores. Today's children are lured by around-the-clock television programming that is targeted at them. While television has its benefits, too much time in front of the television results in children not getting enough exercise, becoming overweight, and not spending enough time on other activities. **Parents need to set limits on television viewing so that children have the opportunity to become their best selves.**

Although giving children some time to watch television is acceptable, allowing them to watch television for many hours each day prevents them from getting enough physical activity. Children and adolescents need an hour or more of physical activity each day to get the aerobic exercise and bone- and muscle-strengthening exercise they need to be healthy. Of course, there are other reasons that children cannot play outside as much now, including a more crowded, urbanized world. But parents must do everything they can to encourage whatever types of physical activity are available and not let the television dominate a child's free time.

Furthermore, watching excessive amounts of television contributes to poor eating habits. Children often eat snacks while sitting in front of the television. Additionally, many television commercials that air during children's shows promote unhealthy foods. Parents can help their children avoid all of the problems that come with obesity, including body image issues, cardiovascular problems, and diabetes, if they strictly limit the amount of time that their children spend watching television.

Finally, when children are watching television, they are not involved in other activities, such as homework, social interactions, creative play, or reading. The brain develops during childhood, so depriving a child of these interactions could limit his or her emotional and intellectual development. After all, children should do as much learning in their homes as they do in school, and if they simply sit in front of their televisions all day, they will miss out on valuable life experiences.

In conclusion, I support parents setting strict limits on television viewing. Children's physical development and health depend on parents knowing when to turn off the television.

# Integrated Writing Task 11

PASSAGE

Contacting one's friends using electronic messaging, such as text messages, Facebook, and email, is becoming increasingly common. However, these means of communication, which seem to keep people in touch with one another, actually make people feel lonely.

One way that electronic messaging makes people less connected to one another is by eliminating the need for face-to-face interactions. For example, there is a marked decrease in recent years of young people getting drivers' licenses. Experts say that young people have less motivation to get together to chat in person. Other studies have shown that people have been gradually spending more money on electronic devices they can use at home, such as computers, and less money on restaurants, travel, and going to the movies. These statistics indicate that people are making less of an effort to see each other face-to-face.

Social networking sites in particular promote interactions that are shallow and that leave people feeling less connected. For example, compared to spoken conversation, typed comments convey very little nuance. Receiving a "like" on Facebook or a smiling "selfie" does not make a person feel connected. Another reason that social media leads to shallow interactions is that people carefully choose the photos and comments that they share, which leads to an artificial presentation of constant happiness. One study found that the people who spent the most time on Facebook faced depression because they were envious of the happy times that their friends were apparently having.

Paradoxically, electronic communication also makes people lonelier because it requires constant self-presentation. Whether people are texting during dinner or posting a picture of a pretty sunset at the beach, they are never able to forget about themselves. Instead of focusing on dinner or the sunset, people are thinking about how to present the experience. The process leads to self-absorption. In the long term, such narcissism deepens feelings of loneliness.

🔊 Now listen to part of a lecture on the topic you just read about.

**Notes**

| P: | L: |
|---|---|
| | |
| | |
| | |

**Prompt**

Summarize the points made in the lecture, being sure to explain how they oppose specific points made in the reading passage.

_____

_____

_____

_____

_____

_____

_____

_____

_____

_____

_____

_____

_____

_____

_____

_____

_____

_____

_____

_____

# Model Answer

Contacting one's friends using electronic messaging, such as text messages, Facebook, and email, is becoming increasingly common. However, these means of communication, which seem to keep people in touch with one another, actually make people feel lonely.

One way that electronic messaging makes people less connected to one another is by eliminating the need for face-to-face interactions. For example, there is a marked decrease in recent years of young people getting drivers' licenses. Experts say that young people have less motivation to get together to chat in person. Other studies have shown that people have been gradually spending more money on electronic devices they can use at home, such as computers, and less money on restaurants, travel, and going to the movies. These statistics indicate that people are making less of an effort to see each other face-to-face.

Social networking sites in particular promote interactions that are shallow and that leave people feeling less connected. For example, compared to spoken conversation, typed comments convey very little nuance. Receiving a "like" on Facebook or a smiling "selfie" does not make a person feel connected. Another reason that social media leads to shallow interactions is that people carefully choose the photos and comments that they share, which leads to an artificial presentation of constant happiness. One study found that the people who spent the most time on Facebook faced depression because they were envious of the happy times that their friends were apparently having.

Paradoxically, electronic communication also makes people lonelier because it requires constant self-presentation. Whether people are texting during dinner or posting a picture of a pretty sunset at the beach, they are never able to forget about themselves. Instead of focusing on dinner or the sunset, people are thinking about how to present the experience. The process leads to self-absorption. In the long term, such narcissism deepens feelings of loneliness.

## LECTURE

These days, people under the age of 30 tend to be most comfortable contacting others with a short typed message or a photo. As evidenced in the reading, this has sparked fear among many social commentators. But there's really no convincing proof that today's modes of communication are making people lonelier.

To start, there's no compelling evidence that electronic communication causes people to stay home more and not get drivers' licenses. There're many other possible explanations. For example, with unemployment being high, young people may be less able to afford driver's training courses, let alone cars, gas, and car insurance. For the same reason, many people may be unable to afford dining out at restaurants. These trends may not be permanent, and they may be completely unrelated to modes of communication.

Secondly, there's no good evidence that social media encourages shallow communication. Communication has probably always been a mix of polite small talk and intimate conversations. For example, when a neighbor walks by and says "How are you?" the expected response is, "Fine, and you?" Only close friends expect more detail. Meanwhile, the majority of people who use social media such as Facebook probably understand these social conventions and don't come to the irrational conclusion that everyone but them is happy. Relying on Facebook for fulfillment may be a symptom of depression, not a cause.

Finally, the fact that some people never put down their electronic devices doesn't mean that everyone is constantly thinking about themselves. Adolescents of every era tend to be more self-conscious than older people, but that doesn't mean they're becoming narcissistic. In fact, having constant access to others through texting and social media might have the opposite effect, encouraging more understanding of others' viewpoints and more appreciation for their humor and creativity.

**Notes**

| **P:** electronic communication causes isolation | **L:** no proof of elec. comm. causing isolation |
|---|---|
| discourages face-to-face comm. | no link b/w driv. lic. & elec. comm. |
| promotes shallow comm. | much comm. has always been shallow |
| promotes self-absorption | elec. comm. may encourage understanding |

The lecture counters the negative attitude that the reading expresses toward digital communication such as text messaging and social networking via the internet. The lecture refutes each of the points presented in the reading.

First, it may be true that, as the reading says, people are staying home more, and that fewer young people are getting drivers' licenses than in the past, but the lecture points out that there are many explanations for these trends. For example, a weaker economy forces people to focus on paying their bills, so they cannot spend money on entertainment or even driving. If people are seeing each other less, it may not be the fault of their laptops and smartphones.

Next, the shallowness of many conversations conducted through websites and texts does not indicate that communication has become shallower. The lecture points out that formulaic polite conversation did not begin with social networking sites, as it has long been a normal part of social life. Moreover, it is probably not true that Facebook causes people to feel envious and sad, because users understand the context of the website. The study mentioned in the reading might be showing that depressed people turn to Facebook for comfort, not that Facebook causes depression.

The lecture also questions the passage's claim that people are focusing on themselves too much because they can never stop thinking about how to convey their every thought and action on social media. The lecture claims that self-consciousness is a symptom of teenagers from every generation, not a phenomenon produced by social media. Ultimately, the lecture claims that constant communication via social media encourages people to focus more on others, not less.

# Independent Writing Task I

**Prompt**

Do you agree or disagree with following statement? Parents today understand their children better than parents 50 years ago did. Use specific reasons and examples to support your answer.

## Brainstorm

_____

_____

_____

_____

_____

_____

_____

_____

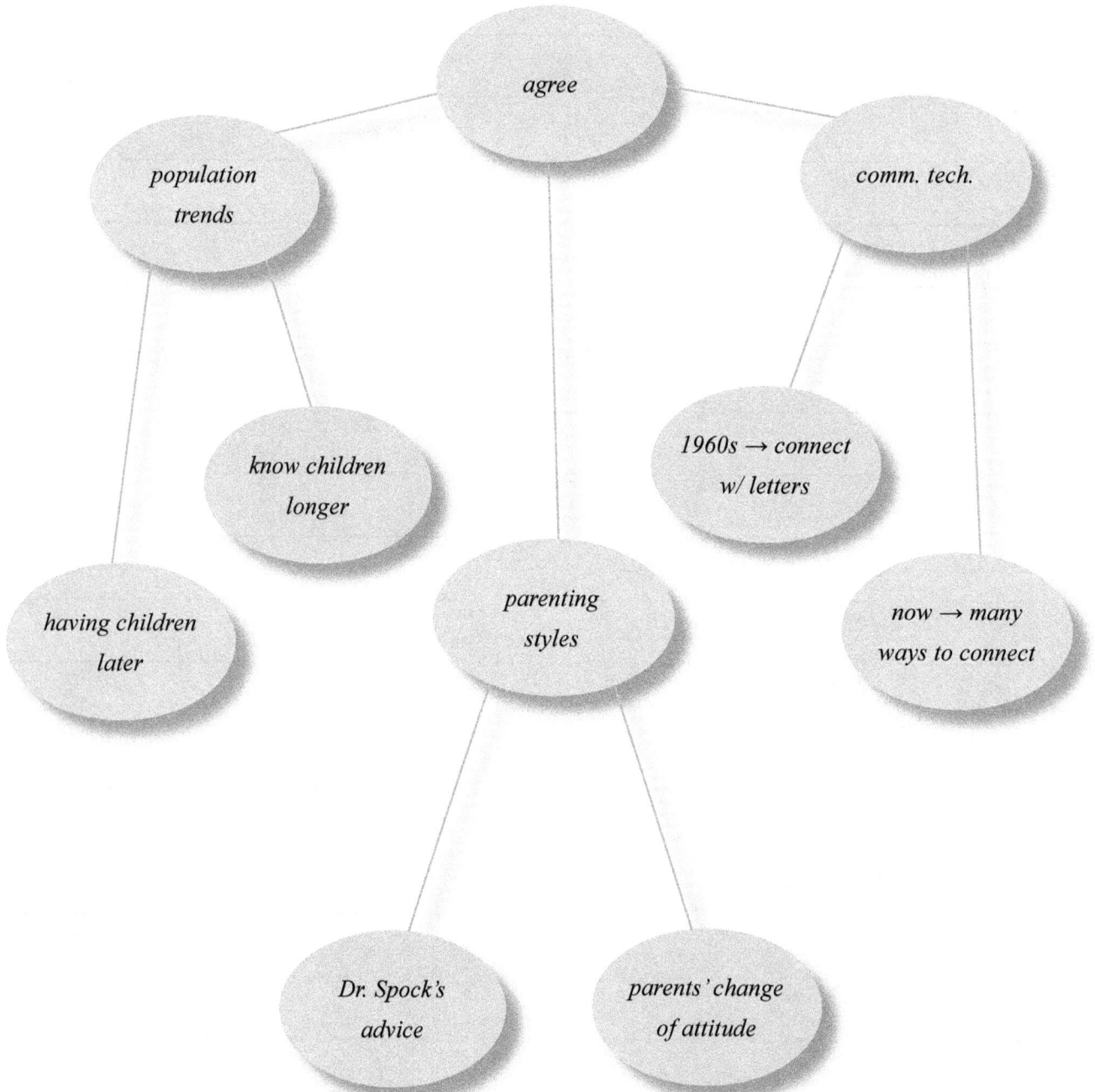

# Model Answer

**→ Prompt ◄**

Do you agree or disagree with following statement? Parents today understand their children better than parents 50 years ago did. Use specific reasons and examples to support your answer.

## Brainstorm

agree

population trends

comm. tech.

know children longer

1960s → connect w/ letters

having children later

parenting styles

now → many ways to connect

Dr. Spock's advice

parents' change of attitude

Parents have probably always spent much of their time thinking about their children. Worrying, complaining, and bragging about one's offspring is an age-old way to pass the time, but nowadays, most parents are more sympathetic toward their children than parents of past generations were. **Parents today understand their children better than parents did even 50 years ago for numerous reasons.**

It is undeniable that population trends have made a difference in the attitudes of parents today. Life expectancies have increased, with people tending to live longer and healthier lives. Fifty years ago, my grandparents married and had children in their teens and early twenties. Nowadays, people expect to live longer, and as a result, they can put off becoming parents until they are a little older and wiser. Even though they have children later, today's parents can expect to know their children for 50 or 60 years, so they have more motivation to build close relationships with them.

Shortly after World War II, parenting styles began changing for the better. Before the war, many parents felt that immediately meeting a child's needs caused them to become spoiled. But by the late 1940s, a book by Dr. Benjamin Spock advised parents to respond to children's needs, give them plenty of love and affection, and not punish children by hitting them. This caused a revolution in parenting styles, and meant that gradually many parents became more accustomed to considering their children's reasons for misbehavior rather than using fear to control them.

Lastly, parents understand their children better these days because of the growth of communication technology. When my grandmother was married and moved away from her family in the 1960s, the only contact she had with her parents was a weekly letter. Long-distance phone calls were so expensive that they were a rare treat. When my father was young, he could be gone on his bicycle all day, and his parents had no expectation of contacting him. Now, children and parents can be in constant contact through cellular phones, texting, email, and social networking. More communication naturally leads to more understanding.

In short, because of changes in lifestyle, attitude, and technology, parents today are in touch with their children and know them better than did the parents of one or two generations ago.

# Independent Writing Task II

**Prompt**

Do you agree or disagree with the following statement? The best way for a child to learn about responsibility is by caring for an animal. Support your answer using specific details and reasons.

**Brainstorm**

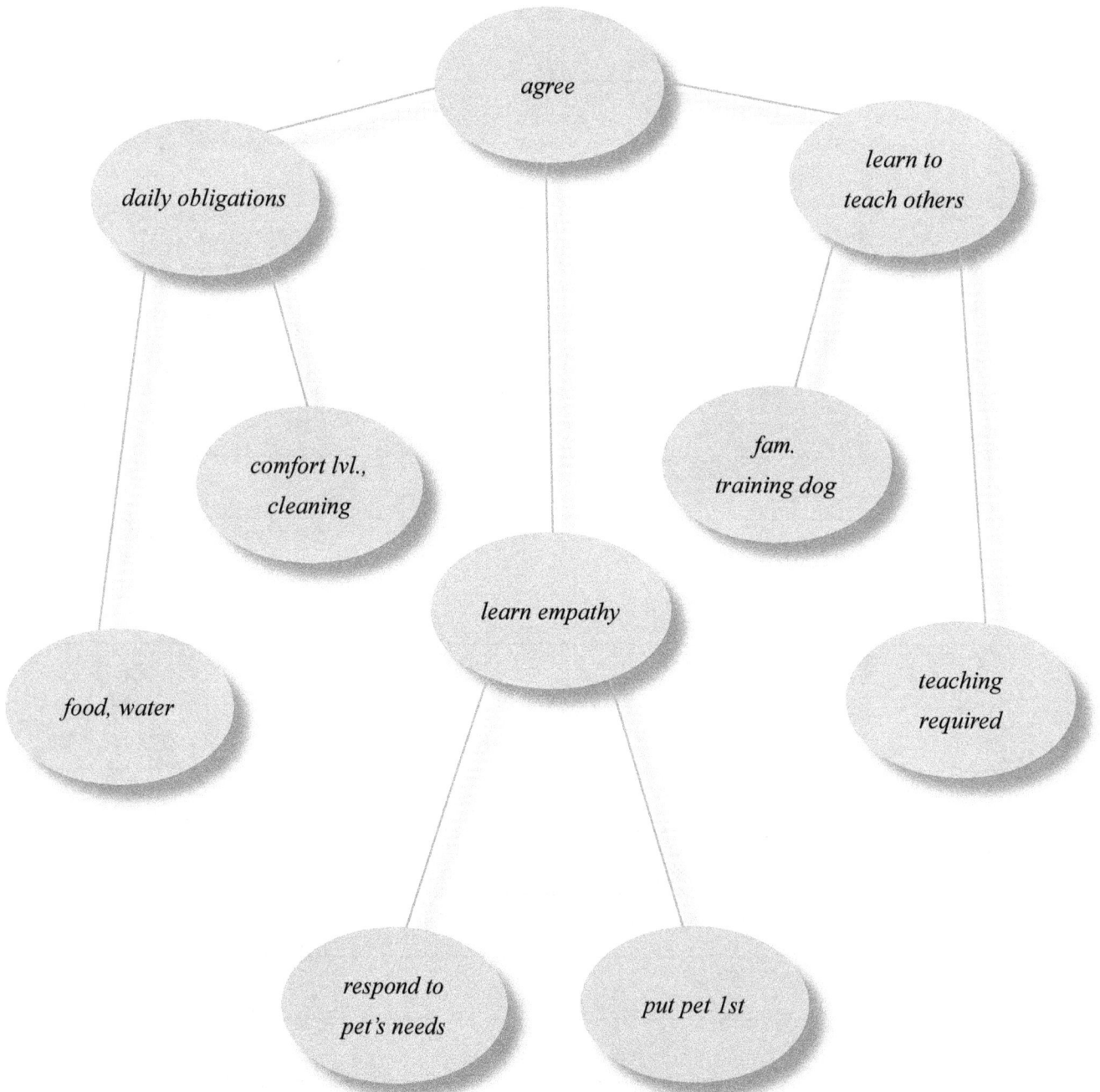

# Model Answer

▶ Prompt ◀

Do you agree or disagree with the following statement? The best way for a child to learn about responsibility is by caring for an animal. Support your answer using specific details and reasons.

## Brainstorm

- **agree**
  - **daily obligations**
    - comfort lvl., cleaning
    - food, water
  - **learn empathy**
    - respond to pet's needs
    - put pet 1st
  - **learn to teach others**
    - fam. training dog
    - teaching required

There is an old saying that a dog is "man's best friend" because of its constant loyalty and affection. And naturally, a person is quite motivated to take care of a friend. **Children tend to form strong bonds with dogs and other pets, so caring for a pet is often the best way for a child to learn about responsibility.**

Children can learn to meet routine obligations by caring for animals that they love. For example, a child can learn about the importance of consistency by providing for a pet's daily food and water needs. Of course, parents should remind children of their obligations, but hopefully children can gradually learn to meet their pets' daily needs without reminders. Children can also learn about maintenance and cleanliness by brushing or bathing their pets.

By taking charge of the well-being of a beloved pet, children can also learn empathy. A child may learn to recognize signals from a pet that the pet feels bored, tired, or hungry, and how to respond to that need. The child can learn to put aside his or her own feelings and consider the pet's needs first. This may include recognizing that a puppy is too tired to keep playing and needs a nap.

Animal care also teaches children to teach others. For example, if a dog barks excessively at people, a child can take part in family efforts to teach the dog not to bark. The family may introduce a command that the dog can learn, such as "No barking," and the child can learn to provide small treats and praise when the dog succeeds. Through taking part in training the dog, the child will learn that teaching others requires patience and commitment.

In summation, animal care teaches children much about compassionate responsibility. Through pet ownership, a child can learn to recognize and meet the needs of others, and also to become a patient teacher.

# Integrated Writing Task 12

Zoologists have debated the intelligence of various animals for many years. Most people know about the intelligence of primates such as gorillas and chimpanzees. But fewer know about the intelligence of dolphins. Dolphins have been proven to be one of the world's most intelligent animals.

One area in which dolphins demonstrate their intelligence is through self-recognition. A common test used for self-recognition in animals is the "mirror test." With this test, zoologists paint a bright dot on one part of an animal's body and then set up a mirror; primates will show that they know they are looking at a reflection because they will look at their body to find the dot. Dolphins tend to use their noses to touch the reflection of the dot in the mirror and swim in circles. They may be trying to see the dot on their body, demonstrating that they too understand that they are seeing themselves in the mirror.

Another domain in which dolphins are able to establish their intelligence is through complex play. For example, captive dolphins have been observed making "bubble rings" underwater. To do this, dolphins push air out of their mouths to make rings in the water. They then examine their creations and seem to enjoy biting them. The whole process requires higher thought processes including evaluation and planning.

A final area in which dolphins exhibit their intelligence is through the use of tools. The bottlenose dolphin in particular is known for this characteristic. To protect its long beak while feeding on the ocean floor, a bottlenose dolphin tears pieces of sponge and wraps the pieces around its beak. This protects them from cuts and abrasions. Of all the other animals, only primates and crows demonstrate tool use of this sophistication.

Now listen to part of a lecture on the topic you just read about.

Notes

| P: | L: |
|---|---|
|  |  |
|  |  |
|  |  |

**Prompt**

Summarize the points made in the lecture, being sure to explain how they oppose specific points made in the reading passage.

_____

_____

_____

_____

_____

_____

_____

_____

_____

_____

_____

_____

_____

_____

_____

_____

_____

_____

_____

# Model Answer

PASSAGE

Zoologists have debated the intelligence of various animals for many years. Most people know about the intelligence of primates such as gorillas and chimpanzees. But fewer know about the intelligence of dolphins. Dolphins have been proven to be one of the world's most intelligent animals.

One area in which dolphins demonstrate their intelligence is through self-recognition. A common test used for self-recognition in animals is the "mirror test." With this test, zoologists paint a bright dot on one part of an animal's body and then set up a mirror; primates will show that they know they are looking at a reflection because they will look at their body to find the dot. Dolphins tend to use their noses to touch the reflection of the dot in the mirror and swim in circles. They may be trying to see the dot on their body, demonstrating that they too understand that they are seeing themselves in the mirror.

Another domain in which dolphins are able to establish their intelligence is through complex play. For example, captive dolphins have been observed making "bubble rings" underwater. To do this, dolphins push air out of their mouths to make rings in the water. They then examine their creations and seem to enjoy biting them. The whole process requires higher thought processes including evaluation and planning.

A final area in which dolphins exhibit their intelligence is through the use of tools. The bottlenose dolphin in particular is known for this characteristic. To protect its long beak while feeding on the ocean floor, a bottlenose dolphin tears pieces of sponge and wraps the pieces around its beak. This protects them from cuts and abrasions. Of all the other animals, only primates and crows demonstrate tool use of this sophistication.

## LECTURE

*There's no doubt that dolphins are intelligent animals, but the reading's claim that dolphins are one of the smartest animals is a bit extreme, to say the least. The brain remains a poorly understood organ, and scientists still have no way to accurately measure the intelligence of humans, much less the intelligence of animals. And ultimately, dolphins aren't the only animals that display the signs of intelligence described in the reading.*

*Over the decades, many animal species have "passed" the mirror test by showing signs of self-recognition. These self-aware animals include the chimpanzee, the orangutan, the Asian elephant, and the European magpie—the only non-mammal to pass the test. And in the end, the mirror test is not a perfect measure of self-recognition, as many researchers have pointed out that the mirror test only gauges visual self-recognition, so it excludes all animals that might use scent, sound, or another sense to recognize itself and others.*

*Furthermore, as a new study published in Applied Animal Behavior Science found, many animals exhibit play behavior and do things just for fun. For example, ravens will playfully perform aerial acrobatics during flight and slide down snowbanks when on land purely for enjoyment. Even electric fish seem to give each other pleasant shocks just for the sake of it. So dolphins' playful behaviors don't set them apart from the rest of the animal kingdom.*

*Finally, the reading implies that dolphins are exceptionally intelligent because they use objects from their environment as tools. But the dolphin is just one of many types of animals that use tools. Many primates use tools, such as sticks and stones, to access food sources. Asian elephants use long sticks to scratch otherwise inaccessible areas. And even several species of octopuses have been observed building shelters out of discarded coconut shells.*

## Notes

| **P:** dolphins most intel. ani. | **L:** dolphins smart, but not most intel. ani. |
|---|---|
| mirror test → dolphins recog. selves in mirror | many ani. pass mirror test (primates, Asian elephants, Euro. magpie) |
| dolphins play → blow bubble rings | ravens play in sky, on land; electric fish shock e/o for fun |
| use sea sponges to protect beak when feeding | tool use → primates (for food), elephants (scratch) , octopuses (shelters) |

Although the lecture claims that dolphins are intelligent, it refutes the reading's claim that dolphins are the smartest members of the animal kingdom. The lecture provides examples illustrating that many animals demonstrate the same signs of intelligence as dolphins.

First, the lecture points out that many animal species have "passed" the mirror test, not just dolphins. The lecture mentions that animals such as chimpanzees, elephants, and even magpies have demonstrated self-recognition. Moreover, according to the lecture, the mirror test only tests self-recognition in visually oriented animals. Thus, the mirror test may be an inaccurate way to test animal intelligence among animals that rely on senses other than vision.

Second, the lecture cites a study revealing that many animals exhibit play behavior. According to the lecture, ravens play games while flying and when on the ground. And even electric fish will shock each other just because it feels good. Thus, the lecture provides evidence proving that dolphins are not the only animals that appear to be having fun because they are smart.

Third, the lecture refutes the reading by explaining that many animals use tools. The reading implies that dolphins are the most intelligent animals because they use sea sponges as tools when feeding. However, the lecture reveals that primates use sticks and rocks to get food; elephants use sticks to scratch themselves; and octopuses use coconut shells to build shelters.

# Independent Writing Task I

**Prompt**

Do you agree or disagree with the following statement? Young people in the past were more dependent on their parents than young people are today. Use specific details and reasons to support your opinion.

**Brainstorm**

_____

_____

_____

_____

_____

_____

_____

## Model Answer

> **Prompt**
>
> Do you agree or disagree with the following statement? Young people in the past were more dependent on their parents than young people are today. Use specific details and reasons to support your opinion.

### Brainstorm

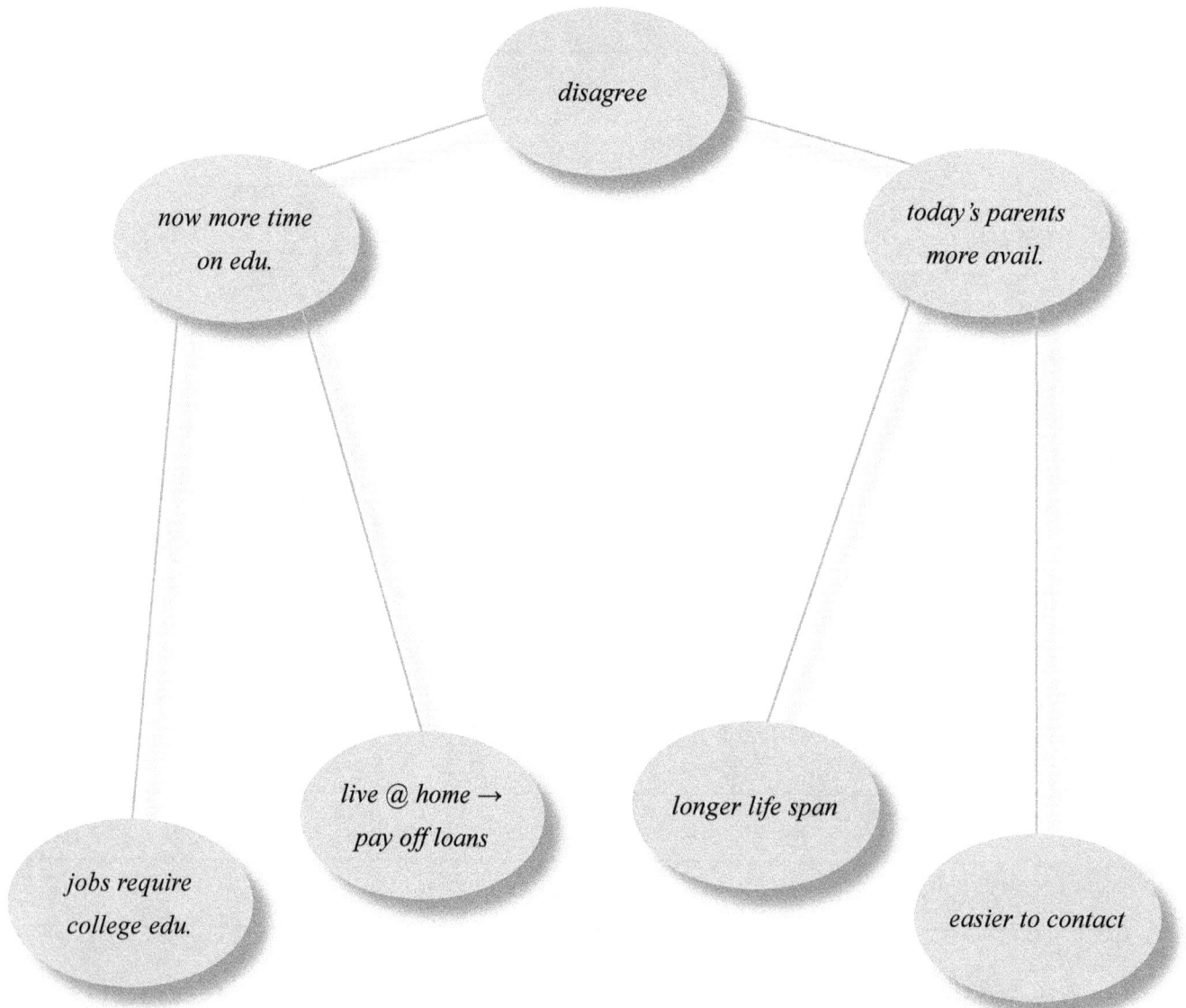

For much of human history, moving away from home was an adventure into the unknown. For the young people of previous generations, leaving home could mean never seeing their parents again. They had to be completely independent. Even if young people stayed with their parents, they usually took on adult responsibilities from a young age, such as planting crops on the family farm. **Therefore, I believe that young people today tend to be more dependent on their parents than young people were in the past.**

For one, <u>young people today usually spend a longer time on education and training than young people did in the past.</u> In the past, even teenagers could support themselves and their families through farm work or other physical labor. In today's economy, most people need to go to college or receive professional training in order to get a good job. Today, people must often rely on their parents for support until they are at least 22. Young people need help with college tuition as well as food and housing while they study. After college, they may have to live at home and depend on their parents even longer while they pay off their student loans.

In addition, <u>today's young people can usually count on their parents living longer and staying in touch.</u> In the past, life expectancy was shorter, and young people often had no choice but to become self-supporting after their parents died. Before modern medicine, including antibiotics, heart medications, vaccinations, and effective mental health care, young people were more likely to lose their parents to illness or injury. Another reason that young people had to make do without their parents was that long-distance travel and communication were so difficult. For instance, if a young person went to settle a frontier or simply moved far away from home, it would be difficult to communicate with family regularly.

Therefore, I believe that these days, young people depend on their parents much more than in the past. Many young people today are lucky that they can still rely on their parents for financial and emotional support, even if it means being dependent on them and staying close to home a few years longer.

# Independent Writing Task II

Do you think that people who live in rural areas take better care of their family members than people who live in the cities do? Use specific reasons and examples to explain your position.

### Brainstorm

**⇢ Prompt ⇠**

Do you think that people who live in rural areas take better care of their family members than people who live in the cities do? Use specific reasons and examples to explain your position.

## Brainstorm

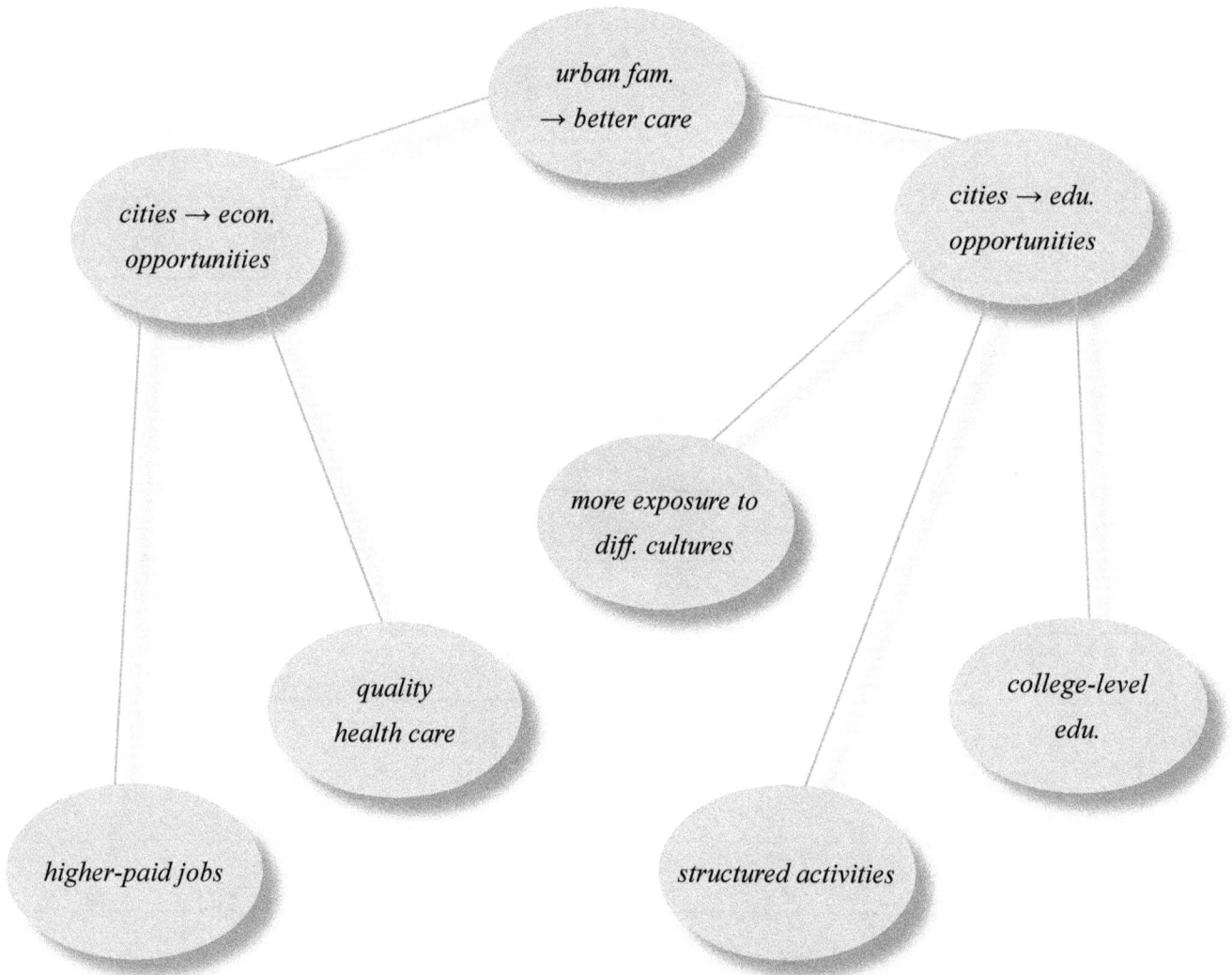

urban fam.
→ better care

cities → econ.
opportunities

cities → edu.
opportunities

more exposure to
diff. cultures

quality
health care

college-level
edu.

higher-paid jobs

structured activities

Providing the best care for one's family members is not necessarily tied to one's geographical location. How family members care for one another is more important than where a family lives. **However, in rural areas, resources and opportunities may be quite limited, so people from urban areas can often provide better care for family members.**

First, <u>cities usually offer a greater number of skilled job opportunities with higher pay than rural areas do.</u> Higher income can mean access to a wider range of high-quality services, such as health care, dental care, and mental health services for family members. Moreover, most medical facilities are located in highly populated areas, so families who live in cities have more immediate access to crucial health services. People living in the countryside may not be able to take advantage of as many services without long drives, even if they can afford them.

Second, <u>cities may provide children and all family members with a greater number of educational and social opportunities, including better schools, music lessons, athletic training, and art classes.</u> For one, living in a city often provides more exposure to people of different cultures. By interacting with people from different cultures, a person can develop a globally minded attitude that will be useful throughout life. Moreover, structured activities, such as art and music lessons, keep children stimulated and prevent them from becoming involved in potentially harmful activities. Educational opportunities for adults such as community colleges and university programs are also more likely to be available in cities. Often, these resources help adults earn higher incomes for their families.

In the end, each family is unique and living in any region has both benefits and disadvantages. Living in the countryside provides a family with opportunities for peace and relaxation. But ultimately, the medical and educational resources, as well as the employment opportunities, available in urban areas make a city the more desirable place to raise a family.

# Integrated Writing Task 13

People who are looking to get into better shape may receive conflicting advice about which form of exercise is most effective. Some physical fitness experts claim that swimming is the ideal exercise, as it works all of the muscles in the body. But unless a person has trouble with his or her joints, or is prone to injury, walking and running are superior to swimming.

Meter for meter, walking and running provide a comparable cardiovascular workout to swimming. However, walking and running put stress on one's bones, which signals the body to build up the density and strength of the entire skeleton. Exercising in water is a bit like exercising in space, where the absence of gravity causes astronauts to lose bone density. Human bones are adapted to develop against the pull of gravity without the buoyancy provided by water.

For most people, walking and running are more accessible than swimming. People are more likely to walk or run frequently than they are to swim. A person needs only a pair of athletic shoes to step outside and go for a walk or a run. A person who relies on swimming has to drive to a pool, where the swim time may be limited, or to a beach, where the water may be too cold or choppy to swim for long periods of time.

A final reason that walking and running are superior forms of exercise is that most people can walk or even run for a much longer period than they can swim. Certainly, a person who goes on a day-long hike will burn more calories and work his or her heart more than a person who swims laps for 30 minutes.

◀)) Now listen to part of a lecture on the topic you just read about.

Notes

| P: | L: |
|---|---|
| 1 | 1 |
| 2 | 2 |
| 3 | 3 |

**Prompt**

Summarize the points made in the lecture, being sure to explain how they elaborate on specific points made in the reading passage.

_____

_____

_____

_____

_____

_____

_____

_____

_____

_____

_____

_____

_____

_____

_____

_____

_____

_____

_____

_____

_____

# Model Answer

People who are looking to get into better shape may receive conflicting advice about which form of exercise is most effective. Some physical fitness experts claim that swimming is the ideal exercise, as it works all of the muscles in the body. But unless a person has trouble with his or her joints, or is prone to injury, walking and running are superior to swimming.

Meter for meter, walking and running provide a comparable cardiovascular workout to swimming. However, walking and running put stress on one's bones, which signals the body to build up the density and strength of the entire skeleton. Exercising in water is a bit like exercising in space, where the absence of gravity causes astronauts to lose bone density. Human bones are adapted to develop against the pull of gravity without the buoyancy provided by water.

For most people, walking and running are more accessible than swimming. People are more likely to walk or run frequently than they are to swim. A person needs only a pair of athletic shoes to step outside and go for a walk or a run. A person who relies on swimming has to drive to a pool, where the swim time may be limited, or to a beach, where the water may be too cold or choppy to swim for long periods of time.

A final reason that walking and running are superior forms of exercise is that most people can walk or even run for a much longer period than they can swim. Certainly, a person who goes on a day-long hike will burn more calories and work his or her heart more than a person who swims laps for 30 minutes.

*Although swimming can provide a good workout, research continues to support claims that regular walking and running are better forms of exercise for most people. Let's take a look at why the points made in the reading are valid.*

*The reading states that weight-bearing exercises such as walking and running are better than swimming for building bone density. Indeed, a study at one university compared the bone densities of college athletes across many different sports. The study found that female competitive swimmers had 10 to 15 percent lower bone density than the average for the other athletes. Some of the female swimmers were even at risk for osteoporosis, a dangerous thinning of the bones as the body ages. Other studies have shown that walking and running build up bone or slow its loss, which becomes especially important later in life.*

*The reading also points out that swimming is usually less accessible than walking and running. People may have more difficulties getting to a pool or a relatively warm body of water than they would finding a suitable place to run. Another factor is that many public pools use intolerable amounts of chlorine to keep the water clean. Also, lakes or ocean waters may be polluted, especially after rain. So even if a person has access to a pool or other body of water, swimming may still be undesirable simply because of the quality of the water.*

*There are several reasons that most people can walk or run for longer than they can swim, as the reading mentioned. For one, water is much denser than air, so moving through water takes more energy. Swimmers tend to lose their breath and experience fatigue sooner. In addition, swimming for a long period can be difficult mentally, as it tends to be boring. Watching the bottom of the pool slip by is much less interesting than walking through almost any landscape, or even running on a treadmill while watching television.*

*So the points made in the reading are exactly right. Walking or running is preferable to swimming because you'll probably strengthen your bones and work out more often and for longer periods.*

| **P:** run/walk best exercise | **L:** agree with reading |
|---|---|
| strengthen bones | bone strength = impt. later in life |
| accessible (more so than swimming) | water quality may be bad for swimming |
| walk/run longer than swim | walk/run more interesting than swim |

The reading makes a strong case for why walking and running are better exercises for most people than swimming. The lecture supports these claims by adding some important information to the argument.

First, the reading lays out several very good reasons that walking and running are better forms of exercise than swimming. For one, walking promotes greater bone density than swimming. Bone density, the reading points out, is an important indicator of fitness, especially as we get older. Additionally, walking and running are much more convenient forms of exercise than swimming. People can walk or run almost anywhere; swimmers have to drive to a pool, find a place to park, and then fit into the pool's schedule. Swimming in the ocean can be limited because of weather conditions. Finally, the reading points out that walking or running are better exercises than swimming because people can almost always walk or run for longer than they can swim.

The lecture agrees with the arguments from the reading. The lecture cites a study showing that competitive college swimmers have lower bone density than other college athletes, and some competitive swimmers even show signs of osteoporosis. Furthermore, the lecture points out that pool water often contains excessive chlorine, which is very unhealthy, and that lake and ocean water may be polluted, especially after a storm. Finally, the lecture points out that walking and running are preferable to swimming because most people can walk or run for longer than they can swim, and both of these exercises are less boring than swimming.

# Independent Writing Task I

## Prompt

In your opinion, is it better to have a career similar to or different from your parents' jobs?
Support your response using specific details and reasons.

**Brainstorm**

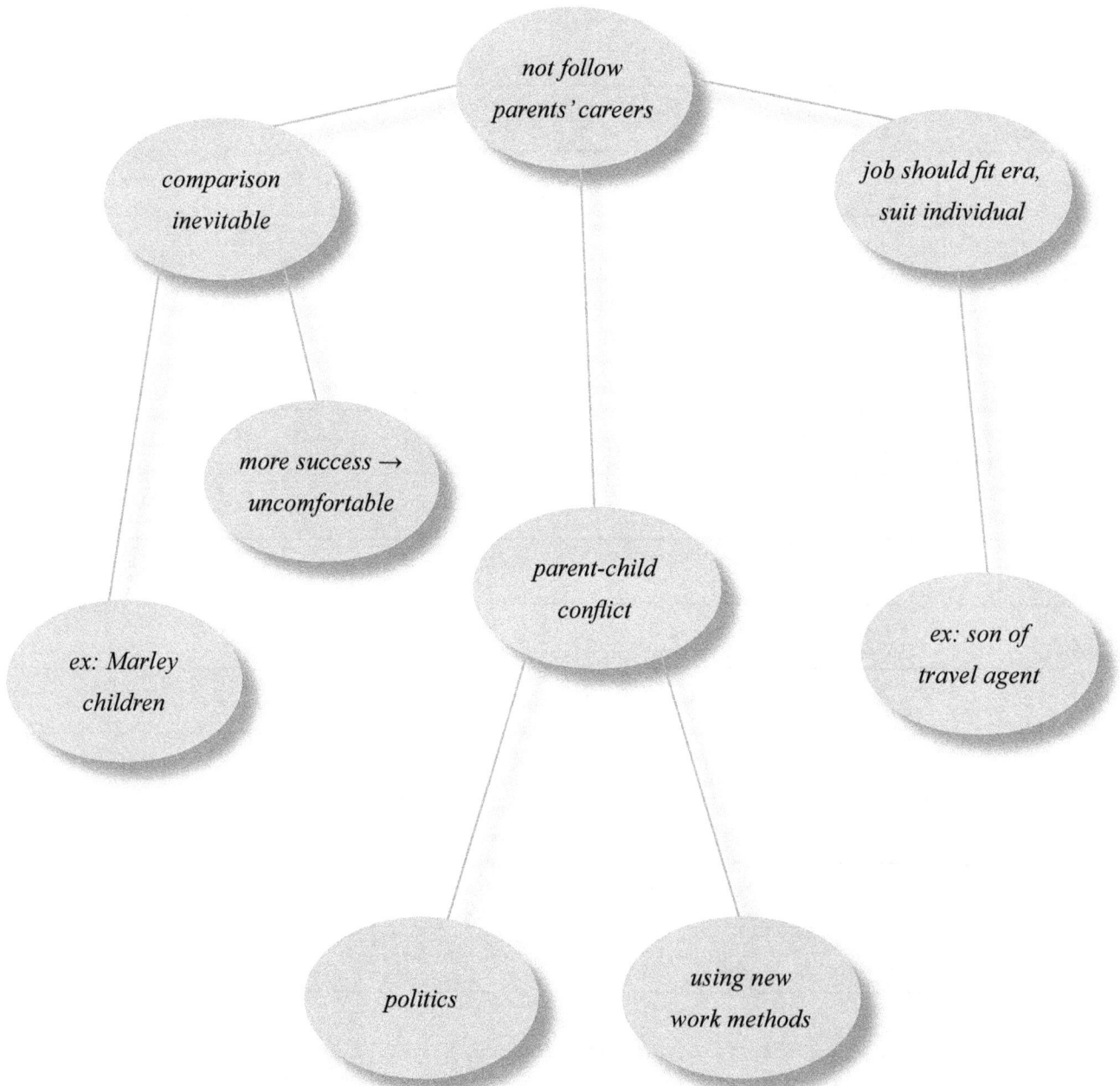

# Model Answer

---

▷ **Prompt** ◁

In your opinion, is it better to have a career similar to or different from your parents' jobs?
Support your response using specific details and reasons.

---

**Brainstorm**

```
                    not follow
                  parents' careers

  comparison                              job should fit era,
  inevitable                               suit individual


        more success →
        uncomfortable
                          parent-child
                            conflict
                                                    ex: son of
  ex: Marley                                        travel agent
  children


              politics          using new
                               work methods
```

Choosing a career is a huge decision. It is often tempting to tread the known path and pursue a career that has been familiar since childhood: the same career as one's mother or father. **While that may be an excellent choice for some people, I believe that choosing a different career path leads to stronger family bonds and more personal success and satisfaction.**

When people enter the same profession as their parents, they are risking a nagging, life-long feeling of self-doubt from comparison. Some children even "live in their parents' shadows," as they can never be recognized for their own talents. For example, legendary reggae musician Bob Marley had several children who have become successful musicians, but they may always be compared to their famous father and endure criticisms that they did not become successful on their own. On the other hand, a child becoming more successful than his or her parent in the same job may cause the parent to resent the child's success.

Pursuing the same career as one's parents may create conflict within the parent-child relationship, as each may be more likely to criticize the other's choices. If a child follows a parent into politics but does not see eye-to-eye on every issue, the relationship may become strained. Alternately, family conflicts may ensue if a child learns new methods for performing a job that conflict with methods the parent prefers.

The most important reason for people to create their own career paths is that they are more likely to end up in a job that is perfectly suited to their personalities and goals. For instance, one of my friend's grandparents owned a successful travel agency. My friend's father grew up enjoying travel, but he disliked paperwork. At the same time, travel agencies were becoming obsolete as people began using the internet to make their travel plans. He ended up closing the agency and becoming a photojournalist instead.

Ultimately, selecting a different career from one's parents can be incredibly beneficial. Doing so often results in improved confidence, a better parent-child relationship, and a satisfying job.

# Independent Writing Task II

**Prompt**

Some people believe that young people today can learn nothing of value from their grandparents.
Do you agree or disagree? Use specific examples and reasons to explain your opinion.

## Brainstorm

> **Prompt**
>
> Some people believe that young people today can learn nothing of value from their grandparents. Do you agree or disagree? Use specific examples and reasons to explain your opinion.

**Brainstorm**

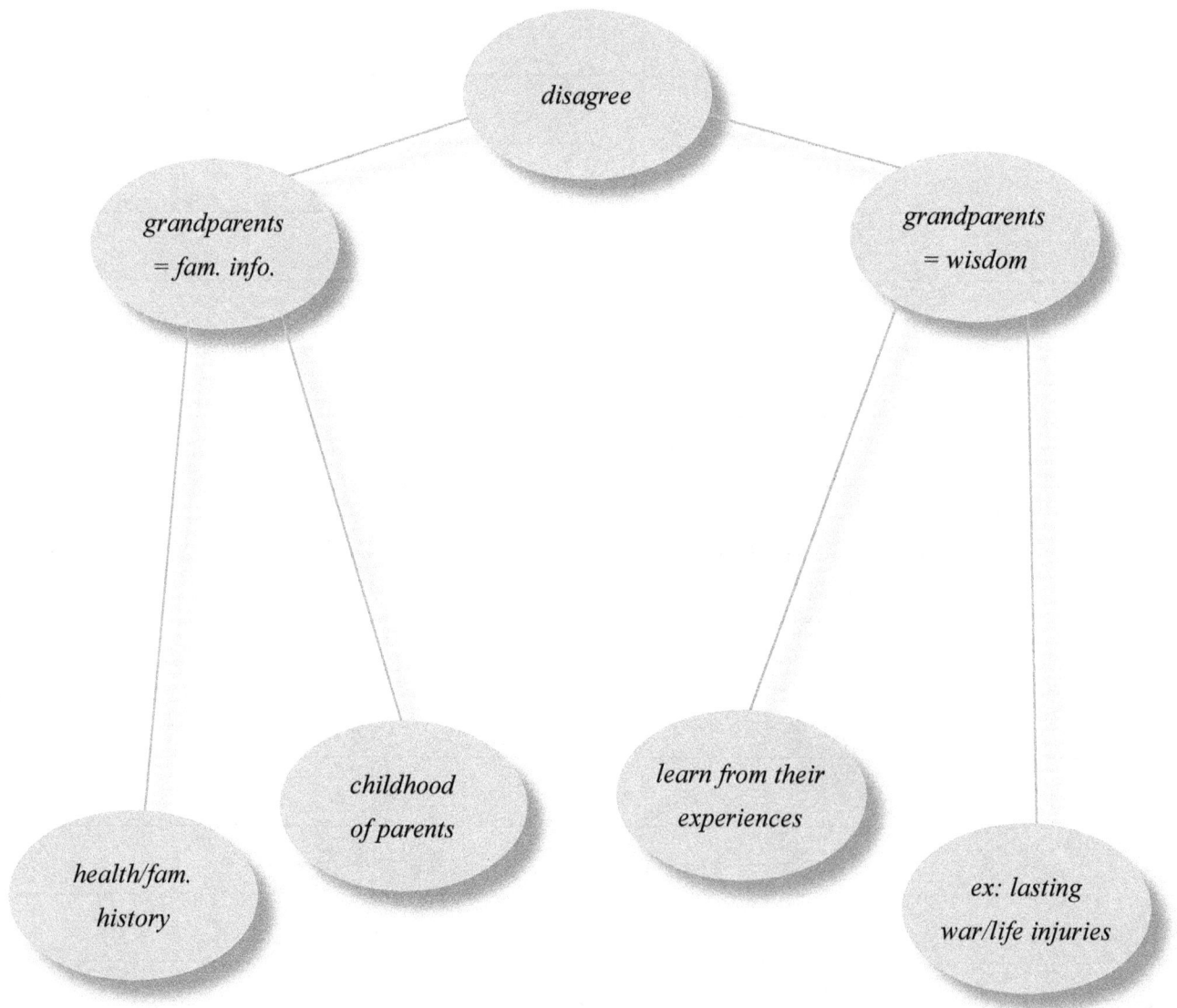

disagree

grandparents = fam. info.

grandparents = wisdom

health/fam. history

childhood of parents

learn from their experiences

ex: lasting war/life injuries

Elderly people tend to know less than their grandchildren about cutting-edge technology and popular culture. As a result, some grandchildren may conclude that their grandparents have nothing of value to convey to them. **However, they are absolutely mistaken, as grandparents can serve as sources of information and wisdom for young people.**

For one, <u>grandparents are often the best sources of family history, from information about health background to customs and traditions.</u> For example, my grandmother used to sing me a lullaby before I went to sleep. When I asked where she learned the song, she told me that her grandmother, who immigrated from Vietnam, used to sing her the lullaby. Additionally, grandchildren can learn about their own parents by listening to stories from their grandparents. After all, parents often know more about their children than children know about their parents. Thus, grandparents can give grandchildren valuable insights into the grandchildren's own experiences, personalities, and values.

<u>Many grandparents can be role models to their grandchildren by offering them life lessons and advice.</u> When grandparents describe obstacles and challenges that they have faced during their lives, their conclusions reflect years of thought. It is inspiring to discover that people who are not perfect can still lead fulfilling lives. Once, when I was complaining about a disappointing birthday, my grandfather stated that on his twenty-second birthday, he was in a military hospital having a leg amputated. I had never paid much attention to his false leg, but his comment led to a conversation about his war experiences. I realized that self-pity was not part of his life, and learned from his wisdom that day.

In summary, each generation of young people assumes that they are conducting their lives in unique times, but there is much to be learned from previous generations. People who are lucky enough to be able to talk with their grandparents may gain information that can enrich their lives.

# Integrated Writing Task 14

PASSAGE

Businesses are constantly looking for ways to improve employee motivation. One new method, "the Google Approach," is named after the work ethic promoted by the managers of the internet search engine Google. The approach uses a combination of on-site investments and management philosophies to maintain employee interest and motivation year-round.

One way that a business using "the Google Approach" might try to maintain employee motivation is by hosting weekly social events. These events may be casual, such as getting together for food and drinks after work, or they can be more formal, such as weekend trust-building seminars. In these seminars, employees engage in activities meant to instill a sense of lasting trust in one another. This prevents employee conflicts and promotes work efficiency.

Another part of the approach may involve incorporating an indoor gym and outdoor "playground" as part of the company itself. The "playground" may include basketball, tennis, and volleyball courts. Employees may use the gym or outdoor areas before or after work, or they can take short breaks during the day to blow off steam and stimulate their brains by using the areas.

Most radically, the approach allows employees to manage their own daily work schedules. So once an employee is given a project and a deadline, he or she is not hounded by managers to complete the job. For Google, this method of management has produced happier, more productive employees.

🔊 Now listen to part of a lecture on the topic you just read about.

Notes

| P: | L: |
| --- | --- |
| | |
| | |
| | |

**Prompt**

Summarize the points made in the lecture, being sure to explain how they oppose specific points made in the reading passage.

_____

_____

_____

_____

_____

_____

_____

_____

_____

_____

_____

_____

_____

_____

_____

_____

_____

_____

_____

_____

# Model Answer

Businesses are constantly looking for ways to improve employee motivation. One new method, "the Google Approach," is named after the work ethic promoted by the managers of the internet search engine Google. The approach uses a combination of on-site investments and management philosophies to maintain employee interest and motivation year-round.

One way that a business using "the Google Approach" might try to maintain employee motivation is by hosting weekly social events. These events may be casual, such as getting together for food and drinks after work, or they can be more formal, such as weekend trust-building seminars. In these seminars, employees engage in activities meant to instill a sense of lasting trust in one another. This prevents employee conflicts and promotes work efficiency.

Another part of the approach may involve incorporating an indoor gym and outdoor "playground" as part of the company itself. The "playground" may include basketball, tennis, and volleyball courts. Employees may use the gym or outdoor areas before or after work, or they can take short breaks during the day to blow off steam and stimulate their brains by using the areas.

Most radically, the approach allows employees to manage their own daily work schedules. So once an employee is given a project and a deadline, he or she is not hounded by managers to complete the job. For Google, this method of management has produced happier, more productive employees.

---

**LECTURE**

*No business plan, even one as successful as "the Google Approach," will work in every setting. Let's look at what happened when a brand-new, medium-sized hospital adopted "the Google Approach" in an attempt to improve employee motivation. Hospital administrators thought it would solve all manner of employee problems, but the result was a nightmare for everyone involved.*

*To start, the social events seemed like a good way to encourage employee bonding. However, the hospital quickly ran into many problems. Namely, there were few spaces large enough to accommodate all the employees at one time. And when employees did get together, there were so many people in attendance that very few coworkers got to know one another well. They quickly developed social groups based on jobs, age, and even ethnic background.*

*The hospital also built basketball, tennis, and volleyball courts for employees to use during their breaks. But these facilities proved problematic as well. Employees frequently abused their break privileges, especially in the gym, where they often stayed longer than scheduled and neglected some of their essential work duties. Worse, some employees became so competitive during court games that conflicts arose. These outside conflicts escalated into arguments that affected the working environment inside the hospital.*

*Finally, the hospital took a less-structured approach when managing nurses, secretaries, cafeteria workers, technicians, and dieticians. However, this style of managing employees proved impossible in the hospital environment. First, because patients and their needs were constantly changing, it was inefficient and even dangerous not to actively manage each employee's schedule. Likewise, doctors were annoyed when medical teams weren't up to date with their patient care.*

| P: *Google approach motivates employees* | L: *disagree → hosp. ex.* |
|---|---|
| *weekly social events* | *sub-groups formed, not much mingling* |
| *exercise areas → get rid of work stress* | *waste time in gym, sports created conflict* |
| *employees manage own schedules* | *patients' needs changed too often for self-schedule* |

The reading introduces "the Google Approach" to business management, which gives employees more freedom than traditional time-management methods. The lecture questions the effectiveness of "the Google Approach" at motivating employees in every work setting. In fact, when used in a hospital setting, the approach resulted in complete failure.

First, weekly social events did not motivate hospital employees. The reading says that these events made Google employees more connected and better able to work together. However, there were too many hospital employees for effective social gatherings. Moreover, when social gatherings did occur, people often stayed together in small groups based on their jobs, ages, and ethnicities instead of attempting to form new friendships.

Second, the athletic facilities only created problems for hospital employees. The reading says that these facilities help Google employees release stress. But at the hospital, the gym became a place for employees to waste time and ignore work duties. Team sports also created physical and emotional conflicts, which seeped into workplace relationships.

Third, the self-management approach was impractical in the hospital. The reading says that this approach made Google employees more productive in the long run. However, the result was the opposite at the hospital. When employees were not kept to a precise schedule, they lacked important knowledge about patients. In addition, it was difficult for doctors to receive necessary information and give directions for patient care.

# Independent Writing Task I

### Prompt

Life sometimes offers hard lessons. Do you believe that parents should interfere or allow their children to learn from their own mistakes? Use specific reasons and examples to support your answer.

### Brainstorm

_____

_____

_____

_____

_____

_____

_____

_____

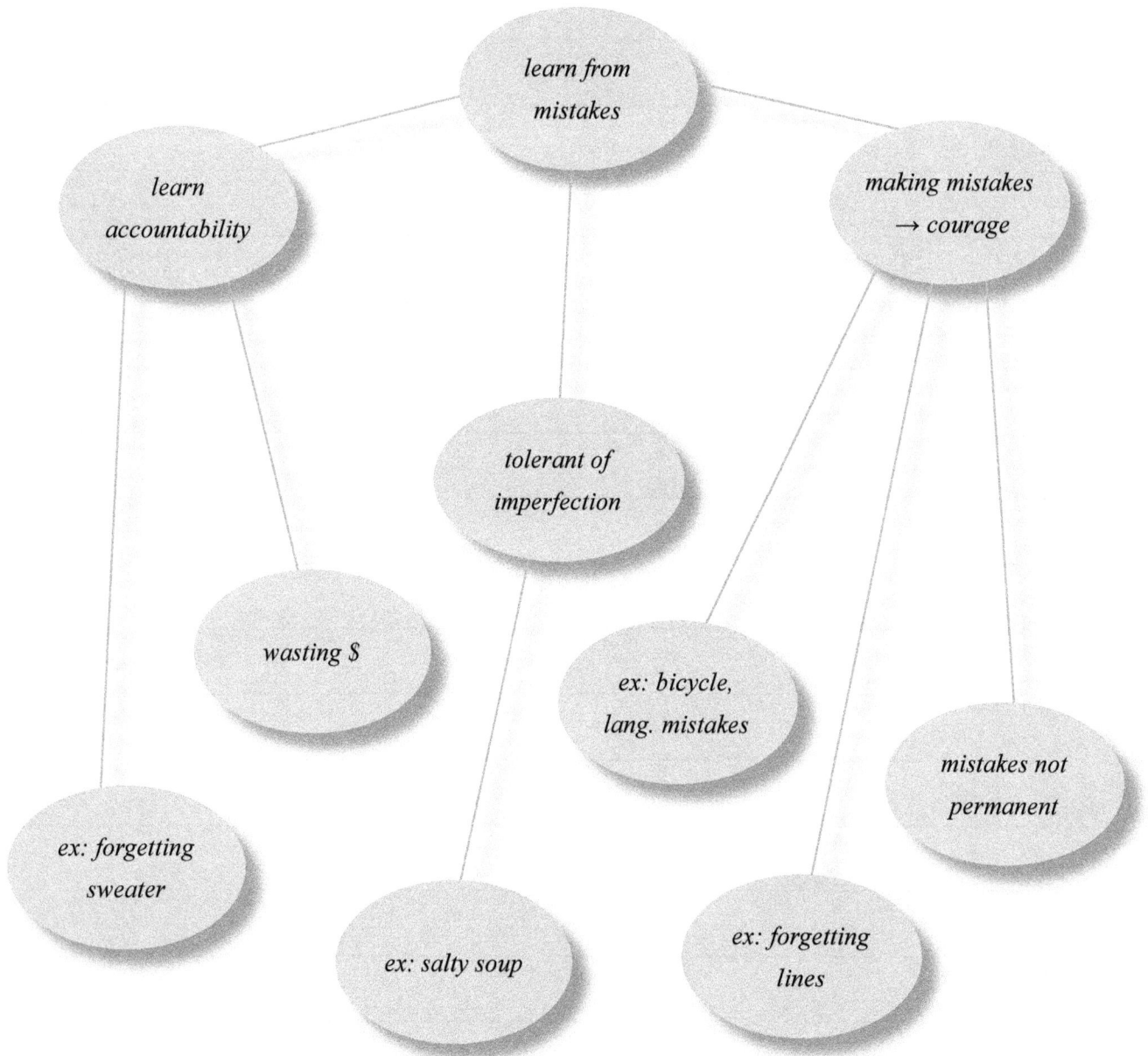

**Prompt**

Life sometimes offers hard lessons. Do you believe that parents should interfere or allow their children to learn from their own mistakes? Use specific reasons and examples to support your answer.

**Brainstorm**

learn from mistakes

learn accountability

making mistakes → courage

tolerant of imperfection

wasting $

ex: bicycle, lang. mistakes

mistakes not permanent

ex: forgetting sweater

ex: salty soup

ex: forgetting lines

When baby birds leave the nest and attempt their first flights, many fall to the ground, still unsure of how to use their wings properly. Indeed, all children must learn through trial and tribulation. **Therefore, parents should allow children to make mistakes so they can learn and grow from their experiences.**

For one, <u>children must be allowed to make mistakes so they learn that they are accountable for their actions.</u> For example, if a child gets cold because he forgot to bring a sweater on an outing, he will remember a sweater next time. Similarly, if a child is allowed to choose how to spend some gift money, and spends it all on candy that is quickly gone, that child will likely feel sad but hopefully wiser. Learning that actions have consequences, and that one is accountable for his or her own decisions, is an important step in learning to act responsibly.

Moreover, <u>making mistakes also helps one tolerate imperfection in others.</u> When I was a child, I once made soup following a recipe that I had written out by hand, but I miscopied the recipe and added so much salt that the soup was inedible. My family made jokes for years about salt, and though I was embarrassed, I was reminded that nobody is perfect. This helps me be patient with children.

Finally, <u>making mistakes helps a child learn to learn and grow from failure.</u> For instance, if a child has a part in a school play and forgets his or her lines, the play usually continues and life goes on as usual. Hopefully, the child will learn to practice harder and be more prepared next time. The same is true of many other challenges that children face, from learning to ride a bicycle and falling down, to learning to speak a new language and making many mistakes. Learning that failure is both acceptable and inevitable is important later in life, and gives people courage to attempt difficult tasks.

In conclusion, it is hard for parents to watch their children make mistakes, yet doing so helps children become more responsible, tolerant, and confident.

# Independent Writing Task II

Writers have claimed, "Clothes make the man." Do you believe that a person's choice in clothing is indicative of his or her character and personality? Use specific reasons and examples to explain your opinion.

**Brainstorm**

_____

_____

_____

_____

_____

_____

_____

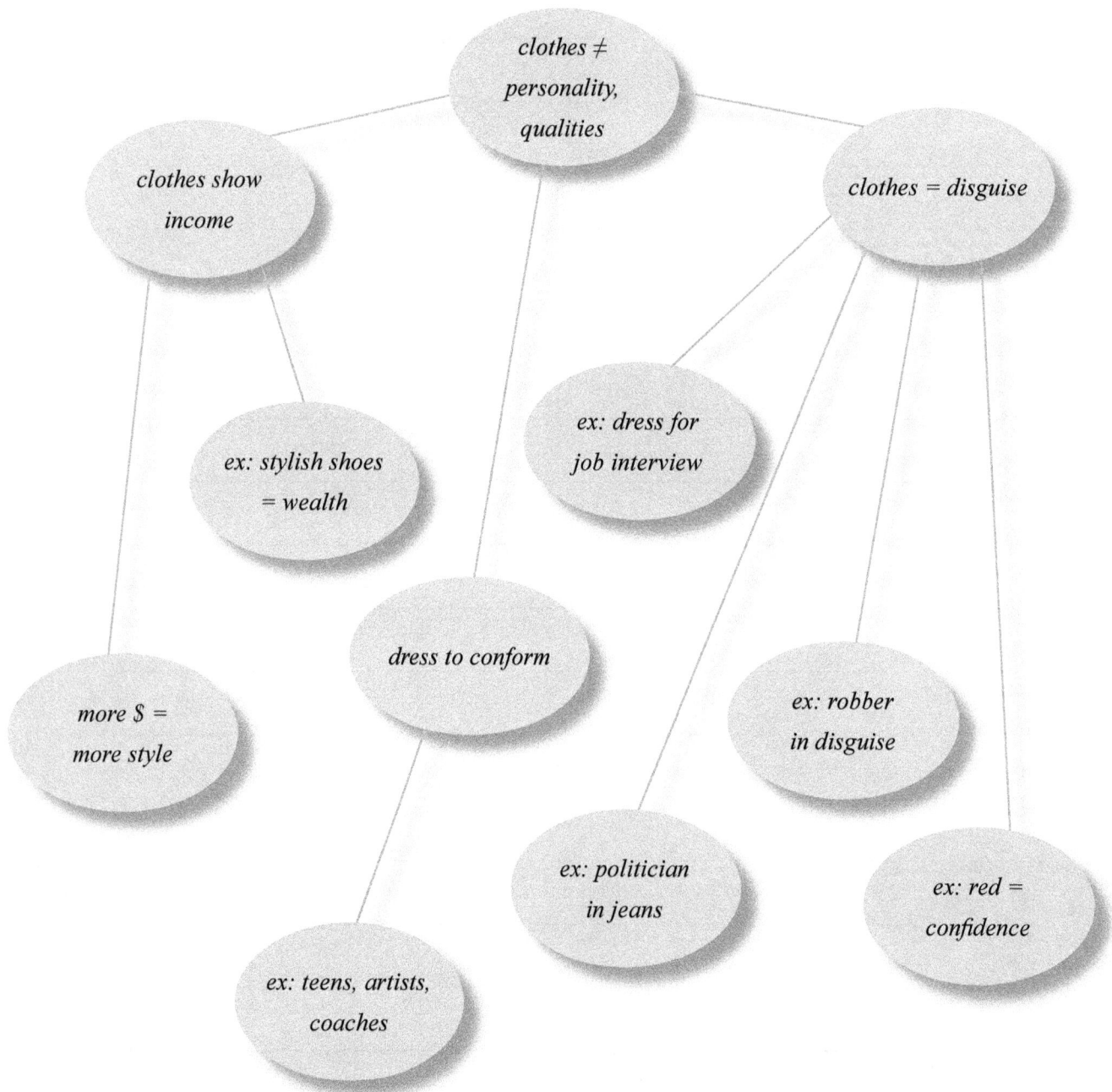

→ **Prompt** ←

Writers have claimed, "Clothes make the man." Do you believe that a person's choice in clothing is indicative of his or her character and personality? Use specific reasons and examples to explain your opinion.

**Brainstorm**

clothes ≠ personality, qualities

clothes show income

clothes = disguise

ex: stylish shoes = wealth

ex: dress for job interview

more $ = more style

dress to conform

ex: robber in disguise

ex: politician in jeans

ex: red = confidence

ex: teens, artists, coaches

The fictional detective Sherlock Holmes can often gather dozens of clues about people's lives by quickly examining what they are wearing. From tiny details, Holmes infers facts about a person's job, habits, and relationships. But in reality, inferences about people based on appearance are often mistaken. **Because people have many different reasons for wearing a particular outfit at a particular time, clothes do not necessarily reveal a person's individual qualities.**

First, <u>clothes tell more about a person's income level than about his or her personality or character.</u> Obviously, having more money allows a person to dress in newer, more fashionable clothing, and to take more risks with unusual colors or styles. In fact, many "fashionable" clothes are designed to show off wealth, such as very high heels, or very shiny shoes, which signal that the wearer does not need to walk far or stand much. Clothes often reveal little more than a person's clothing budget.

Further, <u>people often select the clothing that they wear simply to fit in.</u> For example, teenagers often want to look like other teenagers. Anyone who identifies with a certain social group may tend to dress like other members of that group. As examples, an aspiring artist might sport multiple types of tattoos and piercings, while an athletic coach might always dress in "active wear." Most people have a kind of "uniform" that they put on to look like others with whom they associate. However, a uniform reveals very little about the individual's personality.

Third, <u>nearly everyone occasionally attempts to make a statement with their outfits, even if the statement is not particularly true.</u> For example, an untidy person may dress in neat, ironed clothing when preparing for a job interview. A bank robber may dress like a banker in order to inspire trust. Or a wealthy politician may dress in jeans for an event in order to appear humble. People may even try to fool themselves. For example, a person might wear flamboyant red clothes as a confidence booster when he or she feels nervous.

Overall, clothing does convey information about a person, but the information may be superficial, stereotypical, or inaccurate. As much as possible, it is best to resist drawing appearance-based conclusions about other people.

# Integrated Writing Task 15

## PASSAGE

Between 500 BCE and 500 CE, a group of people called the Nazca, who lived on the dry, windless plains of Peru, drew hundreds of pictures and long, straight lines in the rocky soil. These intersecting lines can extend for kilometers, and some of the lines are interspersed with depictions of animals so large that one can only discern their shapes from high up in the air. Since airplanes had not yet been invented, scholars have long wondered why the Nazca created these expansive images. Although many have concluded that the Nazca Lines had some kind of religious significance, there is little agreement beyond that.

One theory is that the Nazca Lines acted as an astronomical observatory and as places of religious worship. The lines often point to places on the horizon where the Sun, Moon, and other important celestial bodies rise and set. They may also represent shapes made by stars or constellations. Many other ancient cultures built ritual centers based on astronomical observations.

One of the more creative ideas is that the geometric geoglyphs served as patterns for large human looms. In other words, some people would stand on the geoglyph at regular points holding string, and others would walk along the lines, weaving in other strings. In fact, the region is known for its long strings and wide pieces of textile, and the Nazca people used long textiles to wrap and mummify some of their dead.

The idea that is most accepted currently is that the Nazca Lines either symbolized the flow of water or in some other way were meant to serve water deities. It makes sense that people living where there is almost no rain would consider water precious and even sacred. It has even been suggested that the lines might have had something to do with finding underground water or marking wells.

🔊 Now listen to part of a lecture on the topic you just read about.

**Notes**

| P: | L: |
|----|----|
|    |    |
|    |    |
|    |    |

**Prompt**

Summarize the points made in the lecture, being sure to explain how they oppose specific points made in the reading passage.

_____

_____

_____

_____

_____

_____

_____

_____

_____

_____

_____

_____

_____

_____

_____

_____

_____

_____

# Model Answer

Between 500 BCE and 500 CE, a group of people called the Nazca, who lived on the dry, windless plains of Peru, drew hundreds of pictures and long, straight lines in the rocky soil. These intersecting lines can extend for kilometers, and some of the lines are interspersed with depictions of animals so large that one can only discern their shapes from high up in the air. Since airplanes had not yet been invented, scholars have long wondered why the Nazca created these expansive images. Although many have concluded that the Nazca Lines had some kind of religious significance, there is little agreement beyond that.

One theory is that the Nazca Lines acted as an astronomical observatory and as places of religious worship. The lines often point to places on the horizon where the Sun, Moon, and other important celestial bodies rise and set. They may also represent shapes made by stars or constellations. Many other ancient cultures built ritual centers based on astronomical observations.

One of the more creative ideas is that the geometric geoglyphs served as patterns for large human looms. In other words, some people would stand on the geoglyph at regular points holding string, and others would walk along the lines, weaving in other strings. In fact, the region is known for its long strings and wide pieces of textile, and the Nazca people used long textiles to wrap and mummify some of their dead.

The idea that is most accepted currently is that the Nazca Lines either symbolized the flow of water or in some other way were meant to serve water deities. It makes sense that people living where there is almost no rain would consider water precious and even sacred. It has even been suggested that the lines might have had something to do with finding underground water or marking wells.

## LECTURE

*You've just read some interesting theories about the possible purposes of the Nazca Lines. The theories all sound plausible, but there's simply not enough evidence to back up any one of them.*

*First, it's certainly true that many indigenous tribes of the Americas and elsewhere mixed astronomy and religious worship. However, there are hundreds of geoglyphs in the plains. One study found that only about 20 percent of the lines made by the Nazca had any specific astronomical orientation, such as pointing to sunrise on the solstice, which is likely to be by chance. There's also not enough evidence to support the idea that the patterns are meant to copy any constellations—or the dark space within a constellation, as one researcher has suggested.*

*Next, the idea that the lines served as giant looms is unsupported by any evidence. It's true that remains of ancient Nazca people have been found wrapped in long pieces of fabric. But there are no traces of such fabric in or around any of the Nazca Lines. Additionally, there are remains of such fabric on primitive wooden looms, indicating that these wooden looms were used for weaving, not the Nazca lines. Thus, the Nazca Lines probably weren't used as looms.*

*Finally, it's logical to infer that the Nazca Lines represent something water-related, as the Nazca likely wanted to find water, or to find favor with water or rain gods. This theory is based on the idea that the Nazca may have shared cultural practices with nearby Bolivian peoples, who have a tradition of walking in straight lines while praying for rain. But there's no physical evidence of water wells or aqueducts connected with any of the lines. So while the water theories remain our best guess at this time, there's no way to be certain that they're correct.*

## Notes

| P: reasons for the Nazca Lines | L: Nazca Lines' purpose remains a mystery |
|---|---|
| observatory/religious worship | only 20% relate to astronomy; not enough proof |
| huge loom patterns | no evidence of loom activities at Nazca Lines |
| symbols of/for rain deities | best guess — but no evidence |

The lecture calls into question the theories regarding the possible purposes of the Nazca Lines presented in the reading. In fact, the lecture says that there is no strong evidence for any of the theories discussed in the reading.

First, the lecture discounts the theory that the Nazca were trying to chart astronomical data with the placement of their lines, shapes, or figures. According to the lecture, some of the lines do point in directions that could be connected to solstices or other events in the sky, but there are so many lines that this is probably just a coincidence. Also, there simply is not enough evidence that the figures are patterned after constellations.

Second, the lecture contends that the textile theory lacks proof. The lecture agrees that the Nazca mummified their dead with long strips of fabric, but no fabric remains have been found near any of the Nazca Lines. Moreover, fabric remains have been found on primitive wooden devices, suggesting that these were used as looms rather than the Nazca lines.

Finally, according to the lecture, theories about water in connection to the lines are based on inference and on the study of another culture. The Nazca did not leave behind clear clues about their religious practices. Researchers have found no physical evidence of wells or canals near the Nazca Lines. Therefore, the lecture says that scholars have not proven that the Nazca lines were focused on water.

# Independent Writing Task I

**▶ Prompt ◀**

Do you agree or disagree with the following statement? Completing challenging tasks and assignments is more rewarding than completing easy ones. Use specific reasons and examples to explain your answer.

**Brainstorm**

_____

_____

_____

_____

_____

_____

_____

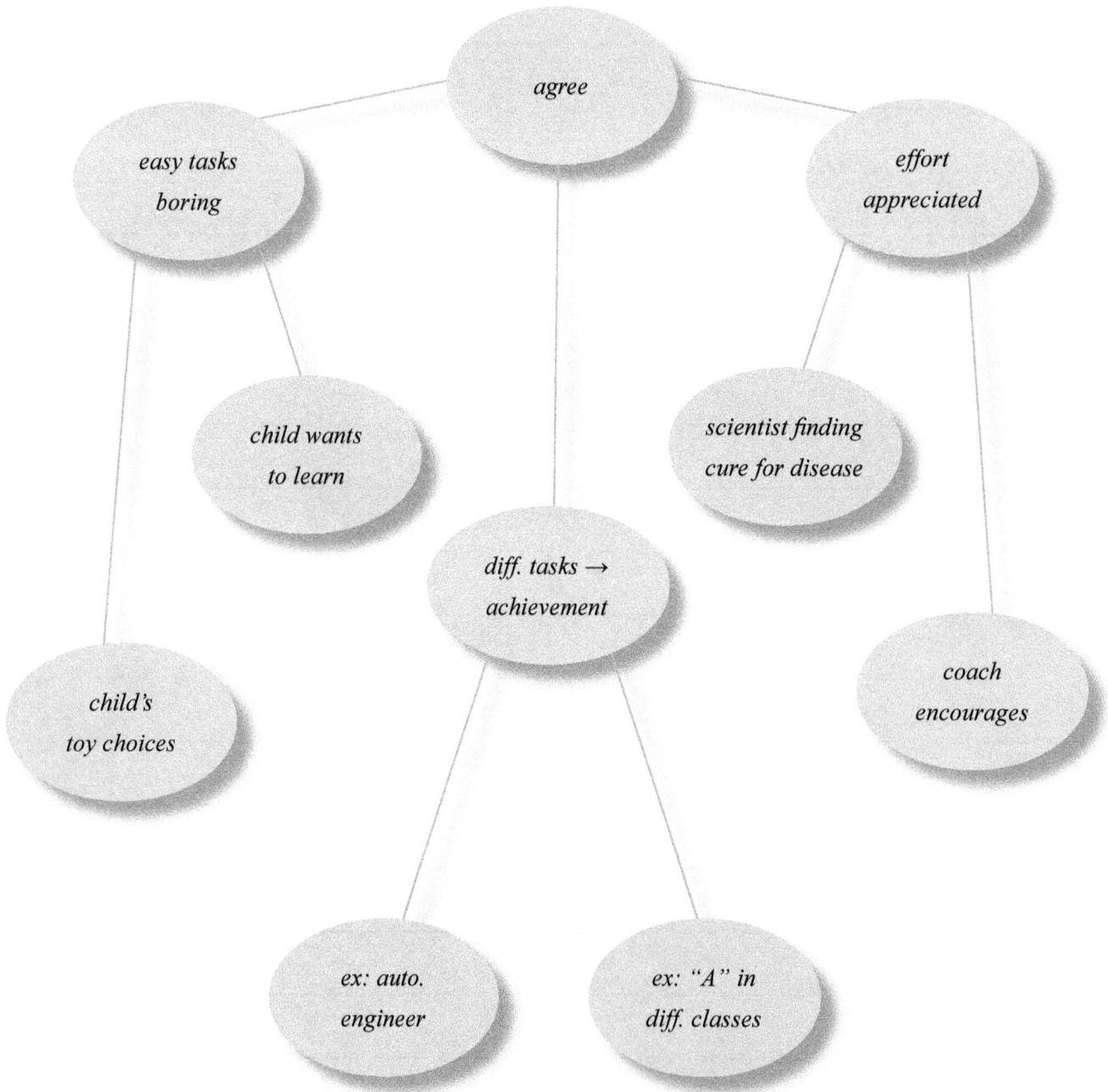

# Model Answer

> **Prompt**
>
> Do you agree or disagree with the following statement? Completing challenging tasks and assignments is more rewarding than completing easy ones. Use specific reasons and examples to explain your answer.

**Brainstorm**

- agree
  - easy tasks boring
    - child wants to learn
    - child's toy choices
  - diff. tasks → achievement
    - ex: auto. engineer
    - ex: "A" in diff. classes
  - effort appreciated
    - scientist finding cure for disease
    - coach encourages

The desire to conserve energy is natural, and it is evident throughout the animal kingdom. For example, a coyote would probably rather catch a few field mice for a meal than try to hunt a fast-running deer. **While it is natural to desire easier work, I believe that people are actually happier when working on and completing challenging tasks.**

One reason that people may become unhappy while doing easy work is that they may become bored. When children are presented with a large selection of toys, they will naturally spend more time with toys that require some thought and effort. For example, a 4-year-old will probably ignore a pull-toy meant for a 1-year-old because pull-toys are predictable and boring by the age of four. Instead, the 4-year-old may spend hours constructing buildings and roads out of wooden blocks, a fascinating task for someone beginning to grasp the basics of three-dimensional shapes and structures.

Moreover, overcoming challenges results in happiness and a sense of accomplishment. An automotive engineer could get an easy, low-stress job doing oil changes. However, the engineer will be happier with the more stressful job of designing car parts, and he will feel a sense of accomplishment when he sees the finished product on the road. Even young students know that earning an "A" in a more difficult class is more satisfying than earning one in an easy class.

Furthermore, people are usually happier when they feel appreciated by others. Patients may express gratitude toward a scientist who discovers a cure for a disease after many years of grueling research. Children and parents may shower a volunteer athletic coach with thanks for inspiring a sense of belonging and teamwork among diverse players. Other people often notice and applaud one's effort to meet challenging goals.

Thus, even though it seems to go against natural inclinations, many people frequently choose tasks that challenge them. They do so because they find such tasks interesting, satisfying, and rewarding.

# Independent Writing Task II

**Prompt**

Should people engage in physical activities and hobbies for relaxation, even when their lives are hectic? Use specific details and reasons to support your answer.

**Brainstorm**

_____

_____

_____

_____

_____

_____

_____

_____

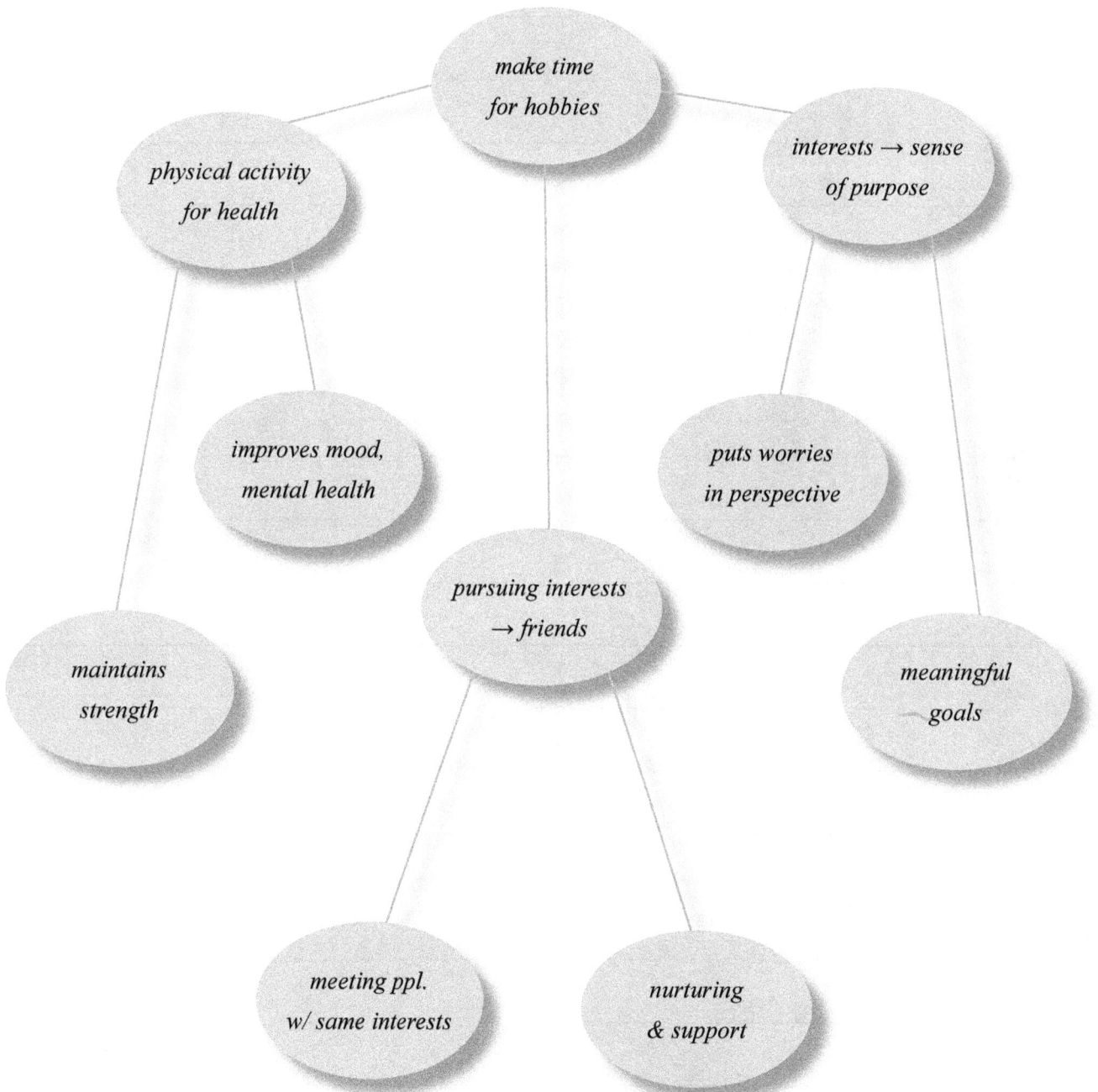

### Brainstorm

*make time for hobbies*

*physical activity for health*

*interests → sense of purpose*

*improves mood, mental health*

*puts worries in perspective*

*pursuing interests → friends*

*maintains strength*

*meaningful goals*

*meeting ppl. w/ same interests*

*nurturing & support*

The obligations of modern life demand much time and energy, and the number of responsibilities that one has tends to increase over time. It may seem selfish or trivial to set aside time in a busy week for engaging in physical activities or hobbies. **Yet relaxing and having fun can encourage people to manage their time effectively so that they can better meet their obligations.**

First of all, <u>relaxing through physical activity offers a recharging period for our bodies.</u> For instance, walking, gardening, or playing a team sport helps maintain overall fitness, preventing injuries and many diseases. Additionally, physical activity may defuse emotional tension and stress, improving people's moods and mental health. Feeling good is essential to keeping up with a hectic life.

Moreover, <u>engaging in hobbies gives one the opportunity to catch up with old acquaintances and meet new people with similar interests.</u> People may meet like-minded friends through activities such as exercise classes, book clubs, and community service organizations. Spending time with acquaintances and friends is another way to boost one's emotional well-being because doing so creates a sense of support.

Finally, <u>pursuing personal interests can give a person a sense of purpose.</u> Sometimes, spending time on a hobby reminds a person that there is life outside of work, and this realization can help a person put problems into perspective. For example, taking time to observe the stars at night may remind someone that there is more to life than simply paying the bills. Personal interests sometimes provide meaningful goals, such as studying a foreign language in order to travel, knitting lap-blankets to comfort people who are sick, or growing flowers favored by an endangered butterfly.

Ultimately, engaging in physical activities and hobbies are important ways to spend one's time. Human beings require time off from work for emotional health and balance. It is important to make time for play and relaxation.

# Integrated Writing Task 16

## PASSAGE

The golden toad was a small, bright orange species of toad that lived in the Monteverde Cloud Forest Reserve in Costa Rica. When the toad was first discovered in 1966, it existed in fairly large numbers. However, the toad has not been seen since 1989 and has been declared extinct. This surprised researchers because the toad lived in a protected park. However, there are several theories to explain the extinction.

One possibility is that the golden toad was especially vulnerable to global warming. Surface temperatures in Monteverde Forest have been increasing since the 1980s, and the area has become increasingly dry over the past three decades. The hotter temperatures and drier climate may have affected the toads' ability to breathe through their skin. Then, in 1987, an unusual weather pattern caused many of the tiny pools where the golden toads laid their eggs to dry up.

A related theory is that the amphibian chytrid fungus killed the toads. This fungus was identified in the 1990s, after the golden toad had already disappeared, but it may have spread before scientists were aware of it. The fungus attacks the skin of frogs and toads, and it has led to species extinctions on several continents. A warmer climate could have supported the fungus' spread to the cloud forest.

Other culprits include the tourists who visited to appreciate the forest's biodieversity. Ecotourism increased by huge margins just before scientists began to notice the decline in the golden toad population. Tourists might have unwittingly brought an invasive species to the habitat. The new organism may have preyed on the toads, out-competed them for food, or changed their environment in some other way. For example, fish introduced to lakes in Yosemite National Park have wiped out local frog populations there. This theory would account for how suddenly the species disappeared.

🔊)) Now listen to part of a lecture on the topic you just read about.

### Notes

| P: | L: |
|---|---|
|  |  |
|  |  |
|  |  |

**Prompt**

Summarize the points made in the lecture, being sure to explain how they oppose specific points made in the reading passage.

_____

_____

_____

_____

_____

_____

_____

_____

_____

_____

_____

_____

_____

_____

_____

_____

_____

_____

_____

_____

# Model Answer

The golden toad was a small, bright orange species of toad that lived in the Monteverde Cloud Forest Reserve in Costa Rica. When the toad was first discovered in 1966, it existed in fairly large numbers. However, the toad has not been seen since 1989 and has been declared extinct. This surprised researchers because the toad lived in a protected park. However, there are several theories to explain the extinction.

One possibility is that the golden toad was especially vulnerable to global warming. Surface temperatures in Monteverde Forest have been increasing since the 1980s, and the area has become increasingly dry over the past three decades. The hotter temperatures and drier climate may have affected the toads' ability to breathe through their skin. Then, in 1987, an unusual weather pattern caused many of the tiny pools where the golden toads laid their eggs to dry up.

A related theory is that the amphibian chytrid fungus killed the toads. This fungus was identified in the 1990s, after the golden toad had already disappeared, but it may have spread before scientists were aware of it. The fungus attacks the skin of frogs and toads, and it has led to species extinctions on several continents. A warmer climate could have supported the fungus' spread to the cloud forest.

Other culprits include the tourists who visited to appreciate the forest's biodieversity. Ecotourism increased by huge margins just before scientists began to notice the decline in the golden toad population. Tourists might have unwittingly brought an invasive species to the habitat. The new organism may have preyed on the toads, out-competed them for food, or changed their environment in some other way. For example, fish introduced to lakes in Yosemite National Park have wiped out local frog populations there. This theory would account for how suddenly the species disappeared.

## LECTURE

*You've just read some of the possible causes for the golden toad's extinction. All of the theories are plausible. But when examined closely, there's just not enough evidence to confirm any of them, and the cause of the species' extinction remains a mystery.*

*Global warming does seem to be an obvious problem for a species that thrives in a damp, cool "cloud forest." But populations of several other toad and amphibian species in the Monteverde Forest haven't declined at all. Moreover, since the temperature of the forest has only been monitored for a few decades, there's still debate over whether the warming that was measured there in the 1980s is part of a normal cycle.*

*The idea that the chytrid fungus caused the toad's extinction is a strong possibility because it has affected so many other amphibian species. But scientists still don't know whether the disease had spread to Costa Rica in the 1980s. And what's more, no one reported seeing diseased golden toads. Normally, when the chytrid fungus attacks amphibians, their skin is visibly afflicted. You'd expect to find diseased carcasses—that is, dead bodies—with such a die-off. Instead, in this case, the toads just disappeared.*

*Finally, there're many documented cases around the globe of invasive species thriving in a foreign habitat. The invasive species can cause the extinction of native species in many ways, predominantly by eating them or by eating their food. So it's tempting to blame tourists for contaminating the beautiful, pristine Cloud Forest with organisms that caused the golden toad's demise. But researchers on the ground hadn't noted the emergence of new or unusual species in the Cloud Forest when the toad population was declining, or since.*

*I'd say that more research is needed before we can know whether climate change, disease, invasive species, or something else entirely caused the extinction of this species.*

**Notes**

| P: | reasons for golden toad extinction | L: | theories lack evidence |
|---|---|---|---|
| | global warming dried environment | | other amphibious species in area fine |
| | fungus killed pop. | | no reports of diseased toads |
| | invasive species | | no reports of invasive species |

The lecture describes the flaws of the reading's explanations for the extinction of Costa Rica's golden toad. In fact, the lecture says that there is little substantial evidence for any of the theories presented in the reading.

First, the lecture claims that the global warming theory cannot be proven. The reading claims that average temperatures rose in the toads' habitat, the Monteverde Forest, and could have dried out their skin. In addition, a warm-weather pattern dried up the water where their eggs usually hatched. However, according to the lecture, other toad species in the forest were unaffected by the temperature change. Scientists are still not even certain whether the warming was part of a normal cycle because they have not observed the forest for long. Thus, the connection between climate change and the disappearance of the golden toad is not at all clear, according to the lecture.

Next, the lecture states that the fungal disease theory presented in the reading has some flaws. The reading says that a fungus that specifically targets amphibians may have killed the toads. However, according to the lecture, the fungus may not have spread to that region of the world at that time. Although the fungal disease usually has visible effects on the skin, researchers did not note any unusual signs of disease on the living or the dead toads.

According to the lecture, there is also not enough evidence to prove the invasive species theory. The lecturer agrees that invasive species can drive native species to extinction in a number of ways. However, no one noted any new species in the Cloud Forest habitat when they noticed the disappearance of the golden toads, nor has anyone reported any new species since then. In the end, the lecture claims that more research needs to be done before a definite cause of extinction can be determined.

# Independent Writing Task I

## Prompt

Do you agree or disagree with the following statement? People who move away from their native villages or hometowns are happier and more successful than people who reside in their native towns for their entire lives. Use examples and specific reasons to support your answer.

### Brainstorm

_____

_____

_____

_____

_____

_____

_____

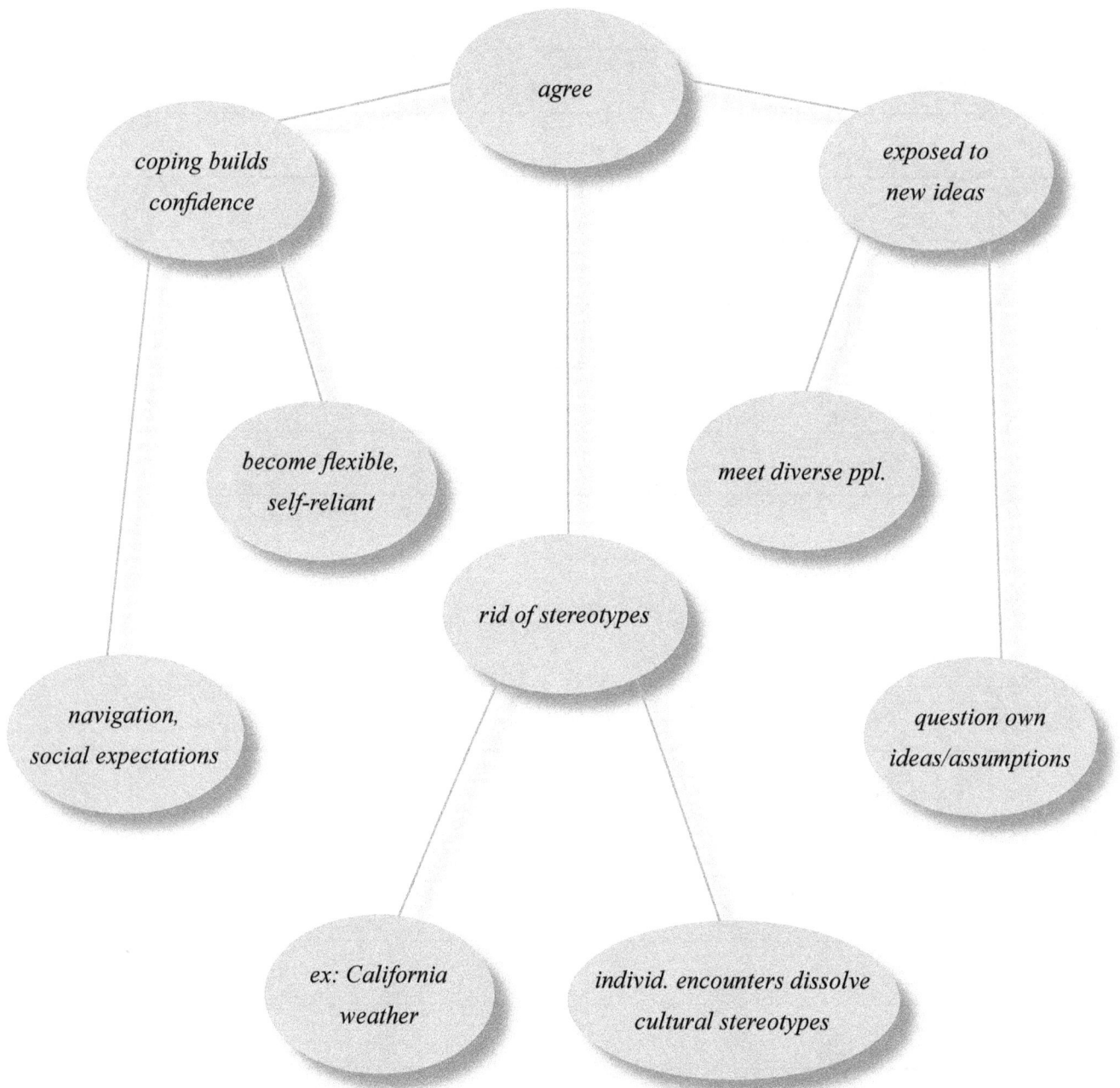

> **Prompt**
> Do you agree or disagree with the following statement? People who move away from their native villages or hometowns are happier and more successful than people who reside in their native towns for their entire lives. Use examples and specific reasons to support your answer.

**Brainstorm**

agree

coping builds confidence

exposed to new ideas

become flexible, self-reliant

meet diverse ppl.

rid of stereotypes

navigation, social expectations

question own ideas/assumptions

ex: California weather

individ. encounters dissolve cultural stereotypes

People who move away from their families and childhood friends are taking a risk. They might find adapting to a new environment confusing or overwhelming at first, and they might feel insignificant and lonely in a place where no one knows them. **However, those who decide to move away from their native villages or hometowns might eventually be happier than those who stay, because those who move away can become more independent and wise.**

First, <u>leaving behind what is comfortable encourages a person to learn about new ways of doing things.</u> By moving to an unfamiliar place, one has to develop methods for coping with daily life. For example, one has to learn the layout of his or her new environment, the social expectations for many situations, and the best ways to cope with different weather. Adjusting successfully to a new environment will make a person more confident and self-reliant. It is challenging and satisfying to overcome a sense of disorientation.

Second, <u>experiencing new people and places undermines stereotypes.</u> For example, people who move to California are often surprised that some regions of the state have extremely cold weather and are quite far from the beach, as the stereotype of California involves sunny beaches. Moreover, most cultural stereotypes are fueled by an ignorance and misunderstanding of that culture. By living among these groups, one is able to understand, and often even appreciate, the customs and traditions of the stereotyped culture.

Third, <u>moving away from a native village or hometown can expose one to different ideas and opinions.</u> Moving often means coming in contact with different ethnicities, languages, religions, and political views. Doing so causes one to question one's own assumptions about large and small issues, such as how to celebrate a birthday or what color to paint a house. Questioning assumptions is a good starting point for wisdom.

Each person who considers moving away from a familiar area will have his or her own unique circumstances to consider. But in general, widening one's perspective of the world is likely to lead to more self-reliance, open-mindedness, and wisdom, creating more success and happiness in life.

# Independent Writing Task II

▶ **Prompt** ◀

Is being similar to others or being unique the surest path to success? Use specific reasons and examples to support your opinion.

**Brainstorm**

**Prompt**

Is being similar to others or being unique the surest path to success? Use specific reasons and examples to support your opinion.

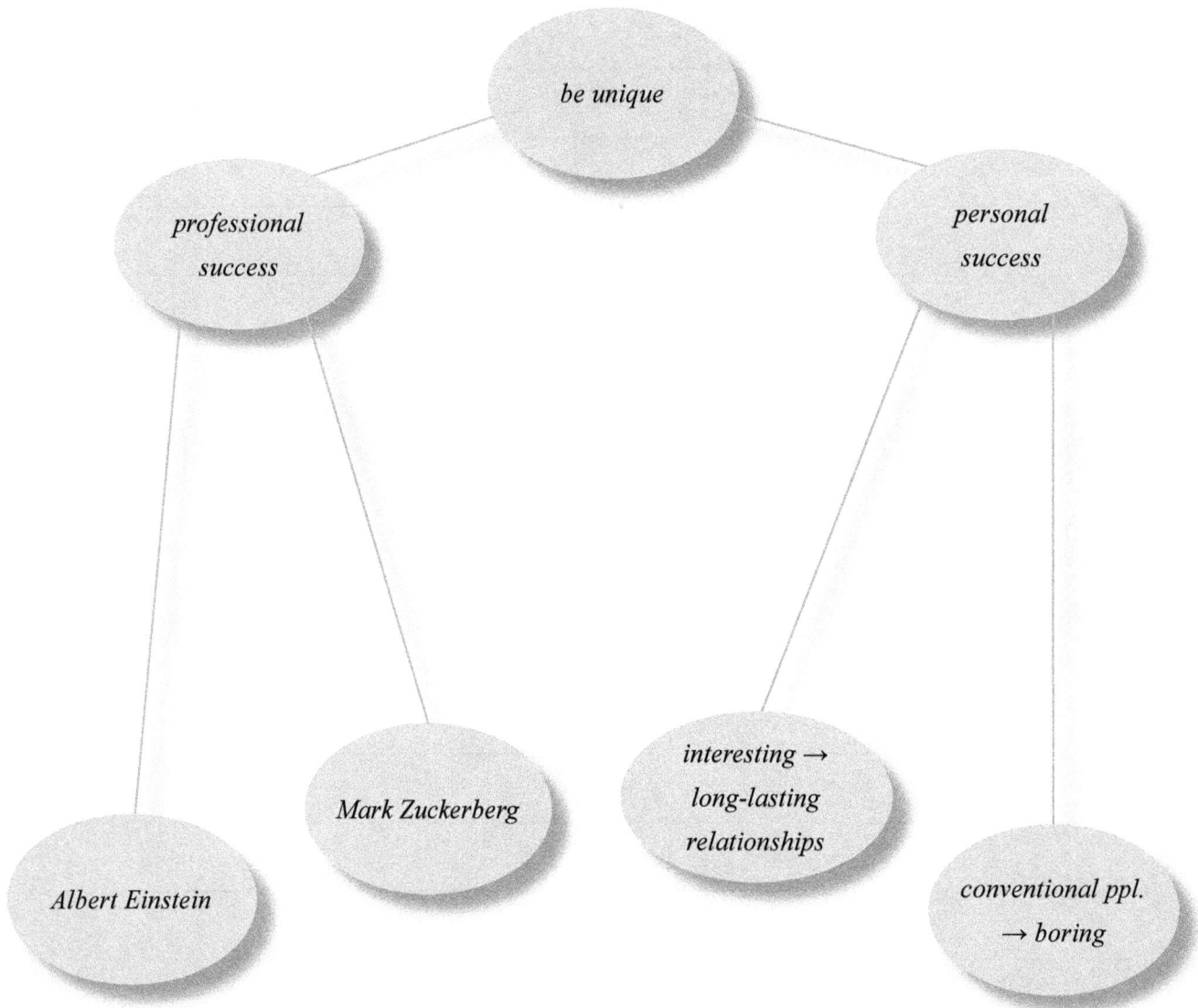

Brainstorm

be unique

professional success

personal success

Albert Einstein

Mark Zuckerberg

interesting → long-lasting relationships

conventional ppl. → boring

People are often torn between a need to conform and a desire to feel unique. Certainly, people consider it positive to "fit in" by meeting others with whom they have much in common. However, people often hope that others notice their one-of-a-kind personality or unusual qualities. **Allowing oneself to be a little different leads to more professional and personal success in life because doing so makes one more interesting.**

There are countless examples of professionally successful individuals who fell outside "normal" bounds for their time and place. Albert Einstein, for example, barely spoke as a child. He refused to wear socks or tidy his hair throughout his life, and he openly opposed racism in American society at a time when it was not popular to do so. More recently, the founder of Facebook, Mark Zuckerberg, has been described as "socially awkward." Yet Zuckerberg had insights into how to make social networking more appealing and accessible. These examples demonstrate that being unique, and even being a bit of a misfit, can give a person a thoughtful, innovative viewpoint.

In the long run, having unusual ideas and being willing to express them may bring more personal success as well. One's "uniqueness" can lead to long-lasting, close relationships because other people will find such a person interesting to talk with. While an attractive or wealthy person may get attention at first, such a person may seem boring after a while. It is human nature to enjoy novelty. Thus, one key to building strong relationships may be to allow oneself to think freely and imaginatively, and to be different.

Ultimately, being unique is more likely to lead to personal satisfaction and professional success than attempting to be like everyone else. Even in a world that loves conformity, there is reward in standing out.

# Integrated Writing Task 17

## PASSAGE

The Tunguska event was a gigantic explosion that occurred over the Tunguska River in central Russia in 1908. The region was uninhabited at the time, so there were no known human deaths, but the shock wave from the explosion knocked down about 80 million trees and caused an earthquake that was 5.0 on the Richter scale. For several reasons, many scientists believe that the explosion was caused by a comet—a large chunk of icy materials from space.

The first piece of evidence indicating that a comet caused the explosion is that researchers did not find a crater at the location of the comet's impact when they visited the site years after the explosion. The lack of a giant indention seems to prove that the object was a comet because its frozen water would have mostly vaporized when it entered the Earth's atmosphere.

Another clue is that, following the comet's impact, much of the hemisphere may have been covered in upper-atmosphere clouds, which an exploding comet would leave behind. Witnesses all over Europe and Asia reported bright clouds in the skies following the explosion. Particles of dust and icy vapor from a comet could have formed the unusual clouds.

Finally, researchers ruled out the idea that the explosion could have been caused by other factors. Scientists have discounted the other main theory, that the cause was a rocky meteorite, because researchers have not found any chunks of space rock in the soil beneath the site of the explosion.

The evidence points to a comet entering Earth's atmosphere and exploding because of the heat and pressure as it hurtled closer to the surface. Luckily, space agencies now track such space objects that come near Earth, and such an incursion is preventable.

◀)) Now listen to part of a lecture on the topic you just read about.

### Notes

| P: | L: |
|---|---|
|  |  |
|  |  |
|  |  |

*Prompt*

Summarize the points made in the lecture, being sure to explain how they oppose specific points made in the reading passage.

_____

_____

_____

_____

_____

_____

_____

_____

_____

_____

_____

_____

_____

_____

_____

_____

_____

_____

_____

_____

_____

# Model Answer

The Tunguska event was a gigantic explosion that occurred over the Tunguska River in central Russia in 1908. The region was uninhabited at the time, so there were no known human deaths, but the shock wave from the explosion knocked down about 80 million trees and caused an earthquake that was 5.0 on the Richter scale. For several reasons, many scientists believe that the explosion was caused by a comet—a large chunk of icy materials from space.

The first piece of evidence indicating that a comet caused the explosion is that researchers did not find a crater at the location of the comet's impact when they visited the site years after the explosion. The lack of a giant indention seems to prove that the object was a comet because its frozen water would have mostly vaporized when it entered the Earth's atmosphere.

Another clue is that, following the comet's impact, much of the hemisphere may have been covered in upper-atmosphere clouds, which an exploding comet would leave behind. Witnesses all over Europe and Asia reported bright clouds in the skies following the explosion. Particles of dust and icy vapor from a comet could have formed the unusual clouds.

Finally, researchers ruled out the idea that the explosion could have been caused by other factors. Scientists have discounted the other main theory, that the cause was a rocky meteorite, because researchers have not found any chunks of space rock in the soil beneath the site of the explosion.

The evidence points to a comet entering Earth's atmosphere and exploding because of the heat and pressure as it hurtled closer to the surface. Luckily, space agencies now track such space objects that come near Earth, and such an incursion is preventable.

## LECTURE

*Let's take a look at more recent research about the Tunguska event, the atomic bomb-like burst over a Russian forest more than a century ago. Scientists agree that a near-Earth object colliding with Earth caused the event. Yet they still debate whether the object that exploded was an icy comet or a rocky meteorite. These days, many people among the scientific community are moving away from the comet hypothesis and toward the meteorite hypothesis.*

*First, the comet hypothesis assumes that the object didn't leave a crater, which is what would be expected from a falling rock. However, some scientists are now investigating whether a certain lake in the area may have started as a crater from the explosion. The lake has a cone-shaped bottom, which is unusual for a lake in the area, and it doesn't appear on maps made before the explosion.*

*Another possible explanation for the apparent lack of a crater may be that even a fairly large meteorite could explode before it hit the ground, just as a comet would. Models show that the heat and pressure from falling through Earth's atmosphere could cause the rock to disintegrate. Such a scenario might explain the strange, dusty clouds after the explosion as well as the lack of a crater.*

*The strongest case for the meteorite may be that there was plenty of space-rock on the ground after the event, but scientists didn't realize it. In the 1970s, some researchers looking in a nearby swamp found some bits of minerals that could've only been formed under intense heat and pressure, but they weren't sure whether the minerals had come from space. Recent studies using new scanning technology determined that the grains of rock did come from space, probably from an iron-rich meteorite. So even if there's no crater and no explanations for the clouds, there's good evidence that a meteorite, not a comet, collided with Earth and caused the Tunguska event.*

Notes

| P: *Tunguska event → comet* | L: *Tunguska event → meteor* |
|---|---|
| *no crater* | *crater may be a lake now* |
| *upper-atm. clouds* | *disintegrating rocks look like clouds* |
| *no space rocks found nearby* | *space rock found in nearby swamps* |

The reading claims that a comet hitting Earth most likely caused the Tunguska event. The lecture, however, describes new and updated research that explains why most scientists changed their minds and now attribute the 1908 Tunguska event to a meteorite rather than a comet.

First, the lecture states that the lack of a crater in the soil below the explosion site is not proof that the object had to be an icy comet that evaporated. A crater may indeed be present, as some scientists are examining one of the lakes in the forest to see if it could have been formed in 1908 by falling rock. Researchers suspect that the lake may have formed as a result of a meteor impact because it has an unusually shaped basin, and it does not appear on older maps of the region.

Second, scientists now reject the idea that only an exploding comet could cause the unusual clouds seen after the Tunguska event. Based on current models, even a large, rocky meteor could completely break apart in the atmosphere during its fall, causing irregular cloud formations. The models could provide an alternative explanation for the strange clouds as well as the seeming lack of a crater.

The lecture provides extra details about how mineral evidence almost conclusively proves that the object was a meteorite. In the 1970s, some researchers found very small bits of unusual minerals in the Tunguska area, but it was only with today's technologies that researchers could take a definitive look at the old samples. They determined that the samples were from space rock.

Thus, newer research, modeling, and laboratory techniques point toward a meteorite causing the explosion over Tunguska.

# Independent Writing Task I

Prompt

Do you agree or disagree with the following statement? The best way to achieve happiness is by letting others be happy. Use specific details and reasons to explain your answer.

## Brainstorm

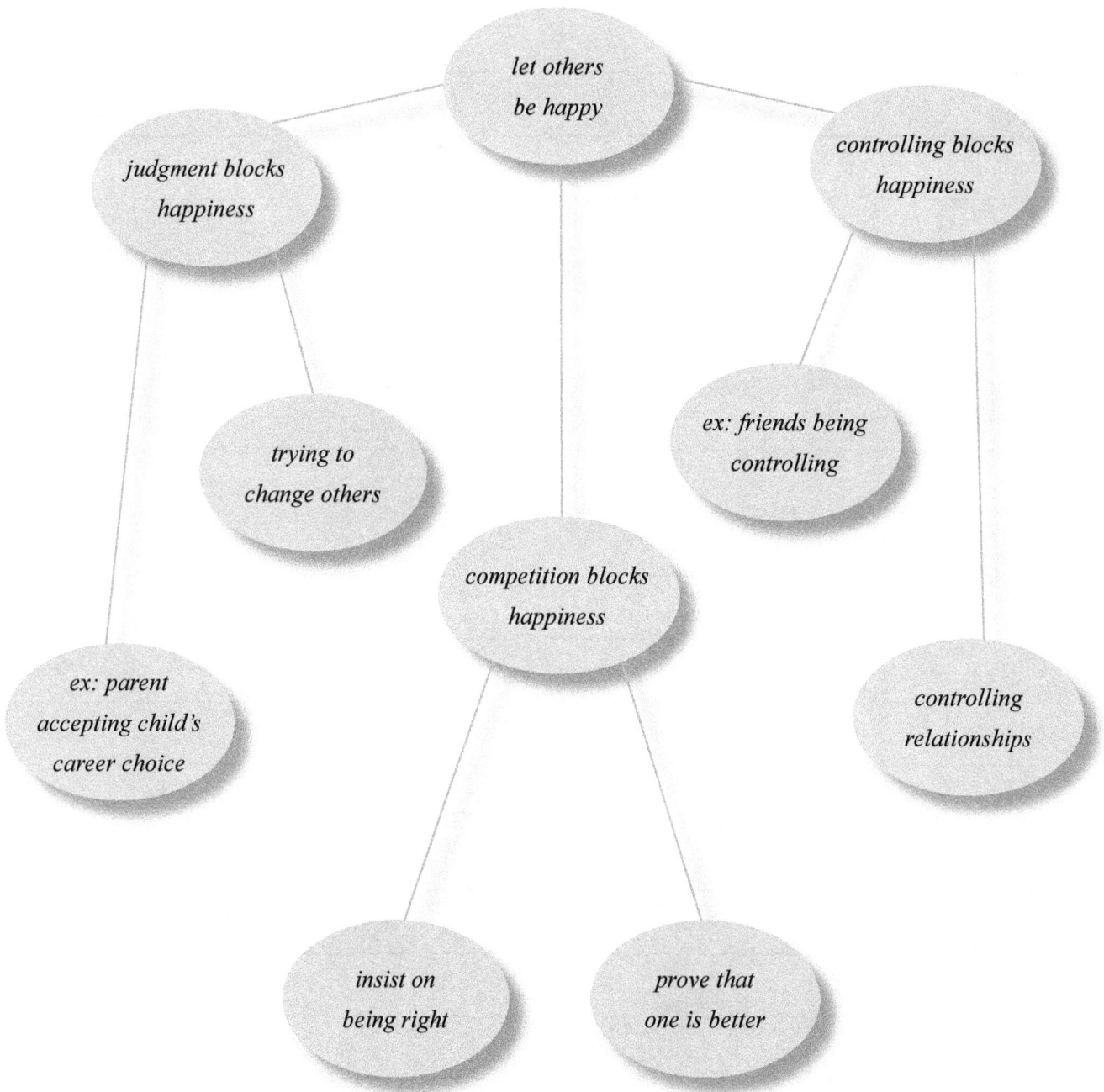

# Model Answer

## Prompt

Do you agree or disagree with the following statement? The best way to achieve happiness is by letting others be happy. Use specific details and reasons to explain your answer.

**Brainstorm**

- let others be happy
  - judgment blocks happiness
    - trying to change others
    - ex: parent accepting child's career choice
  - competition blocks happiness
    - insist on being right
    - prove that one is better
  - controlling blocks happiness
    - ex: friends being controlling
    - controlling relationships

Finding happiness seems like a simple goal, but we all face times in our lives when that goal is difficult to attain. Sometimes, people do not realize that they have isolated themselves because they tried to block the happiness of others.  **So ultimately, the best way to achieve happiness is by examining your closest relationships to make sure that you are letting your loved ones be happy.**

One way to let others be happy is to accept their differences, rather than trying to change them. For example, a college professor who has always enjoyed intellectual pursuits may find it difficult to accept a daughter who would rather work at a horse ranch than go to college. Or a person might feel frustrated that his or her spouse is not more ambitious, romantic, energetic, or organized. But, a healthy approach to such differences is to avoid judging others and to appreciate them as they are. A happy daughter will in turn make her father happier the same way a spouse's happiness will spread to his or her partner.

Another way that people can let others be happy is by avoiding unnecessary competition. Competing with others leads to undue stress between those people. For example, one person may insist upon winning a discussion by getting the other person to agree with him or her, creating a battle of wills. Therefore, everyone will be happier if a relationship does not become a contest, as it allows people to be more relaxed around one another.

A third way to let others' happiness flourish is to avoid seeking total control over them. A young child might say, "I won't be your friend unless you give me your cookie," and that same thinking lasts into adulthood for some people. For example, a person might tell a friend, "If you keep dating that person, I don't think I can hang out with you anymore." Such attempts to control another person's choices lead to resentment, which breeds negativity that affects both people.

Letting others be themselves and pursue happiness in their own way is the surest route to maintaining good relationships. As the old saying goes, "Happiness is contagious." Encouraging the happiness of others builds healthy relationships, making you happier as a result.

# Independent Writing Task II

## ▸ Prompt ◂

Some people say that the personal and work-related challenges that today's young people encounter are not so different from the difficulties faced by their parents and grandparents. What is your opinion? Use specific examples and reasons to explain your answer.

### Brainstorm

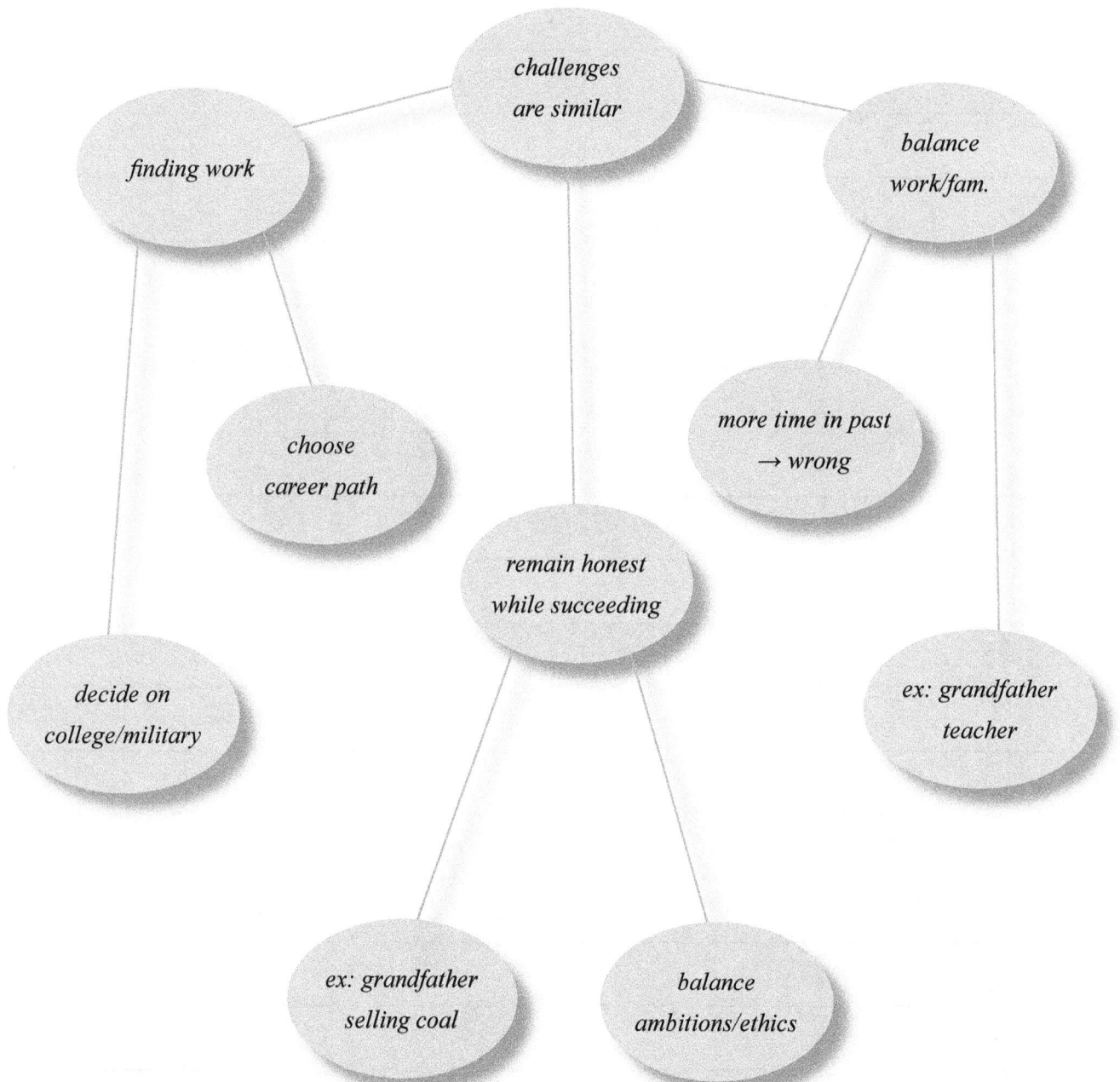

**Prompt**

Some people say that the personal and work-related challenges that today's young people encounter are not so different from the difficulties faced by their parents and grandparents. What is your opinion? Use specific examples and reasons to explain your answer.

**Brainstorm**

challenges are similar

finding work

balance work/fam.

choose career path

more time in past → wrong

remain honest while succeeding

decide on college/military

ex: grandfather teacher

ex: grandfather selling coal

balance ambitions/ethics

With the rise of automation, internet technology, and globalization, many of today's work environments are completely different from those that existed several decades ago. Yet many of the challenges faced by a typical worker remain remarkably unchanged. **Young people have to solve many of the same problems as previous generations of workers did: finding suitable work, competing with others, and balancing one's work and personal life.**

For each individual, finding the best way to make a living has always been a difficult decision. Although the types of jobs available to young people today differ from those available to previous generations, all individuals entering into adulthood have similar decisions to make. One must decide whether to attend college, to join the military, or to begin working right after high school. And later, one must decide upon a career path that will provide both financial and personal fulfillment.

Moreover, each new generation of workers has had to learn how to compete effectively and ethically with others in a work environment. For example, my great-grandfather was a coal salesman. Although he wanted to sell more coal in order to better support his family, he took pride in helping his clients estimate how much coal they would really need. Thus, he had to consider his financial responsibilities to his family as well as his ethical responsibilities to his customers. These days, it is still important for young people to learn to cope with pressures and ambitions while remaining honest.

Furthermore, the greatest work-related challenge in every generation may be balancing work demands with family time. It is tempting to think that today's workers feel more pressure to dedicate themselves both to their work and to their families than did previous generations. Yet one of my grandfathers, who was a teacher, told me that when his children were young, he sometimes cried while getting ready for work in the morning, thinking of all he had to do that day. Each generation must figure out how to divide precious time between domestic and financial responsibilities.

Although the world is constantly evolving, some fundamental work-related challenges persist. Ultimately, what people do for work changes over time, but the challenges they face remain largely the same.

# Integrated Writing Task 18

A number of astronomy groups in various nations are currently involved in the Search for Extra Terrestrial Intelligence, or SETI. There is at least one clue that there may be intelligent life elsewhere in space. In 1977, astronomer Jerry Ehman was checking data from the Big Ear, a radio telescope run by Ohio State University. Next to one recorded signal, he wrote "Wow!" The signal is now referred to as the Wow! signal, and it remains an intriguing hint that life exists elsewhere in the universe. Three characteristics of the signal have fueled speculation that it may have been sent by intelligent extraterrestrial life forms.

The first characteristic is the rise and fall of the signal. A signal originating from a stable source would seem weak as the radio telescope beam came near, strong as the beam focused on it, and weak as the beam moved away. At the rate the beam was moving, the whole process should take about 72 seconds, which is indeed the length of the signal's recording. The appearance of rising and falling makes it more likely that the source was a relatively stable deep-space source, not a passing aircraft.

Moreover, despite intense searches over many years with increasingly sensitive radio detectors, the signal was never found again. A one-time signal rules out the possibility that the signal came from something that was orbiting Earth, such as a satellite or a piece of "space junk." If the signal came from such a device, it would have been detected regularly as the object continued its predictable orbits around Earth.

The signal's most intriguing characteristic is its narrow frequency. As far as scientists know, any object in space that naturally emits electromagnetic energy, including radio waves, emits a broad spectrum. The focused nature of the Wow! signal lends itself to the suggestion that it was not naturally occurring, but rather was created artificially.

◀)) Now listen to part of a lecture on the topic you just read about.

Notes

| P: | L: |
|---|---|
| | |
| | |
| | |

**Prompt**

Summarize the points made in the lecture, being sure to explain how they elaborate on specific points made in the reading passage.

_____

_____

_____

_____

_____

_____

_____

_____

_____

_____

_____

_____

_____

_____

_____

_____

_____

_____

# Model Answer

A number of astronomy groups in various nations are currently involved in the Search for Extra Terrestrial Intelligence, or SETI. There is at least one clue that there may be intelligent life elsewhere in space. In 1977, astronomer Jerry Ehman was checking data from the Big Ear, a radio telescope run by Ohio State University. Next to one recorded signal, he wrote "Wow!" The signal is now referred to as the Wow! signal, and it remains an intriguing hint that life exists elsewhere in the universe. Three characteristics of the signal have fueled speculation that it may have been sent by intelligent extraterrestrial life forms.

The first characteristic is the rise and fall of the signal. A signal originating from a stable source would seem weak as the radio telescope beam came near, strong as the beam focused on it, and weak as the beam moved away. At the rate the beam was moving, the whole process should take about 72 seconds, which is indeed the length of the signal's recording. The appearance of rising and falling makes it more likely that the source was a relatively stable deep-space source, not a passing aircraft.

Moreover, despite intense searches over many years with increasingly sensitive radio detectors, the signal was never found again. A one-time signal rules out the possibility that the signal came from something that was orbiting Earth, such as a satellite or a piece of "space junk." If the signal came from such a device, it would have been detected regularly as the object continued its predictable orbits around Earth.

The signal's most intriguing characteristic is its narrow frequency. As far as scientists know, any object in space that naturally emits electromagnetic energy, including radio waves, emits a broad spectrum. The focused nature of the Wow! signal lends itself to the suggestion that it was not naturally occurring, but rather was created artificially.

*Let's see if we can expand upon th significance of the "alien" Wow! signal that you encountered in the reading material. While of course there are skeptics, the signal has certain features that point toward an intelligent origin, particularly the three characteristics that were covered in the reading.*

*The way the signal rose and fell not only makes it more likely that it was from a stable source, but also that it wasn't just a computer glitch in the Big Ear. After all, a computer glitch is unlikely to produce a radio signal with an ideal rise and fall for an ideal length of time.*

*And as you read, the fact that the signal only occurred once indicates that the signal didn't come from Earth. The signal's singular occurrence also rules out the possibility that the signal was from a naturally occurring celestial object such as an energy-dense quasar. Any naturally occurring celestial body would remain detectable for a very long time, and it wouldn't vanish immediately after an initial detection.*

*As the reading points out, the most interesting aspect of the signal was its narrow frequency. The reading explains that no known natural source emits radio waves within such a narrow range of frequencies. And on top of all this, the Wow! signal's particular frequency is, by international agreement, off-limits on Earth. This frequency remains unused on Earth because it's the precise frequency that scientists suspect aliens would use for inter-planetary communication: 1420 MHz. Intelligent life forms might choose that frequency because it can penetrate atmospheres, and it's generated by hydrogen, the most plentiful element in the universe. Any technological society would recognize it was artificial.*

**Notes**

| P: | L: |
|---|---|
| *Wow! signal = alien* | *agree w/ reading* |
| *rise and fall of signal* | *not a computer glitch* |
| *only heard once* | *not from natural celestial body* |
| *narrow frequency* | *1420 MHz = supposed alien frequency* |

The reading describes the SETI program, which searches for evidence of extraterrestrial life, and the Wow! signal that was recorded in 1977. The reading explains that researchers believe the Wow! signal may prove the existence of extraterrestrials in the universe. The lecture supports and advances this idea with additional information.

The reading states that the Wow! signal, identified by a researcher who wrote "Wow!" in the margin of the data, meets three essential criteria for consideration as a transmission from another intelligent life form. First, the signal fades in and out appropriately. Second, the signal does not repeat, as a signal from a satellite or related space junk might. Third, the signal was recorded on a very narrow frequency, indicating that it was not a naturally occurring phenomenon.

The lecture agrees with the reading, and also extends the argument in favor of classifying the Wow! signal as potentially an extraterrestrial transmission. Further research has ruled out the possibility that the signal may have come from the listening device that made the recording, or as the result of a natural transmission from a quasar or another naturally occurring celestial object. Furthermore, the lecture points out that the recording was broadcast on a frequency that pierces through the atmosphere of planets. This suggests that the transmission may have been purposely designed to reach out across the universe in greeting.

# Independent Writing Task I

## Prompt

Do you agree or disagree with the following statement? Demonstrating rude or disrespectful behavior in social situations is never justified. Use specific examples to support your answer.

### Brainstorm

_____

_____

_____

_____

_____

_____

_____

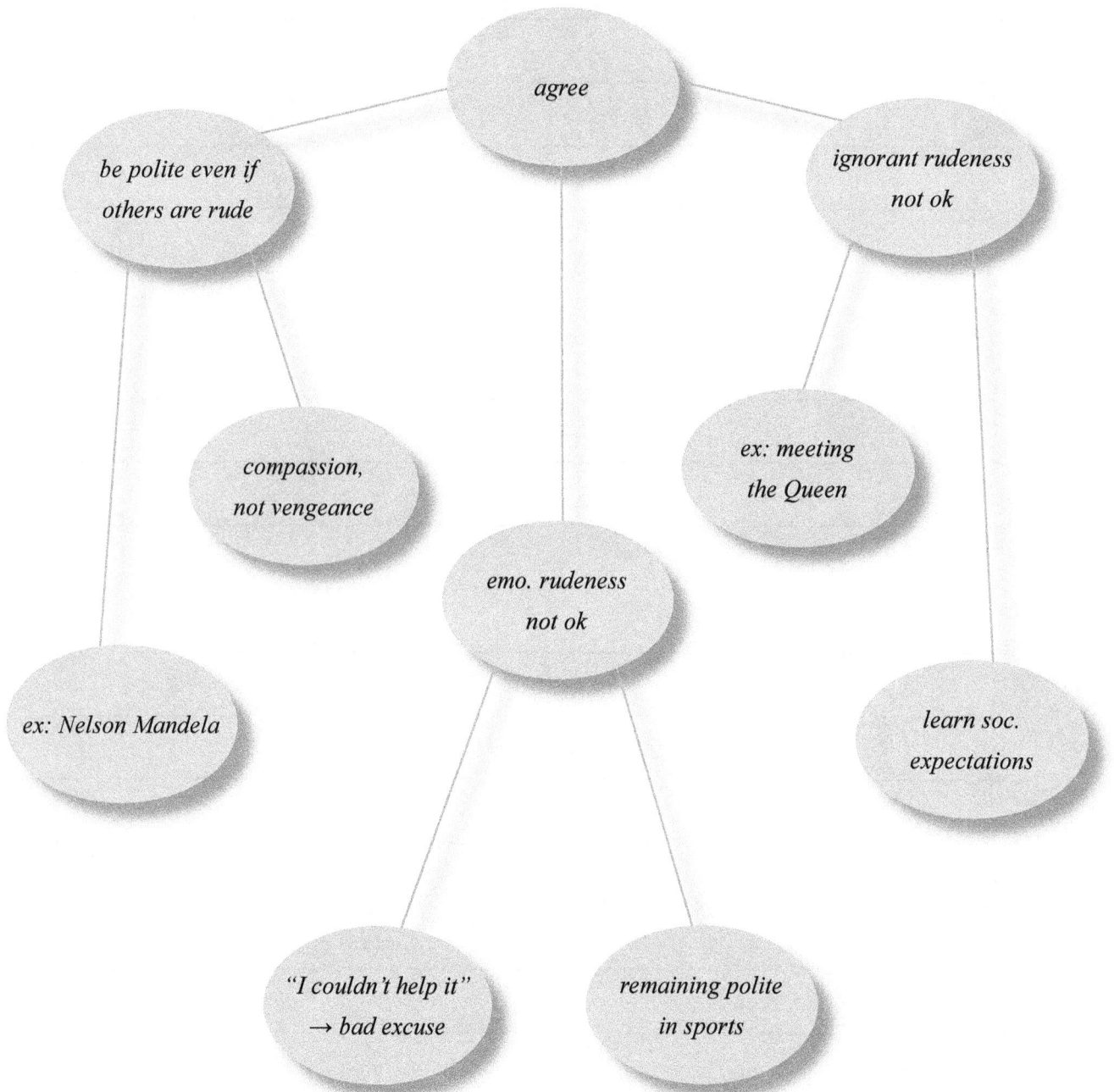

# Model Answer

▶ Prompt ◀

Do you agree or disagree with the following statement? Demonstrating rude or disrespectful behavior in social situations is never justified. Use specific examples to support your answer.

## Brainstorm

*agree*

*be polite even if others are rude*

*ignorant rudeness not ok*

*compassion, not vengeance*

*ex: meeting the Queen*

*emo. rudeness not ok*

*ex: Nelson Mandela*

*learn soc. expectations*

*"I couldn't help it" → bad excuse*

*remaining polite in sports*

No matter what culture people are from, most would agree that it is important to respect other people's feelings. But in some cases, people forget that value and insist that they have good reasons for rudeness. **However, demonstrating rude or disrespectful behavior in social situations is never justified, even if someone seems to deserve it, or if ignorance is the problem.**

First, being disrespected does not give one an excuse to be rude in return. Remaining polite even in an unpleasant situation can help everyone calm down. For example, South African President Nelson Mandela won global admiration because he was considerate to his jailers, even after he was released from prison and gained political power. Mandela modeled the strength that can be achieved by concentrating on one's own caring behavior rather than seeking revenge for someone else's bad behavior.

Second, strong feelings do not justify rudeness. It is not an excuse to say that one "couldn't help it" and had to behave rudely. For example, if a person feels strong loyalty to a certain sports team, and game officials make a call that seems unfair to that team, it is still important to remain civil to the game officials. Name-calling and rude gestures will not solve the problem in that situation or in any other. Rudeness toward the game official will only escalate tensions and create strife.

Finally, being unaware rarely excuses rude behavior. An important part of being considerate to others is to pay attention to them. For example, Queen Elizabeth II meets thousands of people every year, but if someone hugs her or grabs her hand, the action makes international news. Most people learn ahead of time that it is considered impolite to reach out and touch the queen, or they learn by watching how others act around her and then copy that behavior. As they are when meeting the queen, people should be socially considerate during all interactions.

Inevitably, every person makes etiquette mistakes or gives in to strong emotions at some point. But rudeness is not acceptable, and should always be followed by an apology.

# Independent Writing Task II

**Prompt**

Do you agree or disagree with the following statement? The rapid growth of cities is having an overall positive effect on society. Use specific reasons and examples to support your opinion.

**Brainstorm**

_____

_____

_____

_____

_____

_____

_____

> ➤ **Prompt** ◀
>
> Do you agree or disagree with the following statement? The rapid growth of cities is having an overall positive effect on society. Use specific reasons and examples to support your opinion.

**Brainstorm**

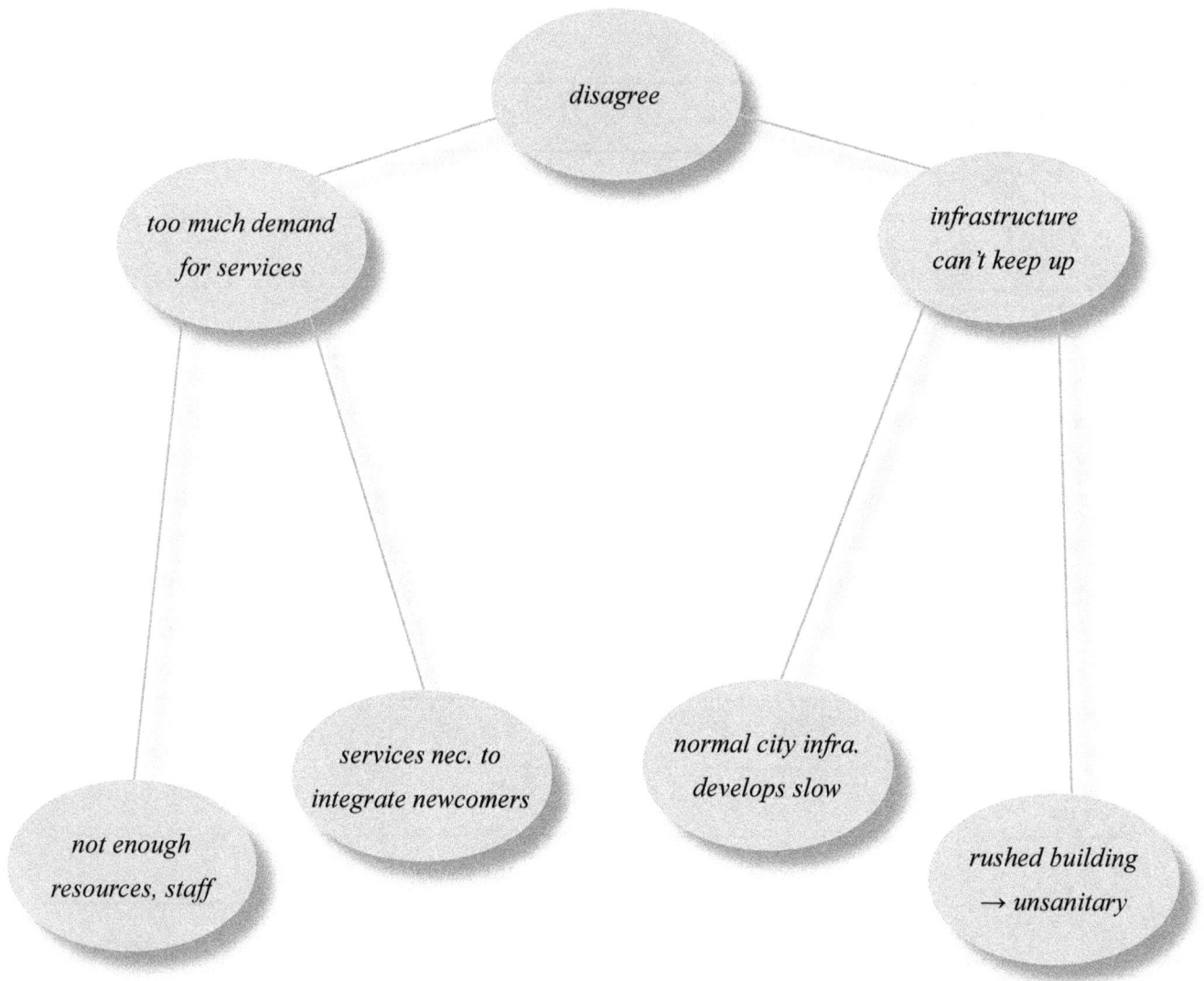

In many developed and developing countries, cities and other urban areas are experiencing major population growth. In some parts of the world, the people are motivated to move into cities by the desire to escape desperate circumstances such as famine or warfare. For these people, any change in location may seem better than their original homes. **However, sudden urban population growth burdens a city's infrastructure, and these changes have a negative impact on society.**

Cities that experience swift population growth do not usually have enough social services to provide for all incoming residents. For instance, a city may not have enough resources to distribute to new residents, and there may not be enough government employees or volunteers to distribute them. Moreover, there may not be enough professionals on hand to handle the medical, security, and educational needs of the population. Yet all of these services help new residents integrate into the economy by finding jobs, purchasing homes, and paying taxes.

Cities also need to expand their physical infrastructure to accommodate population growth. Infrastructure usually develops slowly, so a large influx of residents may overwhelm a city's roads, schools, hospitals, mass transit, housing markets, and water supplies. Furthermore, when infrastructure projects are undertaken without adequate planning, the results are often haphazard and inadequate. For example, people are sometimes forced to set up unauthorized tent cities on private or public land, with unhygienic conditions that may cause the spread of diseases. As a result, all the city's inhabitants suffer, whether they are long-time residents or new arrivals.

Clearly, the heavy burden placed on cities facing rapid growth has a largely negative impact on its citizens. Decentralizing the economy could be an important objective for many governments; doing so might allow people to remain in rural areas, and they would not have to flood into cities.

# Integrated Writing Task 19

## PASSAGE

Charles Darwin's theory of natural selection describes the process by which certain characteristics occur with more or less frequency based upon how well they help a species survive in its particular environment. This theory reshaped how humans understand the development of and interactions between many species. For instance, Darwin theorized that some species coevolve with one another; that is, one species causes cumulative changes in the other, resulting in both of them becoming more fit for survival. The relationship can be one of mutualism, predator-prey, or parasite-host.

In mutually beneficial relationships, coevolution begins when one of the organisms undergoes a genetic change that gives it a small survival advantage. For example, some birds and insects have coevolved with certain types of flowers in a process that benefits both species. Indeed, moths and butterflies have long, tube-like mouths called proboscises that help them extract a flower's nectar. As a result, many flowers have made their nectar more accessible to these insects, as these species spread the flowers' pollen, aiding in the flowers' reproduction.

In a predator-prey relationship, some individuals in the prey species may escape predators more often because of some genetic advantage, such as the production of toxins. As a result, a predator species will avoid attacking members of the prey species that possess the toxin. Over many generations, the toxic prey become the dominant members of the species. However, some members of the predator species may develop a resistance to the toxin, causing the process to begin again.

A parasite-host relationship also results in a process in which each species develops some genetic advantage over the rival species. For example, a host species may gain some extra defense against a parasite, which the parasite species then overcomes. Members of the host species then develop stronger defenses, which the parasite must again overcome.

Now listen to part of a lecture on the topic you just read about.

Notes

| P: | L: |
|---|---|
| | |
| | |
| | |

**Prompt**

Summarize the points made in the lecture, being sure to explain how they elaborate on specific points made in the reading passage.

_____

_____

_____

_____

_____

_____

_____

_____

_____

_____

_____

_____

_____

_____

_____

_____

_____

_____

_____

# Model Answer

Charles Darwin's theory of natural selection describes the process by which certain characteristics occur with more or less frequency based upon how well they help a species survive in its particular environment. This theory reshaped how humans understand the development of and interactions between many species. For instance, Darwin theorized that some species coevolve with one another; that is, one species causes cumulative changes in the other, resulting in both of them becoming more fit for survival. The relationship can be one of mutualism, predator-prey, or parasite-host.

In mutually beneficial relationships, coevolution begins when one of the organisms undergoes a genetic change that gives it a small survival advantage. For example, some birds and insects have coevolved with certain types of flowers in a process that benefits both species. Indeed, moths and butterflies have long, tube-like mouths called proboscises that help them extract a flower's nectar. As a result, many flowers have made their nectar more accessible to these insects, as these species spread the flowers' pollen, aiding in the flowers' reproduction.

In a predator-prey relationship, some individuals in the prey species may escape predators more often because of some genetic advantage, such as the production of toxins. As a result, a predator species will avoid attacking members of the prey species that possess the toxin. Over many generations, the toxic prey become the dominant members of the species. However, some members of the predator species may develop a resistance to the toxin, causing the process to begin again.

A parasite-host relationship also results in a process in which each species develops some genetic advantage over the rival species. For example, a host species may gain some extra defense against a parasite, which the parasite species then overcomes. Members of the host species then develop stronger defenses, which the parasite must again overcome.

LECTURE

*As the reading discussed, coevolution means that two or more species develop characteristics that help them adapt to one another. Let me give you some specific examples that elaborate upon claims made in the reading.*

*In 1862, Darwin described an orchid found in Madagascar called Angraecum sesquipedal that co-evolved with an insect species in a mutually beneficial relationship. The orchid has a 35-centimeter-long spur, the tube that provides a flower's nectar, which hangs elegantly from the star-shaped flower. So Darwin realized that there must be a moth species with an equally long proboscis to access the nectar within the spur. He reasoned that the orchid would've only developed such an extreme trait if it had coevolved with a moth in the manner described in the reading. Forty years later, Darwin was proven correct. A moth with a nearly 35-centimeter proboscis was discovered in Madagascar.*

*An example of predator-prey coevolution is the relationship between the North American garter snake and the rough-skinned newt, a lizard-like amphibian. The garter hunts the newt. As a result, the newt developed adaptations in its skin that make it toxic to garter snakes. The garter snake then developed resistance to the toxins, allowing it to overcome the newt's adaptations. In turn, the newt's toxins became stronger.*

*And finally, coevolution in parasite-host relationships can be seen among certain birds. Some species of cuckoo bird act as parasites by laying their eggs in a host species' nests, tricking the host species into raising the cuckoo's young. Host birds have developed many strategies for overcoming such parasitism. Some host species are able to recognize the parasitic eggs, which they push out of their nests. However, that causes some cuckoo birds to adapt with eggs that more closely mimic the host birds' eggs in appearance, inspiring a seemingly endless cycle of parasitism and retaliation.*

*Thus, studying coevolution offers a window into the development of many ecological relationships.*

| P: coevolution | L: examples of coevolution |
|---|---|
| mutually beneficial relationship: moths/butterflies and flowers | Darwin's Madagascar orchid/moth |
| predator-prey: prey develops toxin, pred. develops resistance | garter snake/rough-skinned newt |
| parasite-host: host develops defense, parasite overcomes | cuckoo bird eggs/host bird nests |

The lecture supports the reading by providing more details and examples to explain coevolution. The lecture helps illustrate how organisms sometimes evolve in response to each other within mutualistic, predator-prey, and parasite-host relationships.

An example of mutually beneficial coevolution involves Darwin's Madagascar orchid. The reading explains how many species of flower evolve features that make them more accessible to moths, birds, and butterflies. The lecture claims that Darwin hypothesized that one species of flower developed a long spur to accommodate the proboscis of a particular species of moth. He inferred this based only on the structure of the flower. Much later, a moth with a long proboscis was indeed found, proving Darwin's hypothesis.

An example of the predator-prey relationship described in the reading is the case of the garter snake and the rough-skinned newt. The lecture says that the newt developed toxins in its skin as a defense against the predatory garter snake. In response, the garter snake developed resistance to the toxin, so the newt's toxin got stronger. Both predator and prey underwent significant genetic changes.

Finally, the lecture describes parasite-host coevolution in terms of bird eggs. A cuckoo bird may lay an egg in a host bird's nest, gaining the survival advantage of not having to take care of its own offspring. The host bird may develop the ability to recognize a strange egg and the instinct to push it out. The parasitic birds who survive will be the ones whose eggs more closely mimic the host's eggs. Thus, over time, the parasite eggs will become harder to distinguish and the host birds will become better at distinguishing.

Overall, the lecture's examples demonstrate the sequential changes that the reading described. The orchid and moth, the snake and newt, and the nesting birds show how coevolution transforms many species.

# Independent Writing Task I

## Prompt

Do you agree or disagree with the following statement? People now are less satisfied with their lives than people were in the past. Use specific details and reasons to develop your opinion.

### Brainstorm

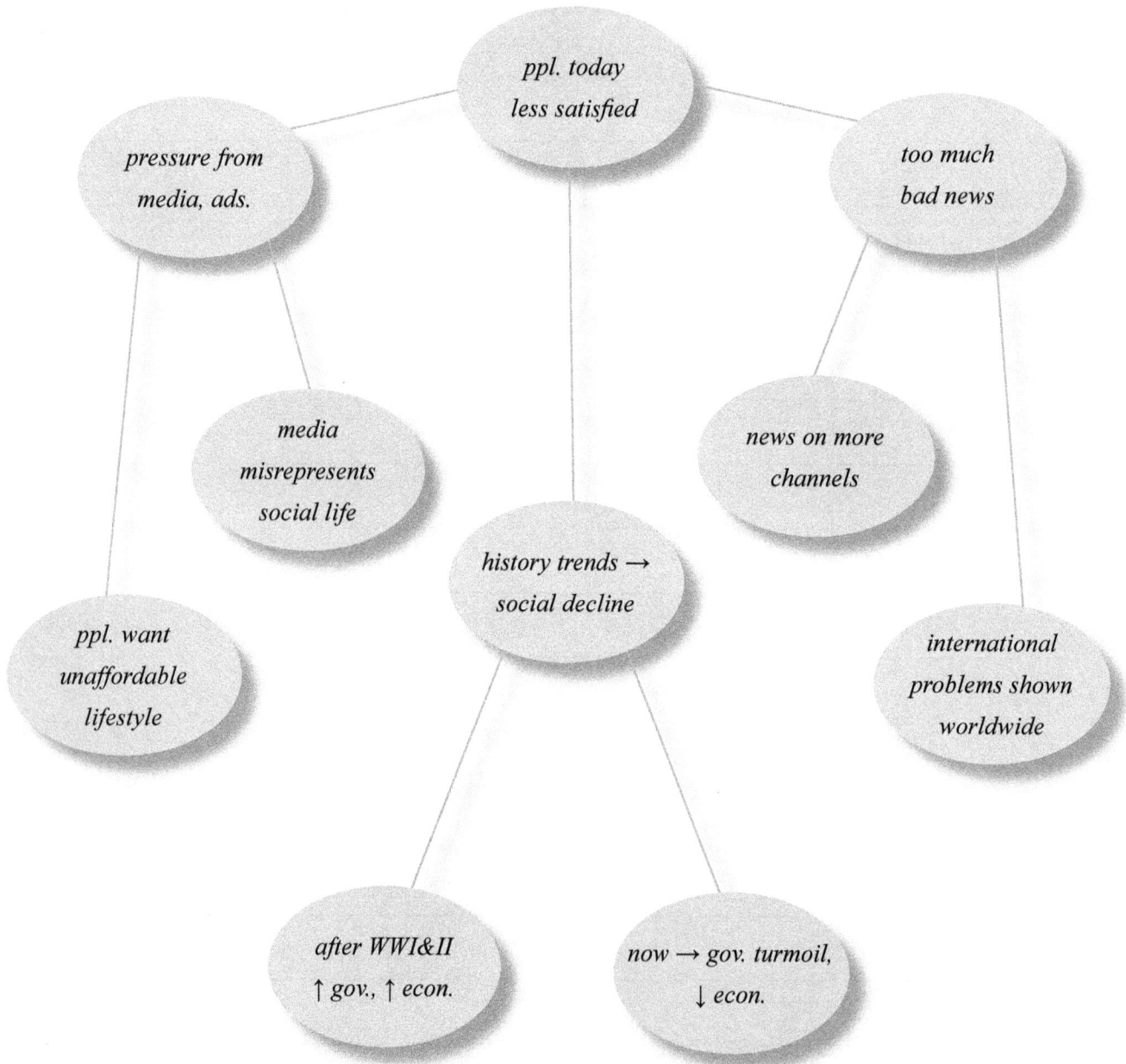

> **Prompt**
> Do you agree or disagree with the following statement? People now are less satisfied with their
> lives than people were in the past. Use specific details and reasons to develop your opinion.

## Brainstorm

**ppl. today less satisfied**

**pressure from media, ads.**

**too much bad news**

**media misrepresents social life**

**news on more channels**

**history trends → social decline**

**ppl. want unaffordable lifestyle**

**international problems shown worldwide**

**after WWI&II ↑ gov., ↑ econ.**

**now → gov. turmoil, ↓ econ.**

It is the best time in human history. People are living longer. Technology is making everyone's life easier and more interesting. Yet people are not happy. First, everyone constantly sees images of what they do not have. Also, global systems, especially the economy, are at a low point. Finally, everyone sees bad news from all media. **For these reasons, people today are less satisfied than people in the past.**

The media shows everyone the things that they should have, including expensive cars, luxury lifestyles, and the best medical care. The truth is that 99% of the world cannot afford the lifestyle and the products shown. Television commercials show images of big groups of friends and big, happy families, gathering together to celebrate the holidays or watch a game on television. Most people do not have that many friends or family members, and they certainly do not have time off from work or school so often. But the advertisements make people feel as though they should. This makes people unhappy.

Another reason that people are less satisfied is because of the natural cycle of history. The human race has reached a temporary peak of progress. After World Wars I and II, the human race enjoyed fifty years of relatively positive change. Growing economies made more things available to more people than ever before, while democracies replaced dictatorships and kingdoms around the world. But that kind of positive economic and political growth was not sustainable. First, the rate of general progress slowed. Then, economic growth recessed, along with the growth of new or more stable governments. In the long history of mankind, it will probably be a short lull. But people living now are dissatisfied. Many people feel that they are failures because they are not moving forward.

Finally, there is too much bad news. News anchors and television personalities constantly deliver bad news, and this bad news is available on more channels than ever before. The problems of the world, from global warming to pollution to war, are being shown to everyone more and more.

For all these reasons, people today are much less satisfied than people were in the past. The unrealistic depictions of life presented in the media make people want things that are unattainable; economic stagnation and political turmoil have people dissatisfied with the present; and the news makes people fear for the future.

# Independent Writing Task II

> **Prompt**
>
> Choose one of the following methods of communication and explain why you think it is the best way to deliver unpleasant or upsetting news.
>
> - email or text    - face-to-face    - telephone
>
> Use specific reasons and examples to explain your position.

**Brainstorm**

_____

_____

_____

_____

_____

_____

_____

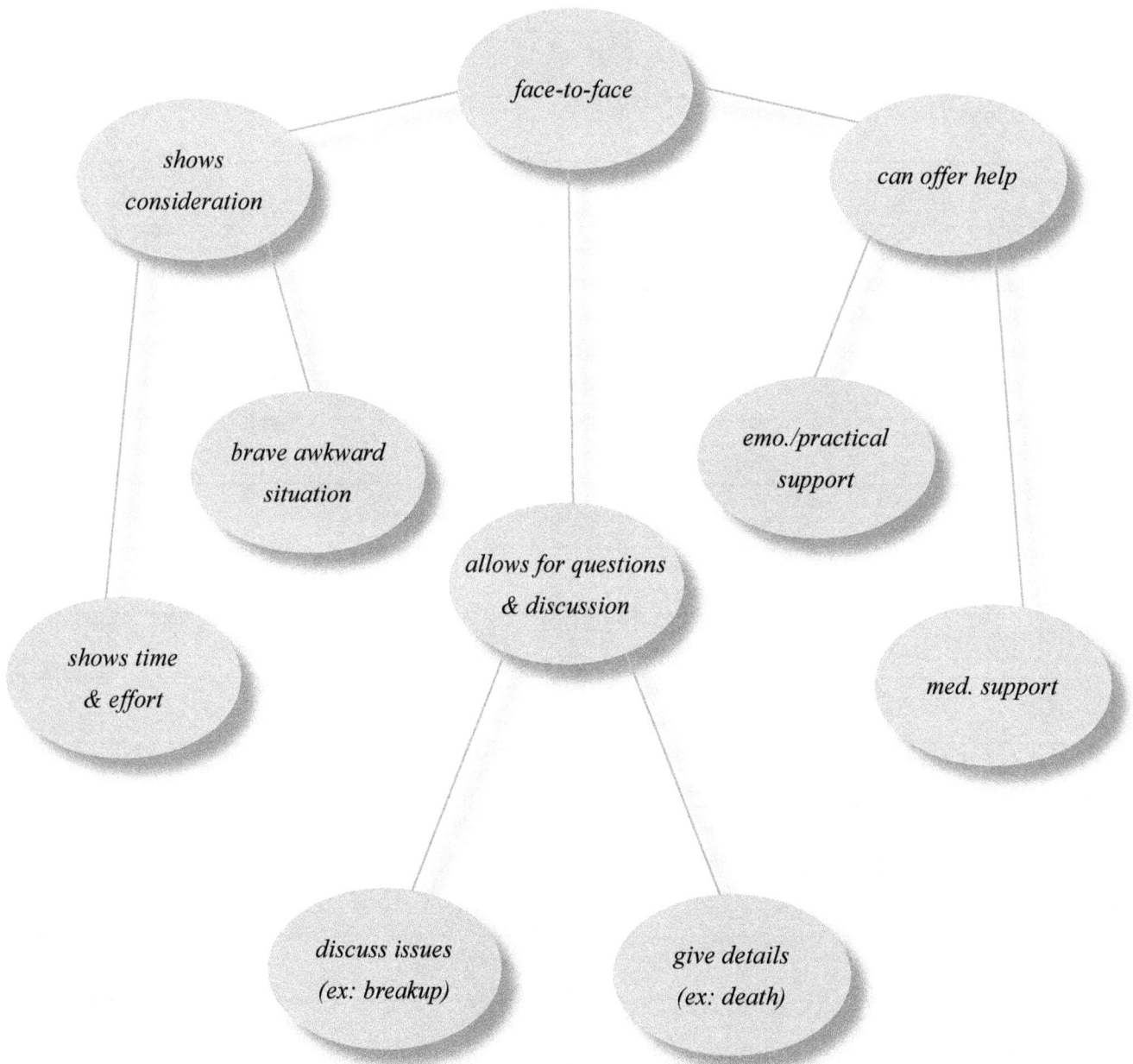

▸ Prompt ◂
Choose one of the following methods of communication and explain why you think it is the best way to deliver unpleasant or upsetting news.

- email or text
- face-to-face
- telephone

Use specific reasons and examples to explain your position.

**Brainstorm**

face-to-face

shows consideration

can offer help

brave awkward situation

emo./practical support

shows time & effort

allows for questions & discussion

med. support

discuss issues (ex: breakup)

give details (ex: death)

When a doctor has to give a difficult or terminal diagnosis, he or she would not email the patient because doing so would be cruel. Patients expect to receive their diagnoses face-to-face. Most people would agree that other methods, such as emailing, texting, or calling, would not be appropriate for the delivery of any upsetting news. **For both emotional and practical reasons, face-to-face interaction is the best way to deliver upsetting news.**

First, <u>providing upsetting news face-to-face shows consideration for the person receiving the news.</u> The bearer of the news has taken time and effort to be with the person when he or she hears the information. Furthermore, everyone realizes that giving bad news can be uncomfortable, and that people rarely feel that they know the right thing to say. Yet by willingly braving an awkward situation to deliver bad news face-to-face, the bearer of the bad news shows that he or she cares for the person receiving the bad news.

Second, <u>delivering an upsetting message in person provides an opportunity to answer questions and discuss issues.</u> For example, if the bad news is that a relationship is over, face-to-face discussions may help clear up misunderstandings, leaving both parties with a clearer picture of the situation. If the bad news is that someone has died, it is natural for people to want to know details about how and why the death occurred. Face-to-face communication offers a chance to clarify anything that needs further discussion.

Third, <u>face-to-face interaction is important because the person receiving the message might need practical or emotional support.</u> This may include a comforting hug, a phone call to family members, transportation, childcare, and so on. There is even a slight chance that the person hearing the news may need emergency medical attention.

In conclusion, delivering upsetting news in person is the best method. Doing so is the only way to ensure that the recipient of the bad news understands the situation. Although relaying a difficult message face-to-face may not be the easiest action to take, it is nevertheless the best choice.

# Integrated Writing Task 20

## PASSAGE

*Fordism* is a term referring to the goals and strategies of Henry Ford, the early 20th century car manufacturer who shaped mass production as we know it today. Ford hired a staff of experts to look for ways to make huge numbers of cars quickly and cheaply. Before Ford, there were other industries using assembly lines, but his assembly-line systems raised workplace efficiency to levels that had never been seen before.

Fordism proved successful because it promoted the continuous flow of production. Ford's engineers sought ways to keep the product moving while workers added parts to it. They used electrically powered rolling systems such as conveyor belts to move cars from worker to worker, and sometimes made use of gravity by means of slides. Some workers focused on keeping assembly-line workers stocked with parts they needed to add. The systems saved time because the line never needed to stop for a worker to set up equipment or carry anything.

Fordism also relied entirely on standardized parts. When parts are handmade, each item is somewhat unique, so it might need to be filed or adjusted to fit another somewhat unique part, a time-consuming process. But if every component of a product has been mass-produced using mechanical equipment and assembly-line production, then there will be no need for adjustment or craftsmanship. Everything will fit together perfectly.

Yet another aspect of Fordism was its new attitude toward workers. Rather than relying on people who had spent years as apprentices learning a craft, Fordism made tasks so simple that they could be performed by unskilled laborers. Ford reshaped the industry by paying assembly line workers high wages. Though most of the business community panicked and predicted that Ford would go bankrupt and ruin the car industry, his profits soared. The higher wages built a stable workforce that was willing to stick with the dull jobs. It was one more strategy to boost efficiency.

🔊 Now listen to part of a lecture on the topic you just read about.

## Notes

| P: | L: |
|----|----|
|    |    |
|    |    |
|    |    |

**Prompt**

Summarize the points made in the lecture, being sure to explain how they elaborate on specific points made in the reading passage

_____

_____

_____

_____

_____

_____

_____

_____

_____

_____

_____

_____

_____

_____

_____

_____

_____

_____

_____

_____

## Model Answer

PASSAGE

*Fordism* is a term referring to the goals and strategies of Henry Ford, the early 20th century car manufacturer who shaped mass production as we know it today. Ford hired a staff of experts to look for ways to make huge numbers of cars quickly and cheaply. Before Ford, there were other industries using assembly lines, but his assembly-line systems raised workplace efficiency to levels that had never been seen before.

Fordism proved successful because it promoted the continuous flow of production. Ford's engineers sought ways to keep the product moving while workers added parts to it. They used electrically powered rolling systems such as conveyor belts to move cars from worker to worker, and sometimes made use of gravity by means of slides. Some workers focused on keeping assembly-line workers stocked with parts they needed to add. The systems saved time because the line never needed to stop for a worker to set up equipment or carry anything.

Fordism also relied entirely on standardized parts. When parts are handmade, each item is somewhat unique, so it might need to be filed or adjusted to fit another somewhat unique part, a time-consuming process. But if every component of a product has been mass-produced using mechanical equipment and assembly-line production, then there will be no need for adjustment or craftsmanship. Everything will fit together perfectly.

Yet another aspect of Fordism was its new attitude toward workers. Rather than relying on people who had spent years as apprentices learning a craft, Fordism made tasks so simple that they could be performed by unskilled laborers. Ford reshaped the industry by paying assembly line workers high wages. Though most of the business community panicked and predicted that Ford would go bankrupt and ruin the car industry, his profits soared. The higher wages built a stable workforce that was willing to stick with the dull jobs. It was one more strategy to boost efficiency.

LECTURE

*Now that you've read about some of the "Fordism" strategies associated with Henry Ford, I'd like to emphasize some of the reasons that the production of Ford's signature car, the Model T, made such an impact when it started in 1914. Ford's strategies contributed to the development of an American middle class, and the production of inexpensive and mass-produced goods, as well as the establishment of an American car culture.*

*To start, the concept of continuous flow described in the reading boosted production to speeds that were astonishing at the time. The process of building an engine and an automobile was broken down into 84 basic steps, each of which had its own work area. A worker stood in one spot and made one small addition, and then the car rolled on to the next worker. The process was so streamlined that each Model T was built from start to finish in 93 minutes, which allowed the plant to produce a million cars a year.*

*The process demanded interchangeable parts, and permitted no frills or options. Even the black color was exactly the same on every Model T. This meant that any of the components made in 1914 could still be interchanged with those on Model Ts made in 1927. It resulted in an unapologetically standard automobile that was also shockingly inexpensive. Fordism meant that owning a car was no longer a luxury reserved for the upper classes.*

*Now let's take a look at why Henry Ford, who was trying to keep costs to a minimum, still paid high wages. In 1914, he announced that his factory workers would earn 5 dollars a day, a huge increase from the 2 dollars and 38 cents they made before. This immediately reduced worker turnover, which saved money. Also, Ford announced that each work shift would be 8 hours rather than 9, which meant workers had more free time and Ford could run three shifts a day, rather than two, and the factory never had to stop. With these moves, Ford increased efficiency and gained excellent publicity. Ford wrote that workers themselves could become enthusiastic customers, able to buy their own Model Ts, which was a powerful symbolic gesture.*

Notes

| P: Fordism changed manufacturing | L: examples to elaborate on reading |
|---|---|
| constant production, worker stations | production → fast (84 steps, 93 mins/car) |
| standardized, mass-produced components | cars all same, but affordable |
| high wages for unskilled laborers | ↑ wages = employee loyalty, more efficiency |

The lecture elaborates on the reading by providing more information explaining the impact of Fordism. The lecture supports the reading by adding details about how the production of the Ford Model T car not only revolutionized production methods, but also changed American culture.

First, the speed with which Ford's assembly-line workers could assemble a car was shocking to people at the time. The process was broken down into many separate stages, and each worker just did one task as the product moved along. The lecture emphasizes that being able to manufacture a completed automobile in 93 minutes made it possible to produce huge numbers of Model T cars—truly a mass production.

The reliance on standardized parts was another factor in the speed with which a Model T could be built. The lecture explains that customers did not have any options, not even the color of the car, because each part on each Model T was exactly the same. The result, though, was the first affordable automobile. According to the lecture, Fordism meant that car culture could spread rapidly as more and more people could afford cars.

Finally, the lecture explains more about the apparent contradiction of saving on production costs by paying workers more for simple, repetitive work. One result was that the factory was able to have a night shift. Also, workers stayed in their jobs longer because of the relatively high pay. In addition, the public praised Ford's policy of paying unskilled workers enough to buy their own Model Ts.

# Independent Writing Task I

## Prompt

Some people like to relax by watching movies and reading, while other people prefer to relax by exercising. Which leisure activities do you prefer? Use specific examples and reasons to explain your answer.

### Brainstorm

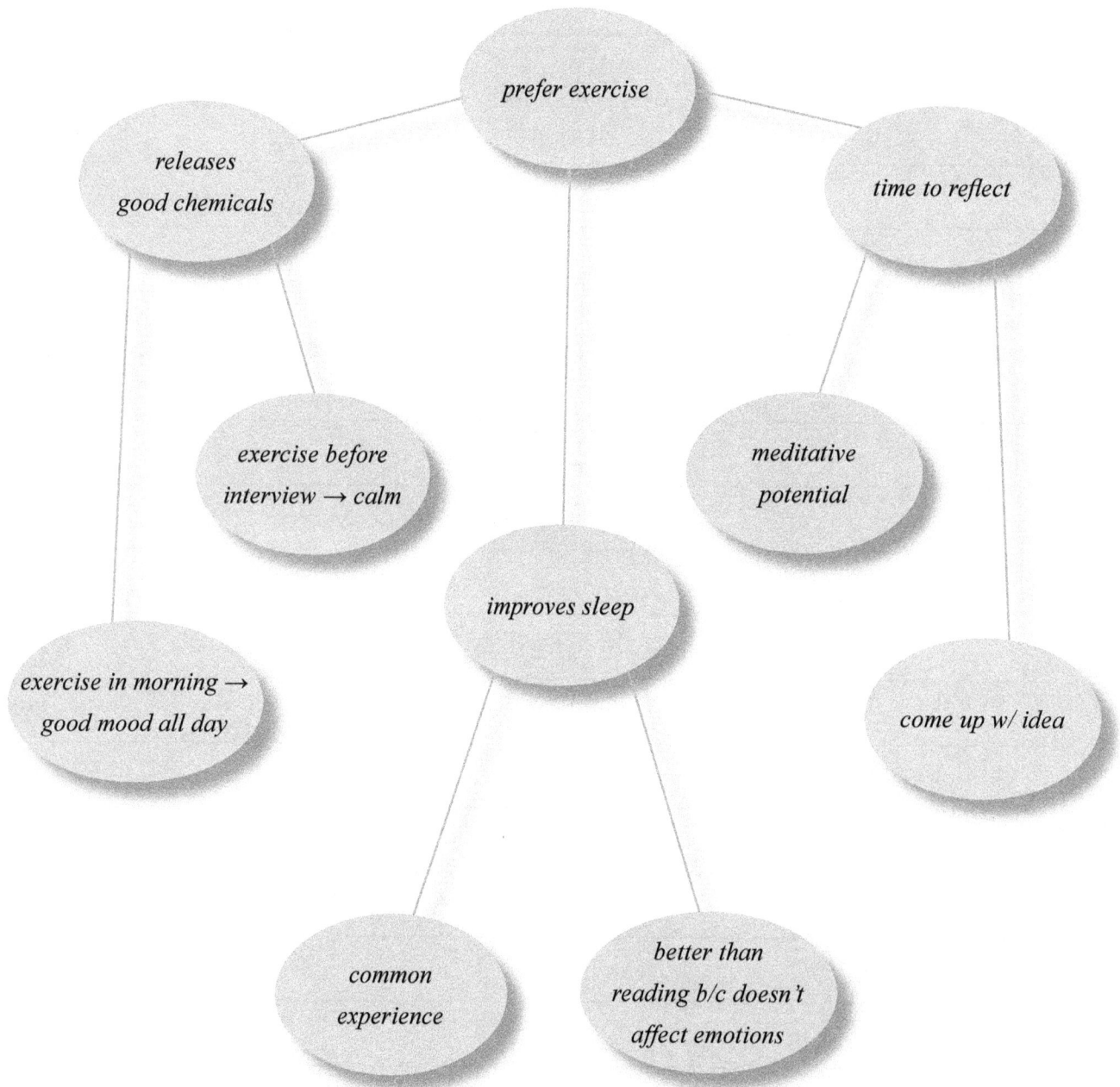

➡ **Prompt** ◁
Some people like to relax by watching movies and reading, while other people prefer to relax by exercising. Which leisure activities do you prefer? Use specific examples and reasons to explain your answer.

**Brainstorm**

*prefer exercise*

*releases good chemicals*

*time to reflect*

*exercise before interview → calm*

*meditative potential*

*improves sleep*

*exercise in morning → good mood all day*

*come up w/ idea*

*common experience*

*better than reading b/c doesn't affect emotions*

Everyone needs an occasional break from daily obligations. A life spent focusing only on work, chores, studies, or worries would be miserable. Of course, the best way to relax at any given moment depends on the person and the situation. One time-honored way is to become immersed in a fictional narrative, whether it is a movie or a novel. **But reading books and viewing films are not always the best ways to relax; most people would benefit from adding more exercise to their routines because doing so has both psychological and physical benefits.**

One of the advantages of physical exercise is that it produces more mood-lifting chemicals than other activities. These chemicals allow people to feel more optimistic, energetic, and calm. As a result, a person's mood improves both during and after exercise. For example, getting up early to walk or run before school may help a person feel confident and positive throughout the school day. Skipping the elevator and taking the stairs before a job interview might help a person remain calm and able to provide thoughtful answers during the interview. In other words, regular exercise can improve the quality of people's lives.

Another benefit of physical exercise is that it promotes sounder sleep. Most people fall asleep quickly and stay asleep longer after an active day. In contrast, relaxing by reading or watching a movie may keep people awake, especially if the plot is especially exciting or scary. Thus, exercising instead of becoming involved in an emotional story provides the benefit of helping someone wake up more refreshed the next day.

Depending on the activity, exercising can give people time to think and reflect. If people always turn to books or movies for relaxation, they lose out on the more meditative potential of walking, running, hiking, or swimming. Sometimes, an energetic but quiet activity is exactly what a person needs in order to make a decision or to come up with an idea.

No one would suggest that people only relax through exercise, but exercise undeniably builds physical and mental health and helps us solve problems.

# Independent Writing Task II

**Prompt**

Do you agree or disagree with the following statement? People nowadays do not know what it means to be happy. Use reasons and specific examples to explain your answer.

## Brainstorm

_____

_____

_____

_____

_____

_____

_____

_____

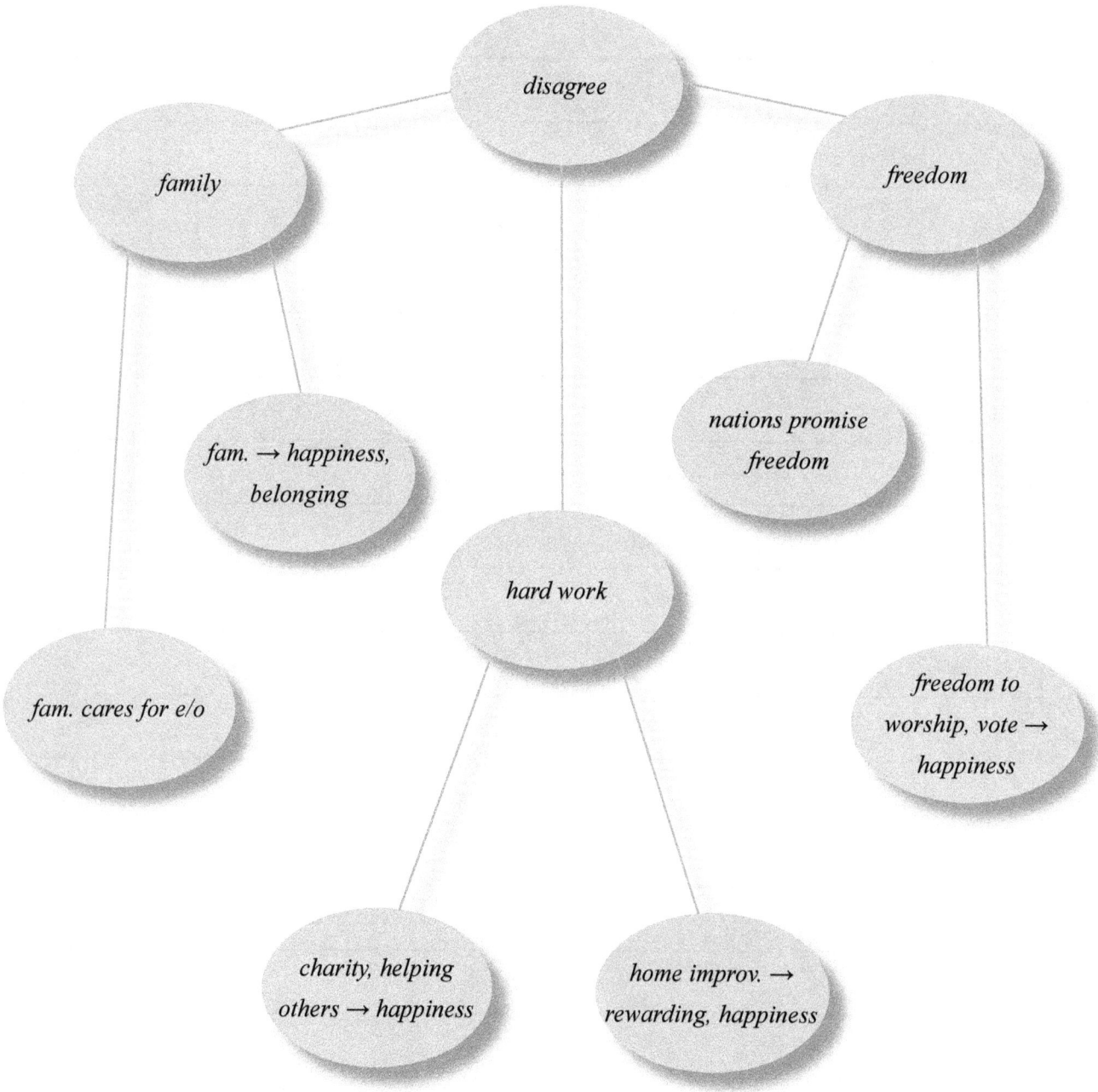

Do you agree or disagree with the following statement? People nowadays do not know what it means to be happy. Use reasons and specific examples to explain your answer.

**Brainstorm**

disagree

family

freedom

fam. → happiness, belonging

nations promise freedom

hard work

fam. cares for e/o

freedom to worship, vote → happiness

charity, helping others → happiness

home improv. → rewarding, happiness

Some will argue that people in the past lived simpler, and therefore happier, lives than do people today. **However, people nowadays still know what it means to be happy, and most people still hold the same values that humans always have: family, hard work, and freedom.**

The key to happiness is contained in a person's core values, and family is almost everyone's first value. Parents make sacrifices to raise families, and eventually, children grow up and take care of their parents. Most people will agree that family—and taking care of family—is the most important thing in life. Spending time with family provides a person with a feeling of happiness and a sense of belonging. When you go to a park, a shopping mall, or a church, you will see generations of families enjoying their free time together.

Another important characteristic of happiness is the value people place on hard work. Many people spend long hours on the job, but the concept of hard work is much the same today as it was in the past. When work is over, people turn to their churches and community groups, working together to meet the needs of others. Such community institutions have been around for ages, and the fact that people today still contribute to these groups is evidence that they are still a modern source of happiness.

Finally, the idea of freedom brings many people happiness. People may disagree about its meaning, but every culture loves freedom. Many modern nations have holidays that celebrate freedom and independence. Furthermore, almost every country today has a constitution that explains the rights of individual citizens. Having basic freedoms, such as the right to worship freely, the right to assemble, and the right to vote, is the essential component of a happy life.

Ultimately, people are able to find happiness in every aspect of daily life: from work, from home, and even from their government. By seeing how much people value family, work, and freedom, one is compelled to conclude that people nowadays know what it means to be happy.

www.ingramcontent.com/pod-product-compliance
Lightning Source LLC
Chambersburg PA
CBHW051115200326
41518CB00016B/2517